CASE STUDIES IN GLOBAL ENTREPRENEURSHIP

second edition

Dianne H.B. Welsh

The University of North Carolina
Greensboro

Shawn M. Carraher

University of Texas at Dallas

Kendall Hunt
publishing company

Kendall Hunt
publishing company

www.kendallhunt.com
Send all inquiries to:
4050 Westmark Drive
Dubuque, IA 52004-1840

Copyright © 2011, 2018 by Kendall Hunt Publishing Company

ISBN 978-1-5249-5076-7

Published in the United States of America

◎ Dedication

Dianne H.B. Welsh

I dedicate this book to my husband Thaddeus J. Shalek, daughter Shannon, grandkids Elin and Collin, and to my co-author.

Shawn M. Carraher

I dedicate this book to my lovely wife Sarah, sons Shawn Jr. & Charles, and to my co-author.

◎ Brief Contents

v

◎ Contents

 Preface

This 2nd edition casebook is the companion book for *Global Entrepreneurship* that was edited by us and published in its 3rd edition by Kendall Hunt Publishing Company. Based on requests from users of the textbook, we have compiled global cases that can be used with the chapters. The book and this companion casebook is a user-friendly, easy to read account of what you need to know about global entrepreneurship. It explains the principles that come from entrepreneurship, international business, cross-cultural management, strategy, exporting, international education, international economics and environmental concerns, and leadership. We have divided the casebook into three sections with the chapters identified on each case that we think best fit the topic of the chapter. The casebook can be used alone or with *Global Entrepreneurship*. We have authored many of the cases based on our experiences around the world, including work in the former U.S.S.R, Afghanistan, Andorra, Angola, Antigua and Barbuda, Australia, Austria, Bahamas, Bahrain, Bangladesh, Barbados, Belarus, Belgium, Benin, Bolivia, Botswana, Brunei, Bulgaria, Burkina Faso, Cambodia, Canada, Central African Republic, Chile, China, Columbia, Costa Rica, Cote d'Ivoire, Czech Republic, Denmark, Djibouti, Dominica, Dominican Republic, Ecuador, El Salvador, England, Eritrea, Estonia, Ethiopia, Finland, France, Gabon, Germany, Ghana, Guinea, Haiti, Hungary, India, Indonesia, Iran, Iraq, Ireland, Italy, Jamaica, Japan, Kenya, Kuwait, Laos, Latvia, Lebanon, Liberia, Liechtenstein, Lithuania, Luxembourg, Madagascar, Malawi, Malaysia, Mauritius, Mexico, Moldova, Mongolia, Mozambique, Myanmar, Namibia, Nepal, Netherlands, New Zealand, Niger, Nigeria, Norway, Pakistan, Papua New Guinea, Paraguay, Peru, Philippines, Poland, Portugal, Qatar, Reunion, Romania, Saint Kitts and Nevis, Saint Lucia, Saint Vincent and the Grenadines, Saudi Arabia, Senegal, Singapore, Slovakia, Slovenia, South Africa, South Korea, Spain, Sudan, Swaziland, Sweden, Switzerland, Taiwan, Tanzania, Thailand, Togo, Trinidad and Tobago, Ukraine, United Arab Emirates, United Kingdom, United States, Uruguay, Vietnam, Yugoslavia, Zambia, and Zimbabwe. In addition, the casebook contains real cases based on the experiences of our contributing authors from around the world. This casebook summarizes what we believe are the most significant core principles put into real cases.

We live in a world with countless opportunities, and the vast majority of those opportunities are international. As electronic mediums expand, ideas that may be opportunities will multiply by the thousands. This casebook was developed with the entrepreneur in mind, especially those that want to identify ideas that can lead to opportunities beyond their borders. We provide hands-on, real cases that provide the essential background information and knowledge that will give the entrepreneur the skills he or she needs to operate globally. The world economy will benefit from entrepreneurs that contribute internationally, both economically and socially.

This casebook presents cases along with accompanying questions that apply the basic principles of global entrepreneurship. Each case includes a teaching note with case overview, learning objectives, relevant courses, data sources, analysis with discussion questions and answers, and references. We have added video links for online courses and to enhance classroom content. These videos focus on real dilemmas, opportunities, and challenges from an entrepreneurial perspective. This casebook was developed due to the lack of accessible material available in one place and from compiling our own materials while teaching the topic for many years. We welcome feedback on the casebook as well as cases for our next edition. We would like to thank our colleagues who contributed to this casebook and to the field of global entrepreneurship.

Dianne H.B. Welsh, Ph.D.
Hayes Distinguished Professor of Entrepreneurship
Founder & Director, Entrepreneurship Cross-Disciplinary Program
441 Bryan School of Business and Economics
The University of North Carolina Greensboro
516 Stirling Street
Greensboro, NC 27402
336-256-8507
dhwelsh@uncg.edu
http://entrepreneurship.uncg.edu

Shawn M. Carraher, Ph.D.
University of Texas Dallas

⊙ Introduction

This casebook is organized in to three sections to coincide with *Global Entrepreneurship*. The three sections divide the chapters in the textbook and the real cases can be used alone or in conjunction with each other. Section One includes the first five chapters in the casebook. The Introduction includes Chapter 1: International Entrepreneurship and International Business and the following real cases: "Jenny Craig Goes Latin" by Don Sciglimpaglia and Massoud Saghafi, and "Entrepreneurial Decision Making Under Conditions of Uncertainty: Boeing vs. Airbus" by Michael Pettus and J. Mark Munoz. Chapter Two: Environmental and Contextual Sources of Global Variation in Entrepreneurial Activities real case is "Shopping for Sunglasses at the Burjaman Center: The Case of a Shady Buyer" by Dianne H.B. Welsh and Ibrahim Al-Fahim. It is about the former student's family business, Paris Gallery and the problem of shoplifting by those on tourist visas. Chapter Three: Global Entrepreneurship Strategy real case is "Starbucks International Enters Kuwait" by Dianne H.B. Welsh, Peter Raven, and Nasser Al-Mutair. The case is a precursor to Starbuck's entering Kuwait a year later. The location for many years was the most profitable location outside the United States. "The Journey of Doorstep Entrepreneurship: A Case on Jaipur Rugs" tells the story of the founding of the company and how its founder is changing the face of social entrepreneurship through his weavers and lifting villages up. Chapter Four: Global Business Plan real case is "Dr. Shingle Goes International: A Roofer's Dream" by Dianne H.B. Welsh. It is a true story that originated from a student's idea at a campus entrepreneurship center that she directed. Chapter Five: Business Opportunities for Global Entrepreneurship has two cases to choose from: "Growing Pains at Growth Cycle Strategies, Inc.," by Dianne H.B. Welsh, is a sales and marketing consulting business that has the challenge of growing with limited resources. The second case is, "Flextronics: Foreign Direct Investment Decisions in Central Europe," by Pavel Štrach and André M. Everett, which takes place in the Czech Republic.

The second section of the casebook focuses on Specialized Topics and includes Chapters Six through Eleven. Chapter 6: Exporting cases include "UNAGRO Corporation: Nothing Is Impossible!" by Flavia Barbery and Janet L. Rovenpor, and "TESY: Exporting in an Uncertain Environment," by Mark Potts. Chapter Seven: Global Economics and Finance includes a true case about a small town and the town's main business and the owner's ethical responsibilities, "Owens Sawmill: A Family Business Facing a Social Responsibility Dilemma," by Dianne H. B. Welsh and David Rawlings. Chapter Eight: Cross-Cultural Customs and Communication Styles includes a real case that describes communication challenges after war, "Al-Bahar & Jacorossi Engineering & Contracting Company: A Study of the Effect of Kuwaiti and Italian Culture on Human Resource Management After the Iraqi Invasion," by Dianne H.B. Welsh and Abdulrahman Al-Bahar and "Badriya's Short Career in Saudi Arabia," by Dianne H.B. Welsh and Mohammed Al-Boluhad. This is a true story of an accomplished U.S. graduate that returns to Saudi Arabia. Chapter Nine: Providing Students with a Worldview: A Competency-Based System for International Entrepreneurship, Education, and Development case is "The Hit and Run Expatriate Employees," by Dianne H.B. Welsh and Ibrahim Al-Fahim. This is a true story about shoplifting in the U.A.E. and how culture influences the law. Chapter Ten: Global Franchising and Other Forms of Entrepreneurship includes two cases: "The Case of the Elegant Shoplifter," by Dianne H.B. Welsh, Peter V. Raven and Faisel Al-Bisher and "To Market, To Market: An Independent Luxury Hotel's Battle for Survival," by Udo A. Schlentrich and Margaret J. Naumes. Chapter Eleven: Global International Alternative Modes of Entry for Entrepreneurial Firms has two cases to choose from, "Crystal Lustry: An Entrepreneurial Company's Entry into the World's Biggest and Most Competitive Market," by Jay Gronlund and J. Mark Munoz and "Fuel Jet Pro: Developing a Market Entry Strategy," by George Puia, and Mark Potts.

Section Three Area Studies includes the last three chapters and focuses on Eastern Europe, Latin America, and China. Chapter Twelve: Entrepreneurship and Security: The State of Entrepreneurship in Eastern Europe case, "The Early Days of 'Perestroika': First-Hand Impressions" by Dianne H.B. Welsh tells the story of Russia in the midst of major changes during Gorbachev's administration in 1990 before the major change heralded in by Yeltsin. "A Romanian Entrepreneur's Success—Florin Talpes—on Hypercompetitive Cyber Security Global Market" by Mariana Dragusin and Raluca Mariana Grosu tells the story of a real entrepreneur and his global success after the defeat of communism in Romania. Chapter Thirteen: Latin America case, "Kurotel Medical Longevity Center and Spa: Setting a Global Standard of Excellence" by Janet L. Rovenpor, Carolyn E. Predmore, and Frederick D. Greene is a real case of a global quality achievement combined with marketing challenges. Chapter Fourteen: China has two cases to choose from: "Corporate Entrepreneurship of Foreign Multinationals in China: A Comparison of Motorola and Nokia in the Cellular Phone Industry" by Nir Kshetri, and "What Works in Beijing, Doesn't Work in Beijing? The Use of Pay for Performance in China," by Sherry E. Sullivan and Shawn M. Carraher. "What Works in Beijing, Doesn't Work in Beijing" discusses how the implementation of human resource management projects in China can influence the effectiveness and outcomes from the project.

In all, we have compiled a diversified set of cases that will provide the reader with a comprehensive look at the issues surrounding going global, while highlighting opportunities that may be applied to their own future. We wish to thank our contributing authors for their enlightening cases and look forward to hearing from you, the reader, on what to include in the next edition.

Dianne H.B. Welsh
Shawn S. Carraher

◎ About the Authors

Dianne H. B. Welsh is the Hayes Distinguished Professor of Entrepreneurship and Founding Director of the Entrepreneurship Programs at The University of North Carolina Greensboro, including the North Carolina Entrepreneurship Center and the Entrepreneurship Cross-Disciplinary Program. She has previously founded two entrepreneurship programs and centers and has held three endowed professorships. In 2015, Dianne was named the Fulbright-Hall Distinguished Chair in Entrepreneurship for Central Europe in 2015. She was honored with the Senior Teaching Award for the University of North Carolina Greensboro in 2015 and was the December Commencement Speaker. She has been a visiting professor in Finland, Poland, Slovakia, and Austria.

Dianne is a recognized scholar in the family business, international entrepreneurship, women-owned businesses and franchising, and has seven books and over 180 publications to her credit. Her research has been published in *Academy of Management Journal, Journal of International Business Studies, Entrepreneurship Theory and Practice, Journal of Business Venturing, Journal of Small Business Management,* and *Journal of Family Business Strategy,* among other journals. She has three new books, *Creative Cross-Disciplinary Entrepreneurship,* published by Palgrave-Macmillan, *Global Entrepreneurship* (3rd edition), besides this one that is now in the 2nd edition, published by Kendall Hunt. She serves on numerous journal editorial review boards and has edited several journal special issues.

She served as the 2015 Chair for the Technology and Innovation Management Division of the Academy of Management with 2,700 members. Dianne is a Fellow in the Family Firm Institute, the US Association for Small Business & Entrepreneurship, the Small Business Institute, and the Pan-Pacific Business Association. She is a Certified Family Business Counselor and holds the Senior Profession in Human Resources certification. She served as a Presidential Appointee to the US Air Force Academy and the Defense Advisory Committee for Women in the Services (DACOWITS). Dianne delivered the keynote address at the U.N.E.C.E. Conference in Azerbaijan in 2012 as well as keynote addresses in five countries. She has conducted research and visited over 40 countries. She has consulted for Fortune 50 businesses, family businesses, franchises, and high growth businesses throughout the world. She has consulted for governments on converting public sector enterprises to the private sector. She also is an expert in no-cost employee reward systems and has worked with businesses across the globe in implementing systems to improve the motivation and performance of the workforce. Dianne has assisted eight universities in implementing programs across campus in the United States and Australia.

Shawn M. Carraher received his Ph.D. in Business Administration from the University of Oklahoma. He has served as the Oxford Journal Distinguished Research Professor and Director of the Small Business Institute® and Clinical Professor in International Business at the University of Texas at Dallas as well as serving at the Undergraduate Research Director. He has served as President of the SouthWest Academy of Management, Division Chair of the Management History Division, Division Chair of the Technology & Innovation Management Division, and PDW Co-Chair and Board member for the Careers Division and the Southern Management Association. He has also served as the President of the Small Business Institute®, the Association for Small Business & Entrepreneurship, and the Association for Entrepreneurship, Family Business, & Franchising as well as an officer of six Divisions of the US Association for Small Business & Entrepreneurship.

He has published over 100 journal articles, which have been cited over 17,000 times. His most recent publications have appeared in the *Journal of Applied Psychology, Journal of International Business Studies, Journal of Occupational & Organizational Psychology, Organizational Research Methods, Decision Sciences, Educational and Psychological Measurement, Journal of Managerial Issues, Journal of Vocational Behavior, Journal of Quality Management, Journal of Applied Management and Entrepreneurship, Career Development International, Polymeric Materials: Science and Engineering, Global Business and Finance Review,* and the *Journal of Business Strategies.*

He has directed research projects in over 130 countries. His research focuses on a variety of behavioral global entrepreneurship topics in the healthcare and tourism industries, and he has worked with over 50,000 SME owners from around the world. Shawn has also worked as a consultant specializing in performance enhancement and management development. He has co-owned a family business which has been in his family since 1893. He has served as the editor of several journals including the *Journal of Management History* affiliated with Division 1 of the Academy of Management and the *Journal of Technology Management in China* affiliated with the China Association of the Management of Technology, the *Cambridge Case Studies Journal,* the *Academy of Strategic Management Journal,* the *International Journal of Family Business,* the *Global Journal of Management and Marketing,* as well as serving as the interim editor of the *Journal of Entrepreneurship Education.*

In November 2015 Shawn was named one of the top 50 Global Business Educators in the world at the Saïd Business School of the University of Oxford. While in 2016 he was named one of the top 12 [#9 based upon academic age] most impactful business professors in Switzerland and in 2017 was recognized as one of the top 30 Professors in the World by three groups in China [Four were in business]. He received the Larry R. Watts Distinguished Service Award from the Allied Academies in 2011 and has been named a Fellow of the Academy of Strategic Management, the Academy of Entrepreneurship, the Academy of Global Business Advancement, the Small Business Institute® and the Direct Selling Education Foundation. On Dec. 6, 2017, celebrating the 100-year anniversary of independence from Russia, Shawn was one of 100 recognized in Helsinki for his contributions to economic development in Scandinavia by the King of Sweden. In the last two years, he has served as the advisor of 106 students who has received grants to support their research. His students have raised over $250,000 to support their travels to present papers at Harvard, Cambridge, and Oxford Universities. They have published 31 peer-reviewed journal articles. His program of educating students with research has received an Innovative Program Award from the Small Business Institute® as well as attracting funders to his programs.

◎ About the Contributors

Flavia Barbery

Flavia Barbery has a Bachelor of Science degree in Business Administration from Manhattan College in Riverdale, NY. She completed a double major in Economics and Management and graduated magna cum laude in May 2010. She has work experience as a project assistant for UNAGRO Corporation in Santa Cruz, Bolivia. She was in charge of developing, analyzing and evaluating feasibility projects for the implementation of a new business unit overseas.

Mariana Dragusin

Mariana Dragusin, Ph.D. is a Professor at the Bucharest University of Economic Studies in Romania, Faculty of Business and Tourism, Department of Business, Consumer Sciences and Quality Management. She is author and co-author of books/manuals, of scientific papers, and was involved in several national and international research projects as a director/team member or a consultant/expert. She attended national and international training courses and was accepted as a Visiting Researcher at The George Washington University in Washington, D.C. and at the University of Tampa in Florida. She has held the positions of chief of university's curricula department, vice-dean, and member of the Managing Board of three trade companies. She is also a member of the European Regional Science Association, the Regional Science Association International, and the Association for Innovation and Quality in Sustainable Business. Her major fields of competence and interest are: management, entrepreneurship, and leadership.

André M. Everett

Dr. André M. Everett is Associate Professor of International Management at the University of Otago, Dunedin, New Zealand, and Adjunct Professor at Huazhong University of Science and Technology in Wuhan, China. His writings on international and operations management strategy have been published or presented in over 30 countries, and he has taught in Argentina, Austria, Brazil, Chile, China, France, Israel, New Zealand, and the USA.

Frederick D. Greene

Frederick D. Greene, Ph.D. is an Associate Professor of Management and Director of the award winning Small Business Institute (SBI) at Manhattan College in Riverdale, NY. He is an active member of the Small Business Institute Director's Association (SBIDA) having served on numerous national committees that include programs, strategic planning and the Board of Directors. He is a Fellow of the SBIDA and is the immediate past president of SBIDA Region 2. Dr. Greene's teaching, consulting, research and writing have concentrated on various aspects of small business management and entrepreneurship.

Jay Gronlund

Jay Gronlund is a marketing professional with over 35 years of senior management experience in large multinationals and recently in international consulting. Jay founded The Pathfinder Group in 1990, which specializes in jump-starting stagnant businesses, including helping U.S.-based clients expand overseas. Gronlund also organizes and conducts customized marketing workshops and ideation sessions in foreign countries and the U.S. Before starting Pathfinder, Jay was the VP, Director of Marketing for Newsweek, Senior VP Marketing/New Business at Seagram, Group Manager at Church & Dwight and a brand manager at Richardson-Vicks. Jay Gronlund is a graduate of Colby College and has an MBA from Tuck at Dartmouth College. In addition he has been teaching a course on "Positioning and Brand Development" at New York University since 1999.

Raluca Mariana Grosu

Raluca Mariana Grosu, Ph.D. is a Lecturer of Entrepreneurship at the Bucharest University of Economic Studies in Romania, Faculty of Business and Tourism, Department of Business, Consumer Sciences and Quality Management. She has been a visiting researcher at the University of Seville, Spain and the University of Bari Aldo Moro, Italy. She works as an assistant editor of the *Amfiteatru Economic* journal and the *Romanian Journal of Regional Science*. She is part of the Romanian Regional Science Association Board and a member of the European Regional Science Association, Regional Science Association International, and Association for Innovation and Quality in Sustainable Business. She is actively involved in national and international research projects and she has published various scientific papers on topics covering her main research interests: entrepreneurship, migration, and regional science.

Hariom Gurjar

Hariom Gurjar is Assistant Professor of Finance at Poornima University in Jaipur, India. He completed his PGCSM from Indian Institute of Management in Indore, his PGDIM from Asia-Pacific Institute of Management in New Delhi, and his MCOM from University of Rajasthan, all in India. He received his Bachelor of Science (B.Sc.) from M.D.S. Ajmer (Raj), India. He has more than seven years of corporate experience and more than four and a half years of teaching experience. He has published research papers in areas of entrepreneurship, technical analysis of Derivatives Trading, and OBS activities in Indian Journals. Currently he is pursuing his Ph.D. programme in Banking and Finance.

Meghna Jain

Dr. Meghna Jain has over 11 years of experience in marketing, training, branding, and consulting. She is the Lead for Marketing & Research at Jaipur Rugs where she works towards luxury branding & investment promotion for sustenance and engagement of a network of 40,000 rural artisans. Her areas of expertise are marketing and communication management, and she is passionate towards emotionally connecting the weavers of exquisite hand-knotted carpets, residing in rustic villages in India with global consumers.

Mahesh Chandra Joshi

Mahesh Chandra Joshi, Ph.D. worked in the industry for six years in the fields of Marketing, Market Research, and Consultancy followed by teaching as a professor for 13 years. He completed his first masters in International Business from M.L.S. University and was a University Gold Medalist. He completed his second masters from Symbiosis Centre of Distance Learning, Pune in Personnel Management.

He has supervised three M.Phil. Scholars and is supervising six Ph.D. Scholars. His research areas of focus are international business, entrepreneurship, and management education. He has attended and/or presented papers at over thirty international, national, and state-level conferences, seminars, and workshops. He has been published in at least thirty books and journals of repute.

Nir Kshetri

Nir Kshetri is Professor at Bryan School of Business and Economics, the University of North Carolina-Greensboro. Nir holds a Ph.D. in Business Administration from University of Rhode Island; an M.B.A. from Banaras Hindu University (India); and an M.Sc. (Mathematics) and an M.A. (Economics) from Tribhuvan University (Nepal). His undergraduate degrees are in Civil Engineering and Mathematics/Physics from Tribhuvan University.

J. Mark Munoz

J. Mark Munoz is a Full Professor of Management and International Business at Millikin University and a former Visiting Fellow at the Kennedy School of Government at Harvard University. He is a recipient of several awards, including four best research paper awards, two international book awards, and the ACBSP Teaching Excellence Award, among others. Aside from top-tier journal publications and book chapters, he has authored seventeen books including: *Contemporary Microenterprise: Concepts and Cases, International Social Entrepreneurship, Handbook on the Geopolitics of Business, Advances in Geoeconomics*, and *Global Business Intelligence*. He serves on several international corporate and editorial boards. He is also the chairman of an international management consulting firm, Munoz and Associates International.

Margaret Naumes

Margaret Naumes is a senior lecturer (retired) in Management at the Whittemore School of Business and Economics at the University of New Hampshire. She received her Ph.D. in Economics from Stanford University and an M.B.A. from Clark University. She is co-author of *The Art and Craft of Case Writing* and cases published in the *Case Research Journal* and elsewhere. She is past editor of *The CASE Journal* and is a Fellow of the CASE Association and of the North American Case Research Association.

Michael L. Pettus

Michael L. Pettus is a former Associate Professor at the Tabor School of Business, Millikin University, USA. He earned his bachelor's degree from Millikin University and his M.B.A. and Ph.D. (in strategic management) degrees from the University of Illinois at Urbana-Champaign, USA. He has published articles in the *Academy of Management Journal* and the *Strategic Management Journal*. He has published two books: first book, *Growth from Chaos*, describes how firms in newly deregulated industries grew over time. His second book, *Strategic Management for the Capstone Business Simulation*, provides the theoretical linkages to the various functional areas within the simulation. He has won several teaching awards. He currently serves on the editorial review board for the *International Journal of Management and Entrepreneurship and Competition Forum*. He has over 30 years of experience working with multinational firms. His research interests are in resource-based view and dynamic capabilities.

Mark Potts, J.D.

Mark Potts, J.D. is Assistant Dean of the College of Business and Management at Saginaw Valley State University. He served as an Economic Development Adviser with the U.S. Peace Corps in Bulgaria (2000–2002) and as speechwriter to the Bulgarian Minter of Foreign Affairs Solomon Passy. He graduated cum laude from the Thomas M. Cooley Law School and holds a bachelor's degree from the University of Michigan.

Carolyn E. Predmore

Carolyn E. Predmore, Ph.D. is a Professor of Marketing at Manhattan College in Riverdale, NY. She is an active member in the American Marketing Association, the Society for Consumer Psychology and Association for Consumer Research. Her research interests cover perceptions of ethical issues by business students, retailing and terrorism, salesmanship, Internet usage and retailing on both a national and international basis. She has published in the *e-learning Digest, Management Decisions, Journal of Business Ethics*, as well as *The Journal of the Association of Marketing Educators*.

George Puia

George M. Puia, Ph.D. holds the Dow Chemical Company Centennial Chair in Global Business at Saginaw Valley State University. He earned a PhD in Strategic Management with concentrations in international business and research methods from the University of Kansas. Dr. Puia's publications focus on contextual differences in cross-national business and entrepreneurship. Puia was named a Distinguished Fellow by the Academy for Global Business Advancement and was selected for the Oxford Journal Global Top 50 Educators Award. He actively consults entrepreneurs and SMEs on foreign market entry strategy. He serves as Associate Editor of the *Baltic Journal of Management*.

Peter Raven

Peter Raven is Professor Emeritus at Seattle University. He previously held the Eva Albers Professor of Marketing and Director of International Business Programs at Seattle University and holds a Ph.D. in Business Administration from Washington State University. His research has focused on cross-cultural consumer issues, export marketing, global Internet marketing, international franchising, and micro-enterprises. He has published in *Journal of International Marketing, Journal of Services Marketing, Transportation Journal, Asian Case Research Journal, Internet Encyclopedia, Journal of Global Marketing, Journal of Consumer Satisfaction, Dissatisfaction, and Complaining Behavior, Journal of Advertising Research*, and others.

David Rawlings

David Rawlings holds a B.B.A. with a major in Management and a concentration in Entrepreneurship from John Carroll University in suburban Cleveland, Ohio. He wrote the case based on a true dilemma his cousin was facing his senior year. He is a Customer Assistance Account Manager at the Bank of America in Beachwood, Ohio. David has also started his own company, DZR Enterprises LLC, through which he sells items on eBay with eBay username Rawl123dzr.

Janet L. Rovenpor

Janet L. Rovenpor, Ph.D. is the Louis F. Capalbo Professor of Business and the Department Chair of the Management and Marketing Department at Manhattan College in Riverdale, NY. She teaches courses in Introduction to Management, Human Behavior in Organizations, and Strategic Management. Her research has focused on business ethics, managerial values and personality traits, women in management, and organizational crises. She has written case studies on JetBlue Airways, Abercrombie & Fitch, Respironics, Wal-Mart, New York Life Insurance Company, Alyeska Pipeline Service Company and Eli Lilly & Company.

Massoud Saghafi

Dr. Massoud Saghafi is a professor of marketing at the San Diego State University specializing in international business and marketing. He received his Ph.D. from the University of Southern California where he was also a post-doctorate scholar in marketing. Massoud has offered academic programs in Albania, China, Taiwan, France, Mexico, Portugal, Italy and Spain and has served as the guest speaker in international conferences worldwide. Dr. Saghafi has extensive consulting experience with the telecommunications and information services industry and has received research awards from the Telecommunication Association for his work on the future of the telecomm industry. He has also published in academic journals, industry and trade periodicals and contributed to popular media.

Udo Schlentrich

Udo Schlentrich is a graduate of the Lausanne Hotel Management School, Cornell University, and holds his Ph.D. from Strathclyde University. He is the Director of the Rosenberg International Center of Franchising and a member of the board of the Educational Foundation of the International Franchise Association. Schlentrich is engaged in advancing the field of franchising and hospitality marketing through applied research, teaching and outreach. He teaches the following courses: strategic management, international franchising, hospitality finance and development, and marketing. Schlentrich has received various awards for his innovative and engaged teaching style.

Schlentrich has held CEO and senior board level positions with leading American and international hospitality organizations such as Hilton International, Loew's, Stakis, Omni International, Preferred Hotels and Steigenberger. He is a regular consultant to international companies and investor groups.

Don Sciglimpaglia

Don Sciglimpaglia is Professor of Marketing and Director of Business Consulting Programs at San Diego State University. He has published in many leading academic journals including *Journal of Marketing, Journal of Advertising, European Journal of Marketing, Journal of Consumer Research and Industrial Marketing Management*. He is an active marketing consultant in the areas of marketing research and marketing planning and has consulted with Hewlett Packard, IBM, McDonald's and many other firms.

Pavel Strach (Bc., Ing., Ph.D. (Prague), Ph.D. (Otago))

Pavel Strach chairs the Institute of Management and Marketing at Skoda Auto University, where he teaches international business and business research methods. Since 2007, he has been Permanent International Visiting Professor in international business at IONA College, Hagan School of Business, New York. Strategies of multinational companies, headquarters-subsidiary relationships, and measurement of customer satisfaction are the focal points of his research interests. His research has been published in more than 25 countries in outlets such as the *Journal of Knowledge Management* and the *Journal of Product and Brand Management*.

Sherry E. Sullivan

Sherry E. Sullivan is the Associate Director of the Reed Careers Center and Fellow of the Southern Management Association. She received her Ph.D. from the Ohio State University and previously taught at Memphis State University. She has received Outstanding Educator Awards from the U.S. Association for Small Business & Entrepreneurship, the Small Business Institute®, the SouthWest Academy of Management, and the Technology & Innovation Management Division of the Academy of Management.

Priyesh Tiwari

Priyesh Tiwari is Assistant Professor of International Business at Poornima University in Jaipur, India. He received his master's degree in Marketing and International Business from Indian Centre for International Business in Pune and bachelor's degree from Rajasthan University in Jaipur. He has more than 12 years of experience spread over corporate organizations like Bennett, Coleman & Co. Ltd. (The Times of India), Music Broadcast India Pvt. Ltd. (Radio City 91.1 FM), Sakaal Media Group, and Poddar Group of Institutions. His areas of interest include international business (specially FDI), entrepreneurship, and strategic management.

Part One

Introduction

Chapter One

INTERNATIONAL ENTREPRENEURSHIP AND INTERNATIONAL BUSINESS

JENNY CRAIG GOES LATIN

Don Sciglimpaglia and Massoud Saghafi
San Diego State University

Learning Objectives

1. *Analyze* market information regarding potential viability of the Jenny Craig business model in Mexico.
2. *Assess* differences in culture as they would impact business viability.
3. *Identify* the health and environmental issues, which are related to social responsibility and may impact business viability.
4. *Discuss* the role of franchising in international market expansion.
5. *Discuss* basic business concepts and functional areas, including recruiting, operations, training, sales development, marketing, and performance management as it relates to the case.
6. *Evaluate* how the strength of a strong business concept or vision at all levels affects the ability for a business to compete in the worldwide marketplace.

Key Words

Obesity

Body mass index (BMI)

Franchising

Master franchise

Noncompete clause

Abstract

Jenny Craig International is a market leader in the weight management industry and an entrepreneurial success story. The company is considering expansion into Latin America. Mexico is of particular interest, based on preliminary market research, access to American media, and the Mexican population's experience with American products. An expert team must assess market information, evaluate Mexico's business and cultural characteristics, and decide if Jenny Craig can succeed in that market. The team must also contemplate the best market entry strategy, assess the pros and cons of various options for the company, and arrive at a viable recommendation.

◎ Problem Statement

Since its inception, Jenny Craig Inc. has provided weight management services to over five million clients. Started as an entrepreneurial venture, it has become one of the leading companies in that industry, both in terms of annual revenues and the number of clients. Headquartered in Carlsbad, California just north of San Diego, it operates in Canada, the United States, Australia, New Zealand, and France. A team of corporate entrepreneurs has just been charged to evaluate Jenny Craig's potential expansion into Latin America.

○ History

Founded in 1983 by Jenny and Sid Craig, Jenny Craig International is now one of the world's leading weight management companies. The entrepreneurial couple had originally founded and expanded a company called Body Contour into 200 centers by 1980, and then sold it to NutriSystem in 1982. Restricted from competing with NutriSystem in the U.S., they subsequently opened a weight control company, Jenny Craig Inc., in Australia in 1983. Their Australian company, using nutritional guidance, pre-packaged food, exercise, and behavior modification, grew to $50 million in revenues by 1985. With the expiration of the "noncompete" clause of their sales agreement with NutriSystem, Jenny Craig entered the North American market, opening twelve centers in the Los Angeles area during their first year in the U.S. Sid Craig's prior experience with another Los Angeles-based weight control business, Gloria Marshall Salons, proved to be an invaluable background for their American expansion.

In 1991, Jenny Craig went public in the U.S. With revenues of over $350 million and with 780 centers by 1999, the company's rapid growth was a phenomenon. Company ownership accounted for roughly eighty percent of the centers in 1999, and the rest were franchised. In a complicated transaction in 2002, Jenny and Sid Craig sold their majority stake in the company to an investor group, of which they were a part, in a take-private transaction. The managing director of ACI Capital, one of the major investors in the transaction, made the following statement at that time: "With well over half of all Americans considered to be overweight or obese, and obesity-related claims costing the economy an estimated $100 billion annually, we realized that Jenny Craig not only possessed huge business growth potential, but that the company could also make a significant positive impact on the health of our nation. We also understood that by strengthening and expanding the company, Jenny Craig could create jobs in communities across the U.S."

Within one year of the 2002 sale, Jenny Craig Centers were in 646 locations in the U.S., Canada, Australia, New Zealand, and Puerto Rico. In 2006 the company was acquired for $600 million by the food and beverage giant Nestle, which subsequently acquired Novartis Medical Nutrition, maker of Boost beverages and nutritional supplements, in 2007. According to the company website, there are now over 800 Jenny Craig Centers worldwide. Approximately 15 percent of centers in North America are franchised, with the Australian and New Zealand markets controlled by a single master franchisee. As of March 2010, the company announced the launch of its *Jenny Craig* weight management program in France, with seventeen *Jenny Craig* centers and an at-home program. Later in 2010, *Jenny Craig* is planning a new national roll-out in the UK since its earlier failure in that market. Other European markets are also likely to be considered and evaluated.

◎ Weight Management Industry and Market Potential

The Need for Weight Management in the United States: Obesity

The U.S. Centers for Disease Control and Prevention ranked obesity as the number one health threat facing America. In the U.S., it causes over 400,000 deaths annually and obesity related costs are between $100 billion and $200 billion annually. The increased risks of developing several serious health conditions, such as cardiovascular disease, hypertension, Type II diabetes, and thyroid disease, are a direct or indirect result of obesity. The growing problem of childhood obesity, defined as individuals under age 18 who are classified as overweight, has grown to more than 15 percent of that age group.

Body mass index (BMI) is a measure of body fat based on height and weight that applies to adult men and women. BMI categories are: underweight (BMI less than 18.5), normal weight (between 18.5 and 24.9), overweight (between 25 and 29.9), and obese (30 or greater). Using these standards, nearly two-thirds of U.S. adults are overweight or obese, with nearly one-third characterized as obese. Less than one-half of U.S. adults are at a healthy weight, and over 15 percent of children and adolescents were overweight in 2000. Additionally, 15 percent of children and almost 15 percent of adolescents were classified as at risk for overweight due to a BMI for their age between the 85th and 95th percentile. Between 1960 and 2000, the prevalence of overweight among U.S. adults increased from 32 percent to 34 percent, and the prevalence of obesity among adults during the same time period more than doubled from 13 percent to 31 percent. From 1988 to 2000, extreme obesity (defined as BMI of 40 or more) increased from 3 percent of the adult population to 5 percent.

The prevalence of overweight and obesity among racial and ethnic minorities, especially women, tends to be higher than that of the White population in the U.S. For example, overweight and obesity among non-Hispanic Black women is over 77 percent, and among Mexican American women is almost 72 percent, compared to a rate of just over 53 percent among White women in the United States. In contrast, almost 61 percent of non-Hispanic Black men are classified as overweight or obese, while almost 75 percent of Mexican American men and over 67 percent of non-Hispanic White men fall into that category.

The Need for Weight Management in the United States: Health Risks

Unhealthy dietary habits and lack of physical activity contribute to more than 300,000 adult deaths in the United States each year. Obesity increases the risk of death from all causes between 50 percent and 100 percent compared with normal-weight individuals, while the life expectancy of a moderately obese person is shortened by between two and five years. The impact of extreme obesity is more striking, shortening life expectancy for White men by 13 years and for White women by up to eight years. Overweight and obesity also contributes to a diagnosis of Type II diabetes, with all its attendant health problems. An estimated 70 percent of diabetes risk in the U.S. can be attributed to excess weight. The ongoing costs to the U.S. health system are dramatically affected by the health risks from the epidemic of obesity in our culture.

Jenny Craig Business Approach

With over 150,000 participants in an average week, the Jenny Craig program charges a fixed enrollment fee and then encourages its followers to buy some of its more than 80 prepared meals and snacks as part of the program. The company makes participation in the program easier and more convenient through an at-home consultation and food delivery option, called Jenny Direct.

The company website indicates that its weight management program combines one-on-one support in nutritional and lifestyle counseling to help clients modify their activities and eating habits. When clients have reached their desired weight levels, they are gradually transitioned away from the prepackaged food and planned menus into the maintenance of a healthy weight and activity level. Jenny Craig offers programs specifically tailored to women, men, teens, senior citizens, and individuals with Type II diabetes.

Jenny Craig participants work with program consultants in individual, private counseling sessions. Although the consultants are not required to be professionally certified as nutritionists or health professionals, they are trained by the company to provide clients with educational and motivational support. Jenny Craig members join one of a number of types of plans and then purchase prepackaged food from their local center. Dry and frozen foods are also shipped by the company directly to clients who have joined the Jenny Craig at Home program. Initially, clients follow a planned menu using the company's frozen and dry foods, supplemented with grocery items such as dairy and vegetables. Participants later learn to customize their menus following the nutritional guidelines of the program. After reaching the halfway point of their weight loss goal, clients begin to use a menu with three or four days of non-program foods.

The company has effectively utilized multiple celebrity clients as spokespeople. This practice started, at the company's inception in Australia, with the use of Jenny Craig herself as the "face" of the company. In early 2000, Monica Lewinsky became a somewhat controversial spokeswoman for the program, but was dropped due to criticism. In 2005, actress Kirstie Alley became the spokeswoman, and was later joined by Valerie Bertinelli, who had slowly gained weight over the years. In 2008, Queen Latifah became a spokesperson, and is continuing to work with the company. Also in that year, comedian Ashley Young joined the program and is serving as an "ambassador" for the company in Australia. In the second half of 2009 Phylicia Rashad, Sara Rue, and Nicole Sullivan became clients or spokespersons and in 2010 Jason Alexander became a spokesman for Jenny Craig. The marketing message, particularly for Queen Latifah and Phylicia Rashad, is to focus on losing 5–10 percent of body weight and leading a healthier lifestyle, rather than to concentrate on a specific weight-loss goal.

JENNY CRAIG INTERNATIONAL	One-on-one consulting Direct to consumer	Improve looks Feel good Lose weight with convenience	Females 25–54 Skewed Caucasian Mid-upper class 20+ lbs to lose
WEIGHT WATCHERS INTERNATIONAL, INC.	Group Program	Attain health Feel good	Females 25–54 Various ethnicities 20+ lbs to lose
NUTRISYSTEMS, INC.	Direct to consumer	Improve looks Lose weight with convenience	Females, males 22–54 Want to "diet in private" 20+ lbs to lose

Weight Management Market and Competitors

Weight management services comprise a complex industry, offering nutritional guidance, products and exercise programs. Top competitors of Jenny Craig include Weight Watchers International, and NutriSystem. Smaller challengers in the market include online services, nutritional weight loss products sold at retail, and "do-it-yourself" diet programs that forgo membership fees and packaged products. These other competitors include Slim Fast, Atkins Nutritionals, Alticor, Bally Total Fitness, ConAgra, eDiets.com, GNC, Heinz, Medifast, Reliv' International, Schiff Nutrition International, and WebMD Health. In the U.S., the total market for weight control programs and products is roughly $3.9 billion. While the market leading companies vary in their consumer-facing models and, to a lesser degree, in positioning, their target markets are very similar (Table 1.1). The 2007 IBIS World Industry Report for Weight Loss and Dietary Centers in the U.S. describes competition in the industry as high, based on the degree to which the industry trades on brand recognition, pricing, and promotions, as well as the large range of substitutes to weight loss centers and programs that exist.

Jenny Craig International Corporate Entrepreneurship: Rationale for Expansion into Mexico

Rationale

Following its success in current markets, Jenny Craig International is looking into expanding its global market. Led by recent MBA graduate, Landry Parker, a corporate entrepreneurship team is beginning to study new markets. Specifically, Parker has steered the company toward considering Latin America, where there are potential growth opportunities in neglected or underserved markets. Of particular interest to Parker, is Mexico, which is known to have increasing obesity levels and improving socio-economic conditions, which may indicate considerable opportunity. Although management is aware that some competitors have already entered the market, the company could gain an advantage by establishing a significant early presence.

Obesity in Latin America and in Mexico

The World Health Organization (WHO) estimated in 2005 that over 1 billion adults were overweight, including 805 million women, and that over 300 million were obese. WHO predicts that the number of overweight people will increase to 1.5 billion and more than 400 million of them will be obese by 2015. Obesity was considered a problem mainly in advanced economies, with the U.S. having the highest prevalence of obesity among all countries. However, it is now rising dramatically in developing countries, mainly in urban areas, primarily related to increasing urbanization and changing lifestyles. As urbanization increases, people are more inclined to consume external food instead of a traditional diet, which includes foods that are high in grains, fruit, and vegetables, and are low in fat.

A decrease in physical activity is another contributor to the obesity problem. As a result, many countries that formerly were fighting with an under-nutrition problem are now faced with an obesity problem as well. Overall, nations in Latin America have seen dramatic increases in obesity; among all countries Argentina ranks third, Mexico ranks fourth, and Chile ranks eighth in prevalence of obesity.

In Mexico, the increase in the prevalence of overweight and obese individuals has resulted from a series of changes in diet, physical fitness, general health, and nutrition. The cultural changes affecting obesity in Mexico include the following:

- Consumers are often provided with a wider variety of food choices at comparatively lower prices;
- Increased access by urban areas to processed and packaged foods imported from more industrialized countries, including the U.S., which tend to be higher in both fat and sugar;
- Less demanding physical work required of workers in service-oriented urban areas.

In 2005, approximately 38 percent of the Mexican urban adult population was classified as pre-obese, and 21 percent as obese, mostly women. The cost of obesity to Mexico's economy was estimated to be $317 million, amounting to roughly 38 percent of national healthcare costs.

Size of Mexican Market

Mexico has a GDP of $1.149 trillion with a real growth rate of 4.8 percent. This translates to a GDP per capita of about $7,300*. Approximately 11 million people earn more than $32,000, with 4.5 million earning more than $52,000 per year. The role of women in the workforce has been steadily increasing and

SMAS	POPULATION	FEMALES	FEMALES, 25–54	NO. OF OBESE & OVERWEIGHT WOMEN	NO. OF HOUSE-HOLDS	NO. OF HOUSE-HOLDS EARNING $52K+
Mexico City	19,231,829	9,895,930	3,580,347	433,863	4,135,877	616,245
Guadalajara	4,095,853	2,107,562	762,516	124,127	1,016,340	161,598
Monterrey	3,664,331	1,885,518	682,180	106,289	916,082	166,727

women currently make up 36 percent of the labor force.

The population of Mexico in 2005 was estimated at 103 million with a growth rate of 1.6 percent. Of the estimated 103 million, 53 million were female, with half under 25. Over 19 million Mexicans fall in the 25–54 age range (the primary age demographic for Jenny Craig in the United States). Almost 10 percent of Mexican women have college degrees. Over 12 million are considered overweight or obese, of which nearly 1.85 million are in the 25–54 age group. The population of Mexico is heavily concentrated in major metropolitan areas. The top three urban centers have a combined population of 27 million.

In Mexico, the average household size is 4.2 persons and does not significantly vary throughout the three markets considered in Table 1.2. In these markets, the top 15 percent of the population has a household income of $52,000. This translates into a purchasing power parity with the U.S. of $70,000.

Cultural Factors

To better understand the Mexican consumers' response to weight-loss programs, one should consider the perceptions of Mexican females about weight loss, appearance and health.

Motivations for Dieting in the U.S. and in Mexico

In the U.S., motivations to diet typically vary by lifestyle stage. For example, younger individuals are more concerned with their appearance, being accepted by society, and attracting potential partners than they are with dieting for health reasons. As both men and women grow older they tend to accumulate weight, which can increase their health risks. Despite cultural differences between the U.S. and Mexico, motivations to diet are similar across these different lifestyle stages as summarized in Table 1.3.

Differences in the Perception of Appropriate Weight

Studies have indicated that societal norms regarding female body image and appropriate weight do vary with culture. In particular, the Mexican culture tradi-

TABLE 1.3 Motivations for Dieting in the U.S. Compared to Mexico

| | COUNTRY | |
MOTIVATOR	UNITED STATES	MEXICO
Health	A motivator for older people who have accumulated weight over their lifetime	
	33 percent think weight is a top health concern	
	49 percent regularly make diet changes to reduce fat, sugar, or calories to improve health	
	14 percent suffer from diabetes	15 percent suffer from diabetes
Appearance	Individuals with higher disposable incomes more motivated in dieting for appearance and confidence	
	Younger vs. older adults more motivated in dieting for appearance and confidence	
Pressure from family and peers		1 in 4 adolescent females feel pressure from peers to lose weight
		3 in 4 adolescent females report having a dieting family member at home

tionally idealizes a more curvy female physique whereas the mainstream Western culture generally values a thin physique. Supporting this theory is evidence from a comparative study of ethnic groups, the goal of which was to examine differences in body image discrepancy and body mass index (BMI) across ethnicity.

Female Hispanic participants in a reported study (20% Mexican, 40% Central American, and 40% Puerto Rican) were significantly slower to report body dissatisfaction than the white American females studied. Additionally, Hispanics did not consider themselves overweight until they reached a significantly higher BMI that the white Americans. In terms of pounds, a 5'6" Caucasian-American female would become dissatisfied at 153 pounds while a Hispanic of the same height would not become dissatisfied until she reached 177 pounds, a 24-pound difference.

Cross-Cultural Differences

Compared to American culture, there are differences that may affect the way that Jenny Craig is perceived and adopted in Mexico. These differences, their implications, and the seriousness of the hurdles they pose are highlighted below.

Studies show that, unlike U.S. citizens, who's ideal female body is uniformly thin, Mexicans prefer women to be heavier, with more curves. Specifically, a typical female adolescent in Mexico City's upper and middle class wants her waist to be thinner but also wants her breasts and buttocks to be more robust.

However, weight loss to accommodate a body image is becoming increasingly more important for Mexican women as they increase contact with the culture of the United States and Europe.

Mexican families, across all socioeconomic groups tend to eat at least breakfast and dinner together. Weekend lunches are also a family affair. Mexican lifestyle does not emphasize fast, convenient meals. Most upper-class women choose not to work full-time because it is not financially necessary. Most upper-class families have a personal cook, while most middle-class families may have a housekeeper. The existence of the personal cook introduces a new dynamic to the method of weight loss for women. Middle-class mothers, who do not have personal cooks, are responsible for preparing meals. Normally, if the mother decides to lose weight, the entire family has to cut its calorie intake.

Many Mexicans add other foods to frozen meals and eat more than the allotted size of the meal. In the United States, there is more of an understanding that maintaining the portion size of the frozen meal is important for weight loss. However, in Mexico, it is common to add spices, breads, tortillas, or other foods to the frozen meal. This extra food consumption may inhibit good weight-loss results.

There is prestige associated with consuming American products. Many Mexicans travel to the United States simply to bring back brand-name clothing and gadgets, and this brand consciousness applies to food as well. Additionally, many Mexican women feel that the U.S. is a clear leader in weight-loss products, and is therefore likely to be trusted before many Mexican services and products.

Marketing and Advertising in Mexico

Rather than turning to family, friends, or doctors for health advice, most middle- and upper-class Mexican females look to magazines, television, and radio sources for information and advice about body image and weight-loss. Due to its media penetration and close proximity to Mexico, the United States is currently the most trusted source of new trends in health and diet.

Other sources of influence include Mexican celebrities, such as the *telenovela*, Mexican soap opera stars. The women on these programs are thin upper-class women who are symbols of beauty in Mexico. Mexican females also receive exposure to celebrities through national publications, especially lifestyle magazines, which are on the rise. The most popular of these are *Quien* (translated as "Who" in Spanish) and *Caras* (translated as *"Faces"*), both of which focus on high society and celebrity lifestyles. While considered trendy among the upper class, they typically offer somewhat superficial content about fashion, celebrities, and entertainment events. Other popular women's magazines include *Vanity Fair, Harper's Bazaar, Vanidades,* and *Marie Claire.* While Jenny Craig's U.S. marketing efforts rely heavily on national television and public relations efforts, the most effective forms of marketing in Mexico are more localized, direct advertising efforts. Localized advertising techniques include the distribution of pamphlets in a store's immediate locality, as well as the placement of ads and articles in smaller local magazines.

Additionally, word-of-mouth and goodwill are incredibly important in spreading the word throughout the community. Evidence of this can be seen in the story of Herbalife's top Mexican distributor, who attributes his personal sales success to understanding that the people he met didn't want "the hard sell," but were willing to "hang around and talk."

◎ Next Steps

The Jenny Craig International corporate entrepreneurship team led by Landry Parker must decide what to do next, based on these data. Increasing obesity levels in Mexico and improving socioeconomic conditions indicate that a considerable opportunity exists. However, a new market in a new country presents unique challenges. Consideration should be given to factors such as size and nature of the market, likelihood of profitability, and cultural attitudes and behaviors that could either inhibit or promote adoption of the Jenny Craig product.

The first major question to address is whether or not the company should consider entry into Mexico. In this regard, the team needs to determine the relative arguments for and against market entry. If it recommends moving forward, should the company consider franchising? In Australia one master franchisee is used. Would that be the best alternative for Mexico? Given the size of the Mexican market, should market entry be limited to major metropolitan areas, or should a larger portion of the country be targeted? What type of marketing approach might be recommended based on prior success in the U.S. and knowledge of Mexico?

Discussion Questions

1. In the U.S., Jenny Craig Inc. was viewed not only as having a positive impact on health, but also as a means of creating jobs in communities across the country. Assess the same situation in Mexico. What potential entrepreneurship and small business opportunities might exist there with the weight-loss market and with Jenny Craig? What other small businesses may develop from Jenny Craig entering Mexico?

2. From the perspective of global corporate entrepreneurs, it is said that companies are involved beyond their country borders either internationally, multinationally, or globally. Based on the case, which characterization best fits Jenny Craig Inc.?

3. As entrepreneurs, Jenny and Sid Craig had experience in Australia and the U.S. How would this experience be different in Mexico? What are the most important cultural difficulties to expect in the Mexican market?

4. The first major strategic question to address is whether or not Jenny Craig Inc. should consider entry into Mexico. In this regard, what are the relative arguments for and against market entry? What are the major potential financial risks involved?

5. Assume the perspective of an international entrepreneur. Do you detect a viable opportunity in the Mexican weight-loss market? Given the competitive land-scape, how should Jenny Craig Inc. position itself in this fast-evolving weight-loss market in Mexico? Given the size of the Mexican market, should market entry be limited to major metropolitan areas, or should a larger portion of the country be targeted?
6. If it plans to move forward, should the company consider franchising? In Australia, one master franchisee is used. What is a master franchise compared to a franchisee? Are franchisees entrepreneurs? Why or why not? Where would you recruit franchisees? In your opinion, what would be the best alternatives for Jenny Craig in Mexico?
7. What is the most promising potential target market for Jenny Craig, Inc.? What types of marketing approaches might be recommended based on prior success in the U.S. and knowledge of Mexico?
8. What would you do? Would you be willing to open a Jenny Craig center in Mexico? Why or why not would you make that decision?

References

International business center, (2012). Mexico Business Etiquette, Culture, & Manners. *Insightly*.

Hensley, S. (2011). Jenny Craig: Winner, Winner, Diet Dinner! *Shots*.

Haupt, A. (2011). Health Buzz: Jenny Craig Ranked Top Diet. *U.S.News*.

Dezember, R. (2013). Nestlé to Sell Jenny Craig Diet Business. *The Wall Street Journal*.

Relevant Videos

Entrepreneur 101 - Potato Chip Business - Mexico City:
https://www.youtube.com/watch?v=kg5aq_eBO6k

Jenny Craig Anywhere:
https://www.youtube.com/watch?v=438NmyBRoy8

JENNY CRAIG'S HEALTHY WEIGHT LOSS APPROACH:
https://www.youtube.com/watch?v=MqtGA3pqC-U

Mexico: Culture and Business:
https://www.youtube.com/watch?v=Od8p65oxVwU

Entrepreneurial Decision Making Under Conditions of Uncertainty: Boeing vs Airbus

Michael Pettus and J. Mark Munoz

Learning Objectives

1. *Understand* that entrepreneurial decisions can have a long-term impact on a firm's position within an industry.
2. *Develop* an understanding of competitive dynamics. Firms make decisions that not only affect their viability/profitability but that also impact competitors.
3. *Explore* decision-making approaches under environmental uncertainty.
4. *Evaluate* decision making in a global duopoly.
5. *Utilize* the information developed in SWOT analysis to make competitive decisions.
6. *Understand* that entrepreneurs can make strategic decisions that are erroneous (i.e., designing an aircraft that has fatal flaws, such as the A380 model with a wingspan that is not compatible with the infrastructure of major international airports.)
7. *Learn* that growth will come from BRIC markets, and that products such as aircraft need to be designed to meet the requirements of airports in foreign countries.

Key Words

Entrepreneurial Decision Making
Global Entrepreneurship
Internationalization

International Strategy
Managing Uncertainty

Abstract

Two entrepreneurs, Phil Conduit of Boeing and Andrew Harrison of Airbus, must predict how the international aircraft manufacturing industry will unfold. This is of significant importance because the development of new models of aircraft is time-consuming and expensive (i.e., substantial R & D investment). A correct prediction will position the company for growth for many years. An incorrect decision could lead to negative returns for many years to come. Global entrepreneurs, such as these leaders of Boeing and Airbus, need to make tough business decisions and grapple with diverse issues under uncertainty.

◎ The Dilemma

Phil Conduit, the entrepreneurial CEO of Boeing, and Andrew Harrison, the entrepreneurial CEO of Airbus, pondered if they had made the right decision in terms of developing the international marketplace. Mr. Conduit had selected the Boeing 787 as the next version of passenger aircraft. The 787 is a mid-range air-

Reprinted by permission of Michael Pettus and J. Mark Munoz.

craft that could be used within many developed markets (i.e., U.S. and EU). The aircraft can also be used along the Pacific Rim.

Andrew Harrison had taken a different approach to developing the commercial aircraft industry. Mr Harrison felt that the growth of the industry would be in long-haul (i.e., in excess of 12,000 miles) in markets such as those from the Pacific Rim to the U.S. or EU.

Which entrepreneur had made the correct decision?

The Decision Process

Entrepreneurship happens because entrepreneurs conceive of new products or services and then develop them through the launch and operation of new ventures. It is anchored on innovation, risk-taking, and proactiveness (Morris & Kuratko, 2001). A key driver in entrepreneurship, especially in a corporate environment, is innovation, and this process can be radical. The emergence of new radical technology and the subsequent development of technological innovation provide opportunities for entrepreneurs to find new organizations and for incumbent firms to explore new markets (Aldrich & Ruef, 2006). Scholars and practitioners have argued that corporate entrepreneurs must not innovate just occasionally, but often quickly and efficiently to ensure future revenue growth generated from customers purchasing new and improved products and services (Wooley, 2010). Firms that offer high-quality products, after radical change is introduced, clarify the opportunity and build market share to gain competitive advantage (Ireland & Webb, 2007). For instance, in the case of Apple, early creation of the iPod and the iTunes music website set the stage for its market domination, proprietary strength, and difficulty of product replication (Ketchen, Ireland, & Snow 2007). In this sense, entrepreneurs truly are the active element in new venture creation (Iriyama, Li, and Madhavan, 2010).

In global corporations, the ability to spot the right opportunity is essential (Morris & Kuratko, 2001). A company's ability to practice corporate entrepreneurship can lead to a path toward business success (Zahra, Kuratko, & Jennings, 1999). One action that corporate entrepreneurs take to better understand the competitive landscape is *environmental scanning*. Managers first scan the external environment to collect data, and then interpret the data by giving them meaning before actions are taken (Smith and Cao, 2007). External scanning enables managers to perceive external events and trends to identify the capabilities necessary for effective adaptation in dynamic markets (Castanias and Helfat, 2001). Indeed, external scanning is considered as the first link in the chain of managerial perceptions and actions that enables an organization to achieve environmental adaptation (Hambrick, 1982).

One way in which environmental scanning can be utilized is by developing a SWOT analysis of your own firm and those of your primary competitors. The global aircraft manufacturing industry is dominated by Airbus and Boeing. No other firm has a significant position within the industry. The SWOT analysis of Boeing, which was directed by Mr. Conduit, resulted in the following matrix:

TABLE 1.4 Boeing

STRENGTHS	WEAKNESSES
Brand recognition and overall reputation	Heavy reliance on suppliers
Entrepreneurial action paves the way in which the industry unfolds	Tarnished reputation due to delays in producing a finished product (Boeing 787)
Strategic alliances/networks for building and maintaining aircraft	Market trends have reduced available capital spending on asset replacement
Lower cost alternative to A-380 (Boeing 777)	Unsure of the 787's final profit margin
Has orders for 863 aircraft	Additional delays causing order cancellations are difficult to foresee
Most airports are not set up to accept an A-380, but they are for a 787	
Provides an aircraft with which Airbus cannot compete	
Minimal competition since barrier to entry for additional contenders is extremely high	

OPPORTUNITIES	THREATS
Most efficient transportation to date will provide buyers with greater revenue potential	Airbus continues to develop and sell directly competing products
Air traffic growth trends in China (8.8% annual) and India (25% annual) favor the 787 over the A-380	Technology used by Boeing suppliers in Japan could also be used by Airbus
Joint Strike Force (JSF) program participation	Potential foreign government contracts favoring Airbus because of their affiliations
Boeing's position within the defense industry	
Marketing a fuel efficient aircraft (787) during a period when countries need to reduce their dependence on foreign oil	

(*Source:* Annual Reports)

From a strength perspective, the 787 was forecast to cost much less than Airbus 380. Another strength that Boeing had over the A-380 pertained to airport runway restrictions. Aircraft were expected to acquire certain clearances while taxiing and on runways. The Boeing 787 had a wingspan of 60 meters. This wingspan is acceptable at virtually all global airports. However, the A-380 had a wingspan of 80 meters. This wingspan was not acceptable at major international airports. Certain airports, such as Heathrow in London, had begun the process of modifying its airport to provide A-380 service. Since this cost was over $100 million, Boeing felt that the issue provided a tactical advantage for Boeing.

The most significant weakness was the extensive delays that both Boeing and Airbus had encountered from a production perspective. This tactical problem could seriously impact the vision of both Conduit and Harrison. In other words, tactical constraints can seriously impact entrepreneurial vision. In addition, the global economic crisis had just begun. As such, capital was more difficult to obtain.

Boeing had a more favorable position within the industry. In 1997, Boeing had acquired McDonnell Douglas. This gave Boeing a solid position within the U.S. defense industry. This position within the military aircraft market provided opportunities for Boeing that were not available to Airbus. In the early 2000s, the U.S. government and the British government agreed to collaborate on the next generation of fighter aircraft. This program was called the Joint Strike Force (JSF) Program. The program was valued at $320 billion. Had Boeing not acquired McDonnell Douglas, it would not have been in position to bid on this program. This is a position that Airbus did not have. From an entrepreneurial perspective, Conduit felt that its core business (manufacturing commercial aircraft) was a cyclical business. He developed positions in other sectors in which Airbus could not establish a position. In addition, the 787 was much more fuel-efficient than the A-380. Further, Boeing felt that India and China were two developing markets that would welcome the mid-range 787.

The analysis that Mr. Harrison's team had accomplished at Airbus is depicted below:

 TABLE 1.5 **Airbus**

STRENGTHS	WEAKNESSES
Repeat customers due to brand recognition and overall reputation	Heavy reliance on foreign governments for funding and components
Large A-380 has no direct competitor with a comparable sized aircraft	Most airports are not set up to accept an A-380, but they are for a 787
Has orders for 121 aircraft	Market trends have reduced available capital spending on asset replacement
Made from advanced composite materials	
Extensive product lines provide revenue from various sources	Profit margins have decreased as the company needs to produce more than 400 A-380s to break even
Develops strong affiliations with many international governments	
Minimal competition since barrier to entry for additional contenders is extremely high	

OPPORTUNITIES	THREATS
Potential foreign government contracts favoring Airbus because of their affiliations	Boeing continues to develop and sell directly competing products
Take advantage of Boeing not having their 787 ready for mass production by selling Airbus alternatives	Technology learned through subcontracting can be used by the Japanese, and other countries in alliance, to directly compete
	Tarnished reputation due to many delays in producing the A-380 and A-350

(*Source:* Annual Reports)

Mr. Harrison felt that one of the primary benefits of the A-380 was that Boeing would not have a competing aircraft. The Boeing 747 was old, and used much more fuel than was expected on the A-380. Another strength of the A-380 was that it was made of advanced composite materials instead of metal. Lighter structure results in a reduction in fuel consumption, an increase in the plane's range, and durability of key parts (Michaels & Lunsford, 2007). In addition, there were many potential international contracts that would be favorable to Airbus because of their affiliations with foreign governments. In many international, developing markets, especially the BRIC markets, the government will decide how the purchase of commercial and military aircraft will evolve. In addition, the A-380 was scheduled to be in service in 2007, before the Boeing 787. The global crisis also was affecting Airbus as much as it was Boeing. Airbus was betting on the growth coming from long-haul markets. Its A-380 would not be suitable for short to medium-range flying. As with Boeing, Airbus had encountered many production delays that put some orders at risk. A related problem was that the cost to produce the A-380 was much greater than expected. This would have an adverse impact on profit margins.

The Way Forward

The case offers an opportunity to review and assess entrepreneurial decision making within a global business platform. The key question is: which entrepreneur would be successful and could provide his firm with long-term growth potential?

Discussion Questions

1. Which aircraft will be more successful, the Boeing 787 or the Airbus A-380? Refer to the Table below for discussion.

Commercial Airline Growth Market Outlook for 2008–2027

Type	Percentage share	Market value
Regional jets	2%	$80 billion
Single aisle	43%	$1,360 billion
Twin aisle	46%	$1,470 billion
747 and larger	9%	$290 billion

Source: Thompson Financial

2. (a) If the A-380 is successful, what position should Boeing adopt? (b) If the Boeing 787 is successful, what position should Airbus adopt?
3. How receptive would major international airports be to the A-380?
4. What other major points need to be considered for this entrepreneurial decision? While the major decision points have been addressed, could there be a few other remaining issues?
5. Which company SWOT analysis is more compelling and why?
6. From an entrepreneurial perspective, how will the aircraft manufacturing industry evolve in 2015 and beyond?
7. What lessons in global entrepreneurship can be learned from the case?

References

Agarwal, R., Audretsche, D., & Sarkar, M. (2007). The process of creative destruction: Knowledge spillovers, entrepreneurship, and economic growth. *Strategic Entrepreneurship Journal*, 1, 263–285.

Airbus. (2017). Passenger Aircraft. *Airbus*. Retrieved from http://www.airbus.com/aircraft/passenger-aircraft.html

Aldrich, H.E., & Ruef, M. (2006). *Organizations Evolving* (2nd ed.). Sage Publications: Thousand Oaks: CA.

Bao, S.R. & Lewellyn, K.B. (2017). The role of national culture and corruption on managing earnings around the world. *Science Direct*, 52 (6), 798-808.

Barkema, H.G. Bell, J.H., & Pennings, J.M. (1996). Foreign entry, cultural barriers, and learning. *Strategic Management Journal* 17 (2), 151–166.

Boeing. (2007, 2008). *Boeing Annual Reports*. Retrieved from http://www.annualreports.com/HostedData/AnnualReportArchive/b/NYSE_BA_2008.pf

Castanias, R., & Helfat, C. (2001). The managerial rents model: theory and empirical analysis. *Journal of Management*, 27, 661–678.

Chang, S.J. (1995). International expansion strategy of Japanese firms: Capability building through sequential entry. *Academy of Management Journal* 38, 383–407.

Dunlop-Hinkler, D., Kotabe, M., & Mudambi, R. (2010). A study of breakthrough versus incremental innovation: Corporate entrepreneurship in the global pharmaceutical industry. *Strategic Entrepreneurship* Journal, 2, 106–127.

EADS (AIRBUS). (2007, 2008). *AIRBUS Annual Reports*. Retrieved from http://company.airbus.com/investors/Annual-reports-and-registration-documents.html

Edmonton Journal. (Dec 8, 2009). New spaceship ushers in astro-tourism, Branson says. Retrieved from http://www.unityinvestments.com/uploads/EJ_Building_Permits_Surge_Dec_2009.pdf

Hambrick, D. (1982). Environmental scanning and organizational strategy. *Strategic Management Journal*, 3, 159–174.

Hambrick, D.C., & Mason, P.A. (1984). Upper echelons: The organization as a reflection of its top managers. *Academy of Management Review* 9, 193–206.

Hamel, G., & Prahalad, C.K. (1985). Do you really have a global strategy? *Harvard Business Review (July–August)*, 139–148.

Ireland, R.D., & Webb, J.W. (2007). Strategic entrepreneurship: Creating competitive advantage through streams of innovation. *Business Horizons* 50:49–59.

Iriyama, A., Li., & Madhavan, R. (2010). Spiky globalization of venture capital investments. *Strategic Entrepreneurship Journal* 16, 128–145.

Johanson, J., & Vahlne, J.E. (1990). The mechanism of internationalization. *International Marketing Review* 7 (4), 11–24.

Ketchen, D., Ireland, R., & Snow, G. (2007). Strategic entrepreneurship, collaborative innovation, and wealth creation. *Strategic Entrepreneurship Journal* 1, 371–386.

Michaels, D., & Lunsford, J. (2007). Airbus faces wide gap in A350 orders. *Wall Street Journal*, 250, 64. Retrieved from: http://biz.yahoo.com/wallstreet/070613/sb118169743230833375_id.html?.v=1

Morris, H., & Kuratko, D.F. (2001). Corporate *Entrepreneurship: Entrepreneurial Development Within Organizations*. Harcourt College Publishers: Orlando, FL.

Morris, M.H., & Kuratko, D.F. (2002). *Corporate Entrepreneurship*. South-Western College Publishers: Mason: OH.

Mutzabaugh, B. (2017). Boeing: 747's future as a passenger aircraft is bleak. *USA TODAY*. Retrieved from https://www.usatoday.com/story/travel/flights/todayinthesky/2017/06/20/boeing-admits-its-747-queen-skies-has-no-future-passenger-plane/412666001/

Smith, K., & Cao, Q. (2007). An entrepreneurial perspective on the firm-environment relationship. *Strategic Entrepreneurship Journal*, 1, 329–344.

Snow, C. (2007). Innovation. *Strategic Entrepreneurship Journal*, 1, 101–102.

Wooley, J. (2010). Technology emergence through entrepreneurship across multiple industries. *Strategic Entrepreneurship Journal* 1, 1–21.

Williamson, P., Zyglidopoulos, S., & Symeou. P.C. (2017) Internationalization as a driver of the corporate social performance of extractive industry firms. *Science Direct*.

Zahra, S.A., Kuratko, D.F., & Jennings, D.F. (1999). Corporate Entrepreneurship and Wealth Creation: Contemporary and Emerging Perspectives. *Entrepreneurship Theory and Practice* 24(2), 5–9.

Relevant Videos

https://www.youtube.com/watch?v=NUsvqtso05s

https://www.youtube.com/watch?v=pEQecnUKOfU

https://www.youtube.com/watch?v=FuVccOroftg

https://www.youtube.com/watch?v=VQg6NOxztZ0

Environmental and Contextual Sources of Global Variation in Entrepreneurial Activities

SHOPPING FOR SUNGLASSES AT THE BURJAMAN CENTER: THE CASE OF A SHADY BUYER

Dianne H.B. Welsh, The University of North Carolina at Greensboro
Ibrahim Al-Fahim, Al-Faheem General Trading Company

Learning Objectives

1. *Examine* shoplifting laws and security device protection.
2. *Respond* to the way the woman was treated by police and store personnel.
3. *Examine* the possibility of a legal action on the retailer's part.
4. *Determine* the proper management response to the situation.
5. *Determine* how management can comply with the law and culture of the country, yet prevent shoplifting.
6. *Evaluate* the current policies and procedures which relate to this situation.

Key Words

Culture

Ethics

Islam

Retail sales

Security

Abstract

This case describes an alleged shoplifting incident. It requires students to consider relevant issues in determining an appropriate managerial response. These issues include: retail store security, shoplifting, employee training, legal regulations, culture, and gender issues.

 Dilemma

A beautiful lady came into the French Gallery, a small specialty shop located in a large mall in the United Arab Emirates (U.A.E.). The store sells colognes, cosmetics, jewelry, watches, sunglasses, and gift items, for men and women. There are five employees working at any one time in the shop. Both men and women are employed as retail clerks in the store. Sales representatives from cosmetic and perfume companies also work in the shop on a varying schedule. Most of these representatives work between one and three days per week. A few representatives work every day but Friday. Friday is honored as a Holy Day, although retail stores stay open in the U.A.E. on Fridays since most people are off of work. The sales representative's wages are shared by the local distributors and the retail store.

A salesman, Mr. Ali, believed he saw a female shopper put something under her jacket, but he was not positive. He told the store manager, Mr. Faheem, about the incident. A couple of weeks later, the same woman returned to the store. This time the salesman immediately alerted the manager. Mr. Faheem and Mr. Ali both watched her. She didn't notice. She tried on various sunglasses, picking up three at a time to try on instead of trying them individually. She slipped some pairs of sunglasses in her purse. When the store manager, Mr. Faheem, and the salesman, Mr. Ali, approached her and accused her of stealing, she started crying. Then she proceeded to accuse Mr. Ali of sexual harassment in a screaming voice. She claimed that he accused her of stealing because she refused his advances. When Mr. Faheem attempted to detain her until the police arrived, she darted to another entrance. The store manager did not want to create a scene by chasing the woman in front of the customers. This would have created a negative image for the store because it is against the culture as well as the religious norms of the Middle East to physically restrain a woman. Before she had a chance to escape, the manager ran to the door and locked it. The mall security arrived within a matter of minutes and waited until police got there. Meanwhile, the customers continued to shop. The door was locked so they couldn't leave anyway. This incident happened on Friday, the busiest day of the week for the store. There were fewer employees working that day because some of the cosmetic and perfume company sales representatives were off.

When the police arrived, they discovered that the suspected shoplifter was a woman, so they went back to the station and returned with a female police officer. After they completed the initial investigation at the store, the officers took the suspected shoplifter back to the station. She vehemently denied stealing any sunglasses, even though Mr. Faheem and Mr. Ali had taken them out of her purse. The police officer searched her purse at the station. He found another pair of sunglasses with the French Gallery price tag on them, a two-week tourist visa, and a passport from Lebanon. The police later searched her hotel room and found more stolen property. The woman was convicted of theft and sentenced to three months in jail. After serving her time, she was sent back to Lebanon.

Later, she was identified as part of an organized crime ring. The ring hired beautiful women, who possessed tourist visas, to steal. In Middle Eastern Countries, where Islam is the predominant religion, it is morally unacceptable, and usually illegal, for a woman to be stopped or held. These women, consequently, take advantage of local shop owners who are inhibited by laws or customs. When their visas expire, these women leave the country with a large amount of stolen goods. There are many of these rings operating now.

Note:

Security devices are seldom used in the U.A.E. because most people consider it offensive to be monitored for theft. Compared to most Western countries, shoplifting and other misdemeanor thefts are relatively infrequent. However, in recent years theft has become more common. Retailers are beginning to explore options available to reduce shoplifting and employee theft.

Discussion Questions

1. Should the law be changed regarding women? Should a male police officer be allowed to detain a woman suspected of committing a crime? Why or why not?
2. Could the incident have been handled differently from a public-relations perspective?
3. Should the visa insurance procedures and regulations be more stringent? Currently, anyone who wants to visit the U.A.E. for two weeks is automatically issued a visa.
4. Could Mr. Faheem, the store manager, have done anything differently?
5. Should Mr. Ali or the other retail sales clerks have proceeded differently? If so, what type of training do you recommend?
6. Could the mall security have done anything differently?
7. What could the store do to improve its security and not offend the customers?

References

Elhais, H. (2014, March 3). United Arab Emirates: Theft article: Punishments. *Mondaq*. Retrieved from http://www.mondaq.com/x/296782/Crime/Theft+Article+Punishments

Human Rights Watch. (2017). United Arab Emirates Events of 2016 World Report. *Human Rights Watch*. Retrieved from https://www.hrw.org/world-report/2017/country-chapters/united-arab-emirates

Ilkkaracan, P. (2016). *Deconstructing sexuality in the Middle East: Challenges and discourses*. Taylor & Francis Group.

OSAC. (2017). United Arab Emirates 2017 Crime & safety report: Dubai. *OSAC*. Retrieved from https://www.osac.gov/pages/ContentReportDetails.aspx?cid=21353

TeachMideast. (2017). Introduction to women and gender roles in the Middle East. *TeachMideast*. Retrieved from http://teachmideast.org/articles/introduction-women-gender-roles-middle-east/

Relevant Videos

Eyeglass Security Glasses Security:
https://www.youtube.com/watch?v=H5IQeKhiG0E&t=1s

Preventing Shop Theft, Employee Training - Take a Good Look:
https://www.youtube.com/watch?v=vwo_GwdtROY

Joe Williams of TRA talks about Organized Retail Crime:
https://www.youtube.com/watch?v=AYqb0AdGEVU

Organized shoplifting rings on the rise:
https://www.youtube.com/watch?v=ID0Ise6_46Q

Busting Organized Retail Crime Rings:
https://www.youtube.com/watch?v=JCncdGb3Lzc

RFID-enabled Store – Overhead:
https://www.youtube.com/watch?v=eQYs6rqGY-k

Chapter Three

GLOBAL ENTREPRENEURSHIP STRATEGY

STARBUCKS INTERNATIONAL ENTERS KUWAIT

Dianne H.B. Welsh, The University of North Carolina at Greensboro
Peter Raven, Seattle University
Nasser Al-Mutair, Seattle University (Student)

Learning Objectives

1. *Evaluate* opportunities in a foreign country.
2. *Understand* various issues to consider when entering a foreign country.
3. *Understand* business culture, customs, and regulations in a foreign country.
4. *Learn* about the Gulf States and their differences and similarities.
5. *Learn* appropriate market entry strategies and methods.
6. *Learn* appropriate business models, such as licensing, franchising, joint ventures, wholly owned subsidiary, etc.

Key Words

Middle East	Strategic Alliance
Gulf states	Franchise
Oman, and UAE	Business model
Gulf War	Starbucks

Abstract

This case describes the situation surrounding the entrance of Starbucks International Coffee into the Kuwait marketplace. It requires students to consider relevant small-business and entrepreneurship issues in determining an appropriate response. These issues include: international joint ventures, culture, gender issues, marketing channels, and cross-cultural management issues.

Professor Raven's teaching interests include Internet marketing, entrepreneurship, international marketing, and marketing research. He taught at Washington State University and at Eastern Washington University before coming to Seattle University as an associate professor. His research interests include export marketing, cross-cultural consumer behavior, international marketing management, global marketing ethics, global e-commerce, and global Internet marketing. He has published in a number of international scholarly journals, including the Journal of International Marketing, Journal of Consumer Marketing, Journal of Marketing Channels, Franchising Research: An International Journal, Journal of Global Marketing, Journal of Advertising Research, *and others.*

◎ Introduction

After a long and tiring flight from Seattle to Kuwait via London, the Kuwaiti Airlines jetliner finally lands and Mr. Howard Behar mentally prepares to meet with Mr. Nasser Al-Mutair. This meeting has been anxiously anticipated by both parties.

Nasser is a young businessman who recently graduated with a degree in marketing from a regional university in the state of Washington. This is where he became familiar with Starbucks Coffee and learned of Mr. Behar, the President of Starbucks International Coffee Company.

Nasser had enjoyed the Starbucks specialty coffees as a student, and had observed how many Americans and other international students also loved to drink this popular coffee. Knowing the fondness that Arab people have for coffee, Nasser thought that a specialty coffee shop might be successful in Kuwait, which has seen an increasing number of Americans and other foreigners since the Gulf War. As a marketing student, however, Nasser realized the importance of planning, obtaining information, and getting expert opinions. This plan would cause for international franchising. According to *The Balance* (2017), international franchising is a strategic way to reduce dependence on domestic demand and grow new, future revenue and profit centers worldwide. He had personally invited Mr. Behar to visit with him in Kuwait City, so that Mr. Behar could see the sites Nasser had selected, and to discuss this possible expansion in person. While the deal was far from complete, Nasser was very confident that his plan would succeed, but was anxious to hear Mr. Behar's opinion.

In fact, Nasser had to persuade not only Mr. Behar that his idea was sound, but also his uncle, Abdul Al-Mutair. Abdul Al-Mutair had long been a prominent financial leader in Kuwait, primarily involved with importing consumer products and trading. He had recently become interested in the service industry. With the increasing number of foreigners living in Kuwait, even for relatively short periods of time, he realized that traditional restaurants were inadequate to meet their desires. After Nasser had returned from the United States with his newly acquired degree, he and his uncle had long talks about what they might do together. Nasser had some interesting ideas and might be a good person to explore new ventures. Abdul Al-Mutair was considering financing Nasser's venture if it seemed feasible and profitable.

Mr. Behar was anxious to meet with Nasser and was also very curious. He had never been to the Middle East, and was uncertain what he would find there. He had had little time to learn about the country or culture, but he had certainly heard about Kuwait and had seen pictures of it during the Gulf War. In addition, Mr. Behar was very interested in expanding his international operations. His main concerns included the image of Starbucks International and profitability. Although curious, he had a number of misgivings about expansion into the Middle East.

As Mr. Behar stepped out of the plane, Nasser met him and escorted him rapidly through customs and the unfamiliar airport. After a brief tour of the city in a chauffeured Mercedes limousine, they arrived at a small restaurant near the center of town for some refreshments. Behar was taken aback by the unique beauty of Kuwait City.

The restaurant was a small, nondescript locale. They began to talk about the trip and other small talk, when Mr. Behar suddenly said, "I really would like to try some of your traditional coffee." Nasser said, "Yes, we have excellent Arabian coffee. This restaurant also serves French Press and Turkish coffees. You should try some Turkish coffee. It will be different from coffees you've had in other places." Mr. Behar said, "Yes. It's been a long time since I have had Turkish coffee." Nasser ordered some for both of them.

While waiting for his coffee, Mr. Behar was able to observe the restaurant, which reminded him of some of the restaurants in Italy where Mr. Howard Schultz, President of Starbucks, first got the idea for Starbucks coffee shops. The coffee was soon served. Mr. Behar had forgotten how good this coffee was and how it resembled straight espresso in texture and strength. He thought to himself, "This is either a very good sign for our coffee-shops—the Kuwaitis already like richer, stronger coffee—or it could be a bad sign in that they might not want another choice. He listened attentively as Nasser spoke, "We love our Turkish and Arab coffees, but I know many of the Kuwaitis who have spent time in the United States, especially the Pacific Northwest; miss their espressos and would like a variety of coffee choices." Mr. Behar and Nasser continued talking for some time. However, they realized that a decision would have to be made quickly, as Mr. Behar had to be in Europe the next day, where he was opening five new stores.

Kuwait and the Middle East

Geography

Kuwait is located in the Northeast corner of the Arabian Gulf. To the south and southeast, it shares a border with Saudi Arabia. To the north and west is Iraq. The distance between the northern and southern borders is about 200 kilometers (124 miles) and the distance between the eastern and western borders about 170 kilometers (106 miles). The total area of the State of Kuwait is 17,818 square kilometers (6,969 miles).

Most of Kuwait's mainland is flat, sandy desert that slopes gradually to the sea. The Kuwait mainland has no mountains, rivers, or other natural features. Historically, it was a crossing for nomadic tribes and caravans.

The weather is characterized by long, hot, dry summers and short, warm winters. Sometimes there is quite a bit of rain. In the summer, there are many dust storms and the humidity increases dramatically.

There has always been a strong connection between Kuwait and the sea. This relationship has shaped the character of the Kuwaitis. The main source of income came from the sea in earlier times, and the sea is still a great source of pride and activity. Many people, including young people, still spend much time fishing. In the evenings, many people can be found on the beaches.

Population

The total population of Kuwait is about 2.1 million. If the current rate of growth remains the same, it will be approximately 3 million by the year 2000. A large percentage of the population is non-Kuwaitis. Since the Gulf War, the country's demographic patterns have been changing. Foreign nationals make up about 55 percent of Kuwait's population. The largest group is from Pakistan and India. There are about 6,200 Americans in Kuwait, mostly military personnel. They compose the largest Western community.

Economy

In the last five to ten years, an increasing number of companies have realized the opportunities that exist in the Persian Gulf markets. This region has often been described as an area where there are many profitable opportunities for the following reasons:

- high purchasing power
- heavy reliance on imported products
- massive consumer demand due to the fast-growing population

Thus, the economic profile of the region suggests increasing opportunities. Although analysts expect that the Middle East will become an extremely important area for business, part of the growth will depend upon peace in the Middle East. For example, Israel has not been able to fully participate in the Middle East market since Arab countries have traditionally not done business with Israel. Whether the Middle East becomes a unified market depends largely on future political agreements.

Many people believe that tourism will continue to grow in the Middle East. Tourism has not been highly developed. Although tourism has continued to increase at an average of 6.5 percent per year since 1983, most of the tourists to the Middle East countries are from other Middle East countries. In 1992, for example, just 27 percent of the tourists were from the Americas or Europe. The most popular tourist place by far is Egypt, with Israel and Bahrain the next most popular places for people to visit.

The Middle East is attracting the attention of such developers as Howard Johnson's Motor Inns, which has just built a 115-room hotel in Dubai, United Arab Emirates (UAE). The chain is planning to do more building in the Middle East in the next few years. Also, in the last several years, many fast-food franchised restaurants have opened in Persian Gulf countries. Some examples include Kentucky Fried Chicken, McDonald's, Baskin-Robbins, Hardees's, Wendy's, Popeye's Fried Chicken, and so forth. Entry into Kuwait might facilitate entry into some of these other countries in the Middle East.

Strategic Alliances

While franchises are a popular way of entering some international markets, strategic alliances are increasingly utilized. In fact, some countries required strategic alliances over other entry modes because they directly involve local firms. A study conducted by U.S. commercial analysts, on the Egyptian and Kuwaiti markets, discovered opportunities for American companies. Its findings suggest that these markets would grow to an estimated $51 million in 1992, and are expected to increase from 10 to 20 percent each year on average over the following three years. Revenues from foreign retail stores in Kuwait totaled about $8 million in 1993 and are expected to rise at an average annual rate of 25 percent through 1996.

Many of Kuwait's residents have large disposable incomes and are likely to buy American products. Although most of the current U.S. firms in Kuwait are fast food restaurants, other opportunities are developing. Kuwaitis are eager to meet with foreign companies. One market characteristic that U.S. businesses should understand is that Kuwaiti tastes tend to change, switching from traditional to new and trendy. Kuwaitis travel frequently and are aware of the latest fashions in Europe and the U.S. As a result, some businesses go out of vogue after about 10 years on average. While its economy is still recovering from the war, average annual growth for all franchise areas is expected to reach 25 percent through 1996, but could reach as high as 60 percent for some franchises.

As indicated earlier, the most common type of franchise is fast food, but there are opportunities in other areas, as well. Based on a recent market research study, some other areas of potential for franchisers in Kuwait include:

- **Automotive Repair and Service;**
- **Recreation.** Travel, sports hobbies;
- **Beauty and Health Aids;**
- **Carpet Dyeing and Cleaning;**
- **Children's Entertainment Services** and educational products and services;
- **Printing and Copying centers;**
- **Coffee Shops;**
- **Florist Shops.**

Although competition in the Kuwaiti market is tough, American companies could do well because a large number of Kuwaitis have studied in the United States and are familiar with U.S. firms. Despite this, Japan has passed the U.S. in the past year as the leading exporter to Kuwait.

Franchises and strategic alliances mainly compete in two ways: through advertising campaigns in the local media and local TV stations; or through promotions, offering free meals for a certain number of purchases or free children's gifts. Kuwait has four main shopping areas, located in Salmiya, Kuwait City Center, Hawalli, and Fahaheel.

Kuwait has a free market with few restrictions on imports. Customs duties are 4 percent across the board. Standards and label requirements apply to some imports. One study advises foreign companies to visit the country to become familiar with the size of the market and its characteristics. In general, to conduct business in Kuwait, every foreign firm should have a local agent, distributor, or representative.

The Coffee Shop Market

In the U.S., there are hundreds of coffee shops, drive-ins, and restaurants that offer specialty coffees. One of the most successful brands of coffee has been Starbucks. Its success in the U.S. may translate to success in Kuwait, if everything is done correctly. Many people in Kuwait drink coffee on a regular basis. In fact, it is considered a high act of hospitality to serve coffee to guests. One of the most popular coffee drinks in Kuwait is Turkish coffee, which is similar to straight espresso coffee served in the Pacific Northwest.

Starbucks Coffee

Starbucks Coffee is a chain of coffee specialty stores that began in 1971 as one small shop in Seattle's Pike Place Market. In the past nine years, it has gone through rapid growth, expanding from 11 stores in 1987 to a total of 500 today.

Mr. Howard Schultz had been a buyer for Starbucks Coffee since the early 1980s. On a coffee-buying trip to Milan, Italy, he noticed that crowds of people gathered each day in coffee bars to drink their specialty coffees. Schultz wondered if the same thing could happen elsewhere. Back in Seattle, he attempted to persuade his bosses to try the coffee bar idea and go beyond just selling coffee beans to restaurants. They refused. Schultz raised $1.7 million dollars and opened his own cafe in downtown Seattle. The first coffee he served was Starbucks. In less than a year, he had opened two more stores. Subsequently, he bought out Starbucks from his former employers for $4 million.

Specialty coffees have slowly taken business away from the traditional canned coffees. The high-quality coffee bean industry created $717 million in sales in 1990, with a 13.5 percent share of the coffee market. By 1991, the penetration was even deeper. Gourmet sales had reached $800 million and their market share rose to 17.7 percent. In the meantime, coffee shops grew at a rapid rate. By 1992, Seattle had 150 coffee bars.

Starbucks' mission statement reads, "To establish Starbucks as the premier purveyor of the finest coffee in the world while maintaining our uncompromising principles as we grow." Some of the principles of the company are treating everyone with respect and dignity, buying the best available coffees, developing loyal customers, contributing to the environment, and making a profit.

While this hardly makes the company unique, what does make the company special is that it seems to understand the connection between delivering a great cup of coffee and treating their employees with respect. One training manager suggests that the quality of everything comes down to the employee experience. The company's culture is built on very strict standards for how coffee should be prepared and delivered, combined with an empowering attitude toward the employees who deliver the coffee to the customers.

Starbucks is opening 150 stores a year in new markets across the United States. Almost two million Americans visit Starbucks coffee shops each week. During 1995, it planned to open 200 new stores and to expand overseas. However, growth is beginning to slow in the American market, due to intense competition. Also, higher coffee prices have hurt the domestic industry. In 1994, Starbucks earned approximately $13 million. International expansion is a strategic plan and occurs through Starbucks International, of which Mr. Howard Behar is President. Starbucks International policy requires strategic alliances in its development of international markets.

Many people believe that Starbucks is the model for growth in a small company. When sales start to take off, many small companies have problems and begin to fail. But it is said that Schultz has placed top quality and experienced managers from larger chains into Starbucks and has invested heavily in personnel, information systems, and facilities. The company is constantly checking its image, its interior design, and locations. Starbucks believes that site selection is a key to success. The real estate division begins working up to nine months before a store is opened. They collect large amounts of information on the income, education, and coffee-buying habits in the new market.

Schultz feels the market is far from saturated. Slow growth in established stores is not a concern. In September of 1994, Starbucks bought its first acquisition, The Coffee Connection, Inc., of Boston, Massachusetts. In 1995, Starbucks planned to team up with foreign partners to open stores in Europe and Asia. However, it is possible that the Starbucks "chic" may not be popular overseas. Starbucks has a joint venture with Pepsi to bottle its iced coffees.

To summarize, Starbucks has a strong reputation for quality because of the following:

- The company goes to extreme lengths to buy the very finest Arabica coffees available on world markets, regardless of price;
- The company's freshness and quality are legendary. Beans that are held in bins for more than a week are donated to charity;
- Every piece of coffee-brewing equipment that is sold has been tested and evaluated;
- Each Starbucks employee is extensively trained to ensure that customers receive knowledgeable service.

During the last 20 years, consumer interest in fine coffees has increased greatly. All over the country, people who used to be content with canned commercial blends are now searching for fresher, more flavorful alternatives. Whole bean coffee is now sold in kitchen shops, delicatessens, grocery stores, and supermarkets. Coffee lovers have learned, however, that buying whole beans does not guarantee great coffee. The freshness standards set at Starbucks in 1971 are still being used today. Over the years, Starbucks has grown to become one of the largest purchasers of high-quality Arabica coffees in the United States. They also have in-store coffee bars that have set the international standards for espresso, cappuccino and drip coffee.

Most of the specialty drinks use espresso, which is a brewing method, a blend of beans, a roast color, and a beverage. Espresso is a rapid method of brewing which uses pressure, not gravity to brew. Starbucks Espresso is a unique blend of Central American and Indonesian coffees that yields a thick, caramel-sweet, and highly aromatic espresso.

A Decision

As Nasser takes Mr. Behar to his hotel for the evening, each has many thoughts and ideas to consider. Tomorrow promises to be a pivotal day, as a meeting is scheduled with Nasser's uncle, Abdul Al-Mutair. Nasser knows that Abdul will ask some very penetrating questions and will expect direct, well thought-out answers. Howard Behar also has mixed feelings and is anxious to get Mr. Abdul Al-Mutair's perspective. He suspects that, with the right contract, a Kuwaiti operation would be very successful. Tomorrow will be Mr. Behar's last day in Kuwait, as he must leave in the late afternoon for his flight to Frankfurt.

Discussion Questions

1. What questions should Mr. Behar ask Mr. Abdul Al-Mutair tomorrow?
2. What questions would you anticipate Mr. Abdul Al-Mutair asking Behar? Nasser?
3. Should Nasser and his uncle invest in a Starbucks International joint venture in Kuwait? Why or why not?
4. What further information would you like to obtain before making the decision for Nasser and his uncle? Where and how will you obtain this information?
5. Assuming the decision is to proceed, what information is needed to select a location? How will this information be obtained? Why is it important?
6. What specifics should Behar insist on in a contract with the Al-Mutair? Why?
7. Assuming all parties agree to a joint venture, how should the coffee shop differ from those in the U.S. in order to satisfy the needs of Kuwaitis?
8. What type of marketing strategy should be adopted?

◎ Starbucks Enters Kuwait Case

Epilogue and Update 2001 (March 2001)

Since this case was written (1996), a number of changes have occurred. Starbucks did enter the Kuwait market and now has six stores in Kuwait. Global expansion has also increased with 3881 stores now open, 643 of which are outside North America. (*Business Wire*, February 1, 2001). Also since expanding to Kuwait, Starbucks has introduced its Crystal Tower store, the first store with a Reserve coffee bar. (Starbucks, 2017). Another major change from Starbucks includes their recent expansion into selling their Starbucks products in grocery stores (Whitten, 2016). CEO Kevin Johnson believes that in order for Starbucks to survive, merchants need to create unique and immersive in-store experiences (Cowley, 2017).

Starbucks Coffee International opened its first store in Kuwait on February 9, 1999, at the Souk Sharq, Gulf Road, Sharq. It is operated in partnership with M.H. Alshaya Co. W.L.L., with whom Starbucks Coffee International has a multi-jurisdictional licensing arrangement (*Business Wire*, May 31, 2000). Kuwait serves as the gateway into the rest of the Middle East countries as, together, the two companies already have or plan to open stores in Saudi Arabia, Oman, Bahrain, United Arab Emirates, Qatar, and Lebanon ("Starbucks Opens Another Store Abroad—In Kuwait," *Seattle Post Intelligencer*, Seattle, WA, February 9, 1999).

As quoted at the time,*

Starbucks Coffee International and M.H. Alshaya Co.W.L.L. announced today plans to expand into the Gulf Cooperation Council (GCC) countries with the opening of the first Starbucks retail location in Kuwait at the Souk Sharq, Gulf Road, Sharq.

At the newly opened store, Starbucks customers enjoy a wide selection of Starbucks authentic, premium coffee beverages, a choice of around 15 varieties and blends of the finest arabica coffee beans, freshly baked and tasty local food offerings and an impressive range of coffee brewing equipment and accessories.

In its multi-jurisdictional licensing agreement with M. H. Alshaya Co.W.L.L. of Kuwait, Starbucks retail locations will also be opened in the other five GCC countries (Saudi Arabia, Oman, Bahrain, United Arab Emirates, and Qatar) and Lebanon.

"We are excited with our opening in Kuwait as it will serve as our gateway into the GCC countries. It will also create wonderful expansion opportunities for us to the rest of the Middle East," said Howard Behar, President of Starbucks Coffee International. "Starbucks is also proud to have found a great partner who not only has expertise in the region's marketplace, but also shares our business principles and people values."

"The people of Kuwait will wholeheartedly embrace the unique specialty coffee experience of Starbucks as the company offers the best of class in everything it does," said Mr. Mohammed Alshaya, CEO Retail Division of M.H. Alshaya Co. W.L.L. "Starbucks will be a success in Kuwait as it stands for uncompromising commitment to people, quality coffee and innovative products."

M.H. Alshaya Co.W.L.L. is one of the largest and most successful operators of leading global retail brands in the Middle East. It is a family-owned business recognized for its leadership role in real estate development, hotel management, warehousing, car dealerships, food services, and retail operations.

Starbucks Coffee International is a wholly-owned subsidiary of Starbucks Coffee Company (Nasdaq: SBUX). Starbucks is the leading retailer, roaster, and brand of specialty coffee in North America. Kuwait represents Starbucks' eleventh international market to open retail locations. Starbucks has retail locations in Japan, Hawaii, Singapore, the Philippines, Taiwan, Thailand, the United Kingdom, New Zealand, Malaysia, China (Beijing), and has signed a licensing agreement in South Korea.

About M. H. Alshaya Co. W.L.L.

Alshaya has become a byword for trading and commerce excellence in the Arabian Gulf. Since its foundation in 1890, they have become a major player within a variety of sectors; initially in the Kingdom of Saudi Arabia and Kuwait and, more recently, throughout the Middle East. Today, they have over 4,000 employees; of these, more than 2,100 work within the retail division (Alshaya Home Page, accessed 3/18/2001, http://www.alshaya.com/leader.htm).

Alshaya Retail operates more than 20 international retail brands throughout the Middle East—the Kingdom of Saudi Arabia, Kuwait, the United Arab Emirates, Bahrain, Qatar, Oman, and Lebanon. These include many of the world's leading clothing, health & beauty, fashion and restaurant names, all carefully chosen to bring the highest brand and label quality to the region's premier retail locations. Alshaya Retail represents a number of lines, including The Body Shop, Mothercare, Liz Claiborne, Laura Ashley, Clinique, Esteé Lauder, and Starbucks and currently operates over 200 stores in seven countries.

Kuwait and Saudi Arabia each have over 60 outlets, with more than 30 in the UAE and a significant presence in Bahrain, Qatar, Oman, and Lebanon. They are also looking at retail opportunities in Egypt, Jordan, and Syria.

Starbucks Coffee International, and M.H. Alshaya Co. W.L.L., celebrated the opening of the first Starbucks retail store in Qatar on August 1, 2000. Qatar represents the fourth country in the Middle East that Starbucks has entered. Following the signing of a multi-jurisdictional licensing agreement with M.H. Alshaya Co. W.L.L. of Kuwait, the first Starbucks store was opened in Kuwait on February 9, 1999. In Lebanon, the first Starbucks store was opened in Beirut on November 29, 1999, while Dubai celebrated the opening of the first Starbucks store on May 31, 2000. "The Middle East is an exciting market for Starbucks," said Peter Malsen, president of Starbucks Coffee International. "In the Middle East market, our partner, M.H. Alshaya Co. W.L.L., has been instrumental in the phenomenal reception we have received in Kuwait, Lebanon, and Dubai. We plan to expand into Saudi Arabia and Bahrain by the end of the year." (*Alshaya Company News*, http://www.alshaya.com/news.htm, accessed 3/18/2001).

"The opening of our first retail store in Qatar is a celebration of Starbucks uncompromising commitment to people, quality coffee, and innovative products," said Mr. Mohammed Alshaya, CEO of M.H. Alshaya Co. W.L.L. "The coffee culture in Qatar will be greatly invigorated with Starbucks entry as the market leader in the country." M.H. Alshaya Co. W.L.L. is one of the largest and most successful operators of leading global retail brands in the Middle East. Its affiliate company, Dareen International Co. (Qatar) W.L.L., will operate Starbucks stores in Qatar (*Alshaya Company News*, http://www.alshaya.com/news. htm, accessed 3/18/2001).

Starbucks Coffee France EURL, a wholly owned subsidiary of Starbucks Coffee International, and Dareen International Co. L.L.C., an affiliate company of M.H. Alshaya Co. W.L.L., opened the first Starbucks retail store in Dubai City, Dubai. Also, through a multi-jurisdictional *licensing* agreement with M.H. Alshaya Co. W.L.L., Starbucks has stores in Kuwait and Lebanon (Cuevas, Li and Darek Johnson, "Methods to Build International Business: Starbucks Demonstrates Successful Expansion Methods," *Signs of the Times,* http://www.signweb. com/management/cont/management0900.html, accessed 3/18/2001).

Starbucks Coffee International is a wholly owned subsidiary of Starbucks Coffee Company, the leading retailer, roaster and brand of specialty coffee in the world. In addition to the Republic of Korea, Starbucks has retail locations in Japan, Hawaii, Singapore, the Philippines, Taiwan, Thailand, the United Kingdom, New Zealand, Malaysia, Beijing, Kuwait, Lebanon, the United Arab Emirates (Dubai), Qatar, Hong Kong, Shanghai, Australia, Saudi Arabia and Bahrain.

References

Anonymous (1994). Franchising Opportunities: Fast Food and More, Part I. *Middle East Executive Reports*, *17*, 2.

Anonymous (1994). Franchising Opportunities, Part II. *Middle East Executive Reports*, *17*, 3.

Cowley, S. (2017). Starbucks Closes Online Store to Focus on In-Person Experience. *The New York Times*, Retrieved from https://www.nytimes.com/2017/10/01/business/starbucks-online-store.html

Delaney, L. (2017). International Franchising: A Global Strategic Initiative. *The Balance*. Retrieved from https://www.thebalance.com/international-franchising-a-global-strategic-initiative-1953329

Dravo, E. (1994). Java Jive. *Financial World*, *94*, 17.

Filipczak, B. (1995). Trained by Starbucks, and Born to be Wired. *Training*, *73*.

Leonidaou, Leonidas, C. (1995). The Saudi Distribution System: Structure, Operation and Behavior. *Marketing Intelligence and Planning*, *13*, 11-27.

Oleck, J. (1993). When Worlds Collide. *Restaurant Business*, *92*, 10.

Saudi Electricity Company, Saudi Electricity (2008). The Saudi Arabian Distribution Code. *Electricity & Co-Generation Regulatory Authority*, *00*, 1.

Scarpa, J. (1995). Java Nation. *Restaurant Business Magazine*, *94*, 13.

Starbucks Corporation. (2017). Starbucks Introduces Unique Store in Crystal Tower, Kuwait. *Starbucks EMEA* News. Retrieved from https://news.starbucks.com/emea/starbucks-store-kuwait

Wang, G. (1995). A Natural Extension: A new name along with a plan for hotels spanning the globe. *Lodging Hospitality*, *51*, 10.

Whitten, S. (2016). Starbucks knows how you like your coffee. *CNBC*. Retrieved from https://www.cnbc.com/2016/04/06/big-data-starbucks-knows-how-you-like-your-coffee.html

Relevant Videos

*Howard Schultz on Starbucks' quest for healthy growth
http://www.mckinsey.com/Videos/video?vid=2340984655001&plyrid=2399849255001

*Starbucks's Schultz on Growth Strategy, Asian Markets
https://www.youtube.com/watch?v=7dlNtUGKkUI

*Howard Schultz on Global Reach and Local Relevance at Starbucks
https://www.youtube.com/watch?v=tTbjDoLQQKw

*Howard Schultz: No Brand Has Accomplished What Starbucks Has in China
https://www.youtube.com/watch?v=G-pO6ubvxek

Howard Schultz- Starbucks' CEO Talks About His Business
https://www.youtube.com/watch?v=0g0VhF4wBo4

The Man Behind Starbucks Reveals How He Changed the World
https://www.youtube.com/watch?v=LnA7n9qSB7E

Howard Schultz on Leadership
https://www.youtube.com/watch?v=K1WmackWSQY

*How Starbucks Built a Global Brand, UCLA
https://www.youtube.com/watch?v=_kAiEO6jP48

*The arrival of Starbucks in South Africa: Howard Schultz
https://www.youtube.com/watch?v=-rz-Q2AUql8

* indicates international content

THE JOURNEY OF DOORSTEP ENTREPRENEURSHIP: A CASE ON JAIPUR RUGS

Mahesh Chandra Joshi, Ph.D., Poornima University, India
Dianne H.B. Welsh, Ph.D., University of North Carolina Greensboro
Meghna Jain, Ph.D. Jaipur Rugs, India
Hariom Gurjar, Poornima University, India
Priyesh Tiwari, Poornima University, India

Learning Objectives

1. *Evaluate* the socioeconomic scenario of a developing country.
2. *Study* social entrepreneurship and entrepreneurial skills.
3. *Explore* business model development and marketing strategy formulation.

Key Words

Developing economy   Entrepreneurship
Business model innovation   Social development
Global design

Abstract

The carpet industry is considered one of the oldest trades in the world. In the twenty first century, carpets are used for aesthetic and functional properties. The post-independence era in India has witnessed an export-led growth for carpets. The export prospect of carpets depends on overseas demand and domestic supply potential.

Jaipur Rugs was founded in 1978, when NK Chaudhary borrowed a sum of 5000 rupees from his father and began his journey with only 9 artisans and 2 looms. Mr. Chaudhary studied India's carpet industry, which lacked innovation, technology, connectivity to global design trends, and efficient production processes.

Over the years, Mr. Chaudhary's humble beginning transformed Jaipur Rugs into a globally conscious brand that connected 40,000 artisans from 600 villages of India with clientele across 40 countries of the world who subscribed to a common philosophy of responsible manufacturing. Jaipur Rugs is a family business that combines the pursuit of profit with the spreading of kindness in a way that benefits all stakeholders.

The Carpet Industry

The carpet industry is considered one of the oldest trades in the world. It is evident that woven forms of floor coverings were present during the Neolithic Age, i.e. about 7000 B.C. Early theories suggest that carpets were used to protect people from adverse weather conditions. Other theories suggest that they were traded for ornamental purposes by the rich and influential. Historically,

Afghanistan, Armenia, China, India, Persia, Turkey, Spain, Bulgaria, France, and England were known for their carpets. Many antique Persian style carpets were easily recognized for their rich weave and decorations.

Carpets from Middle Eastern countries, like Egypt, were fabricated with better quality and in higher quantities. With their unique elegance, these carpets were traded to places in the Far East. Chinese carpet designs included a beautiful mix of flowers as well as abstract geometrical figures that were curvilinear in nature. Turkish carpets were inspired by local culture and tradition.

In the twenty first century, carpets are used for aesthetic and functional purposes. In addition to covering floors and improving the interior design of a home or office, rugs and carpets serve as a protective layer for floors. In regions with a predominantly cold climate, carpets are used to keep the floor from getting too cold. Carpets come in a variety of different weaves: woven, needle felt, knotted, tufted, etc. In terms of materials, they could be made of silk, wool or a wool blend, viscose, nylon, polypropylene, polyester, or acrylic.

The rise of the carpet industry in India can be credited to the Mughal dynasty. It introduced Persian and Turkish weavers to the country to produce carpets for palaces. With the downfall of this Dynasty, the practice of carpet weaving was negatively affected. However, it gained momentum in the form of independent units during the post-British period. Now the industry is glowing with utmost glory across the states of Rajasthan, Kashmir, Punjab, Uttar Pradesh, Andhra Pradesh, and Himachal Pradesh. For centuries, the Indian carpet industry was considered a significant revenue generator and employment provider. Indian carpets were rich with a wide range of patterns, styles, and designs on their bristled surfaces.

The post-independence era in India has witnessed an export-led growth for carpets. The export prospect of carpets depends on overseas demand and domestic supply potential. Employing over 2 million weavers, it is an old and well established de-centralized sector. However, despite being the world's largest producer and exporter of carpets, India is witnessing an unfortunate downfall in the demand for handmade carpets. In comparison to carpet exports worth around 46,602 USD in 1947-48 and 1,708,838 USD in 1970-71, India registered a manifold increase and exceeded 55.92 million USD in 2006-07; but other nations performed well.

An article by Indian Brand Equity Foundation states that India accounts for 61 percent of the global loom age, 22% of the global spindle age, 12% of the world's production of textile fibers and yarn, and a 25% share of the total world trade of cotton yarn. Exports of carpets have increased from $654.32 million USD in 2004-05 to $930.69 million USD in 2006-07, showing a growth rate of 42.23%. During April-October 2007, carpet exports totaled $404.74 million USD. In 2013-14, the total value of hand-made carpet exports was $1,037 million USD. This made India the world leader in carpet exports with 36% of the global market share. Indian handmade carpets are exported to over 100 nations and the U.S. accounts for the largest share. For instance, around 40% of the total carpet exports in 2011-12 were to the U.S.

Indian carpets have a special place in developed countries, which account for 88-90% of Indian carpet exports. The United States and Germany, the two largest and most established markets for carpets, account for 76% of India's exports. Indian carpets are famous worldwide for their magnificent designs and heart-winning workmanship. Hand-knotted woolen carpets, tufted woolen carpets, chain stitch rugs, pure silk carpets, staple/synthetic carpets, and hand-made woolen durries are just some of the floor covering types that have a large market demand in both Europe and the United States.

India is a developing economy and the Indian carpet industry is very labor intensive, with a large focus on exports. Apart from generating foreign exchange, the industry provides employment to many people. Most of the carpet manufacturing in India takes place in the northern part of the country in the towns of Bhadohi, Agra, Jaipur, Srinagar, and Danapur.

◎ Jaipur Rugs

"Let goodness, fairness, and most importantly, love prevail in business; profits will inevitably follow." —NK Chaudhary

Jaipur Rugs was founded in 1978, when NK Chaudhary borrowed a sum of 5000 rupees from his father and began his journey with only nine artisans and two looms. While working in his father's shoe shop as a young man, he decided to combine his love of beautiful patterns and craftsmanship with his quest for social justice and formed his own enterprise. Mr. Chaudhary studied India's carpet industry, which lacked innovation, technology, connectivity to global design trends, and efficient production processes. He saw that the carpet industry in India was infected with atrocious practices like child labor, infringement of money by multiple middlemen, and weavers were treated as societal outcasts and untouchables. Their hand-knotted carpets, however, were sold at phenomenal prices around the globe. This led to the mushrooming of multiple middlemen who intended to usurp the deserved-dues of the weavers.

Mr. Chaudhary seethed with agitation and impatience towards these practices and he harbored within him a deep desire to change the lives of talented weavers. So, with his new-found knowledge of the trade, he setup shop to rescue the art of traditional hand-woven rugs from the brink of extinction. He started to work with the concept of "cultural sustainability" way before academic literature highlighted its growing importance. Mr. Chaudhary had the passion to have the Indian weavers recognized as artisans and started his business on the principles of equity, empathy, and dignity.

Working around the clock to establish his fledgling business, Mr. Chaudhary travelled miles on his bicycle to procure the raw materials, ate with the weavers near the looms, and spent nights at the production center. He learned a lot from the company's weavers and by the end of the third year, he had ten additional looms and more artisans. Over the years, Mr. Chaudhary's humble beginning transformed Jaipur Rugs into a globally conscious brand that connected 40,000 artisans from 600 villages of India with clientele across 40 countries of the world who subscribe to a common philosophy of responsible manufacturing. Jaipur Rugs is a family business that combines the pursuit of profit with the spreading of kindness in a way that benefits all stakeholders.

Results Chain

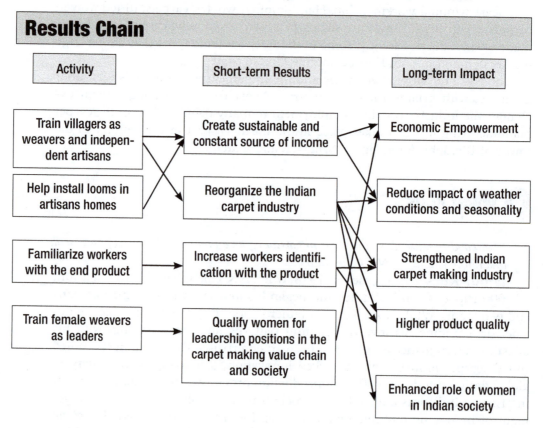

Jaipur Rugs' supply chain follows a disruptive model where the raw materials for carpets are delivered to the homes of the weavers. Mr. Chaudhary understood that bringing change to the supply chain of the carpet industry meant he had to strengthen its weakest link, the weaver community. Thus, a system was set in place to oversee production via rigorous quality control processes, collecting, distributing, and marketing finished products across the globe. Jaipur Rugs' model brings their share of the profits directly to weavers, who receive a minimum of $70 USD per month (compared to $6 USD for seasonal work in agriculture). Mr. Chaudhary continued to expand the business because he put in place a "supportive and nurturing home based creative unit" instead of a machine driven emotionless production line.

With a sales and marketing entity called **Jaipur Living Inc.,** headquartered in Atlanta, Georgia, Jaipur Rugs has grown to become one of the leading providers of hand-woven rugs from India. JLI expanded the company's offerings to include flat weaves, naturals, transitional, and modern collections to serve their U.S. customers. Through their vertically integrated business structure, Jaipur Rugs controls products from conception to delivery. This method allows the group to offer an exceptionally high quality and consistent product while employing tens of thousands of rural handcrafts people around the world.

There are three major areas of innovation in the company:

1. Business Model Innovation—Successful and profitable vertical integration is made possible by enrolling and empowering women as local managers right in the rural communities where products are being made to manage quality control and production.
2. Social Innovation—empowering women into these roles as right people for the job made good business sense since they have the experience, expertise, and connections to the community. In the process, this innovation can shift powerful cultural norms.
3. Community Innovation—Jaipur Rugs offers a whole-spectrum experience to all their stakeholders.

For example, Jaipur Rugs provides opportunities for customers to learn about their weavers who make the products, for the weavers to see photographs of the finished product in the customer's home, and bring the customers in for a rural immersion. These innovations generate financial, social, and community prosperity for everyone in the system, including the families of the weavers, and they have a positive impact on society. The inclusive socioeconomic business of Jaipur Rugs is addressing the key global concerns of poverty, unemployment, gender equity, sustainability, livelihoods, and inclusive growth. The company also works to boost rural India's economy by developing new generations of artisans, quintessentially reviving the traditional craft of rug weaving, eliminating middlemen, and directing the flow of benefits to artisans.

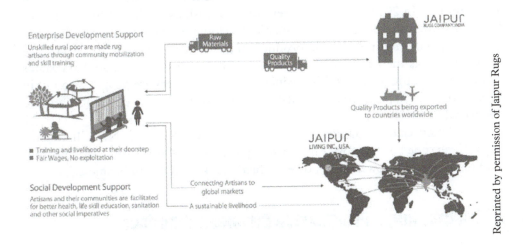

Reprinted by permission of Jaipur Rugs

Jaipur Rugs Foundation is the service arm of Jaipur Rugs Group, which stays connected to the company's grassroots. It was registered in 2004 under the Rajasthan Public Trust Act with the aim of integrating rural people into its value chain by training them to become home-based artisans and giving them a market for their products. Through the foundation, potential weavers are trained in weaving hand-knotted carpets using manually operated looms. Now, ready for work, the artisans develop into independent weavers with the freedom to work for Jaipur Rugs or any other rug company.

Thus, the overall work mandate of the Jaipur Rugs Foundation is to empower the marginalized communities, especially women, living in the unserved and underserved areas. This is achieved by developing their skills and capacities and providing them with an option for a sustainable livelihood. Such weaving of lives is done through two intertwined verticals: "entrepreneurship development'" and "social development." The entrepreneurship development vertical focuses on the economic well-being of the artisans and their communities through skill development and livelihood support. The social development vertical focuses on the artisan's social well-being through interventions, awareness generation, and linkages. The foundation connects them with literacy and financial education, health care, and artisan cards, enabling certified artisans in India to access additional social services. These two complement each other and facilitate the artisans to advance into their development trajectories. The sense of personal worth and recognition worked magically as more and more women artisans were fascinated with this transformation process and decided to be a part of this journey. This created a model of "Inclusive Growth" where the women artisans gained financial and emotional stability. Mr. Chaudhary believes that, "He made the weavers—the weavers made Jaipur Rugs."

In August of 2011, Jaipur Rugs joined the Business Call to Action with a pledge to provide sustainable livelihoods for 6,000 underprivileged women and deliver skills training to 10,000 of the poorest people in rural India. Surpassing these goals by 2015, the company went on to provide management and leadership training to 1,700 women so they could assume managerial positions within the company. In 2016, Jaipur Rugs renewed its Business Call to Action commitment of supporting the global sustainable development goals such as no poverty, gender equality, and responsible production and consumption. With the conviction that this is the beginning of a new era for business, Mr. Chaudhary states that, "I am not the owner of this business. The real owners are people who put in their hard work to produce beautiful carpets which are liked by customers around the world."

Often called "Gandhi of the Indian carpet industry," NK Chaudhary says, "Everyone has the power to transform the world; the key is to search within and discover your power—the power to heal mankind through business."

◎ Jaipur Rugs' Progressive Business Practices

"Business as an agent of doing greater good, most importantly, business as an instrument for human healing." —NK Chaudhary

Jaipur Rugs' business model is artisan centricity and customer centricity which is propagated through a culture of openness and learning.

1. Shifting Mindsets through First-hand Experience

- Bringing awareness amongst employees and workers through observation and exposure.

- Bridging gaps through first-hand knowledge in a decentralized business model across vast geographical locations.

Business Practice:

- Sensing Journey: Jaipur Head Office to weaving villages (1 day engagement program)
- Weavers Engagement Program: Weavers from villages to Jaipur Head Office and carpet finishing facilities
- Rural Field Immersion Program: Immersion from Head Office to village (3 day deeper engagement program)
- Sensing Journey: U.S. Head Office to Jaipur Head Office and weaving village (the engagement program is called Back to the Roots)
- End customers' visit to weaving villages

2. Listening Carefully to the Voices of Frontline

- Deep listening to issues faced by the frontline on the field
- A key growth driver of Jaipur Rugs, built over the years through constant listening to the grassroots people

Business Practice:

- Jaipur Rugs Foundation: formed in 2004 (NKC's link with the weavers was institutionalized as the business scaled up)
  - Socioeconomic development of artisan communities
  - Capacity building of artisan communities (weaving and spinning)
  - Mentoring and coaching of grass root leaders through constant listening
- Conference calls: a revolutionary practice that has resulted in resolving grass root issues with the organizational growth
  - This program gave voices to the unheard people at the grassroots level
  - A two-way feedback mechanism: head office and frontline

3. Creating Grass Root Leadership: Developing Leaders from Ordinary People

- Creating village level leaders for quality manufacturing and timely delivery in a de-centralized network of 600+ villages
- Naturally evolving local leaders as company grew from 2 to 20 looms, to 2000 to 7000 looms

Business Practice:

- Young Women Social Entrepreneurship Development Program (an example is the case of Archana, which is mentioned in the following section)
  - First time village level leadership of women in the carpet industry

- – Women monitoring women weavers: Bunkar Sakhi program
  Artisans are trained and empowered to eventually take over as quality control officers and this aspiration, to move up in the hierarchy, acts as a constant motivation for the artisans.
- Developing leaders in newly developed weaving belts
  - – Developing new generation of artisans, trainers, and leaders through skill development in highly marginalized communities
- Transforming non-contributing family members of marginalized communities into responsible family members and leaders of Jaipur Rugs
- Eventually these leaders take ownership of their own areas (an example is the case of Zareena, which is mentioned in the following section)

4. Innovating to Bridge Industry Gaps

- Disruptive solutions to industry problems that set new standards in the carpet industry
- Seen since the inception of Jaipur Rugs
- Unique supply chain of Jaipur Rugs is also a result of this business practice

Business Practice:

- Artisan Originals: lifting the weaver's mindset beyond wage worker.
  - – Transformation of relationship with the art of weaving, from work to art
  - – Mindset shift: bringing connection to the work, like in the older days when the weavers were fully connected to what they were doing
  - – Customers get the complete information regarding where the rugs came from and information about the weaver and their inspiration for the rug that they created
- Customer-Weaver Postcard Program
  - – Connecting the two ends: the weaver and the consumer communicate through postcards that bring an emotional connect beyond the rug as a mere commodity
  - – Customer is not only sensitized that it is not a machine-made product but also gets a perspective about the artisan community thriving through this art
- Delhi Retail Experiential Store

  Jaipur Rugs plans to continue pursuing its path of sustainable growth. In addition to its existing sales channels, the company aims to increase sales in the domestic market, a strategy supported by the opening of a showroom in New Delhi.

  - – Live demonstrations and storytelling to engage and educate the consumers beyond the idea of a rug as a mere commodity
- Involvement of women in *Gultaraash* process

◎ Social Impact of Jaipur Rugs

Story 1: Archana Devi, Bunkar Sakhi, Mahasingh Ka Bas, Rajasthan

Archana Devi was one of the participants of the Young Women Social Entrepreneurship Development Program (YWSEDP)—Phase 1 in 2014. After the program, she went through the leadership program, called the "Bunkar Sakhi Program," aimed at empowering women weavers. These Bunkar Sakhis are the women weavers who check the quality of carpets made by fellow women weavers in their villages. One of the Bunkar Sakhis, Archana from Mahasingh Ka Bas village says, "I can do anything in the world." Her progress in the last 3 years is incredible; her confidence in expressing herself in front of people has grown tremendously. She has no fear in talking to her reporting Branch

Archana Devi, Mahasingh Ka Bas, Rajasthan

© Jaipur Rugs

Manager and the founder of the organization. Today, she manages the quality of 35 looms in Mahasingh Ka Bas village near by Jaipur. The organization has found that because of Archana, many women were inspired to become Bunkar Sakhis and today there are a total of 7 Bunkar Sakhis—adding a new cadre of women leaders at the villages of Jaipur Rugs.

In her family, there are a total of 8 members including herself, her husband, 3 daughters, and 2 sons. Prior to becoming a Bunkar Sakhi in 2014, she had been weaving carpets for 15 years. When asked why she started weaving during childhood, she said, "I did not like school, though my family members used to force me to go to school. I was afraid of our strict school teachers. I decided to continue weaving because I loved weaving."

Before YWSEDP in 2014, she was working with a contractor for 50 rupees per day from 2002 to 2007. After that, she started working with Jaipur Rugs and the company paid her, and other weavers, 60 to70 rupees per day. Gradually, the rate increased as per design and in the year 2014, each weaver started earning 200 rupees per day for specific design and level of quality. She used to work 20 days per month, earning about 4000 rupees in an average month. If there were any urgent orders, she would work for 25 days a month and would then earn around 5000 rupees for that. When she attended YWSEDP, she was selected as a Bunkar Sakhi and began training in August of 2014. She was appointed as a fulltime Bunka Sakhi in October of 2014 and her initial salary was 5400 rupees, a significant increase in her monthly income. When she joined as Bunkar Sakhi, her husband did not have a job. Listening to Archana's request—as claimed by company sources—her husband also got a job in a store department of a Branch. Today, Archana's monthly income is Rs. 6000 and her husband's income is Rs. 6500

Story 2: Zareena, Weaver, Kubakala Center, Mirzapur

Zareena is one of the tufted carpet weavers from Kubakala village in the Mirzapur District of Uttar Pradesh, India. People in this village mostly engage in breaking stones for construction and farming during the season. The girls and women in this village apparently did not have any employment opportunities except for farming. Jaipur Rugs Foundation intervened in this village and offered skill development training for tufted carpets in the year 2014. Zareena was one of the girls who were surveyed by the Jaipur Rugs Foundation team. After having the burden of debt on the family due to the marriage expenses and health expenses of her sisters, Zareena realized that she needed to support her family financially.

Zareena is a girl who really loves her family. She is always calm and faces life with a positive attitude. When she learned weaving, she thought that she could earn money and learn a skill that could help her become independent. With this dream of independence, she started learning weaving at the center that opened in her village and asked her mother to stop selling bangles in the market as she started earning money and supporting the family. Initially, her parents did not allow her to go to the center as it was far from her house, but still she continued weaving with determination.

© Jaipur Rugs

Zareena, Kubakala, Mirzapur, Uttar Pradesh

Today, she earns 3000 to 4000 rupees per month after completing household works in the home. She wants to support her father and help reduce the debt which her father took for their family. Zareena is happy that she has become independent while working in her own village. When she was asked about her dream in life, she said, "We should face life as it comes with all the problems and happiness. Nobody knows about their life. I just want to see my parents happy. My parents are happy with my weaving work. Whatever is in my destiny will happen to me."

Discussion Questions:

1. What is the Global Entrepreneurship Monitor (GEM) approach? Discuss its various components.
2. How can technology and innovation help an organization to grow and expand? Critically evaluate a developing country like India with reference to technology and innovation.
3. What is "high-level" and "low-level" entrepreneurial activity? Based on your response, which level does Jaipur Rugs belong to?
4. What methods and approaches help a firm to become international in operation?
5. What are some critical areas of Jaipur Rugs which need improvement? Suggest appropriate strategies for improving these critical areas.
6. What are the contributions of an enterprise like Jaipur Rugs to a society and a nation?

References

http://www.gemconsortium.org/

http://www.jaipurrugsco.com

http://thecis.ca/wp-content/uploads/2016/04/GEM-Global-Report-2015.pdf

Ahuja, V. (2012). Success Through Social Responsibility: A Unique Business Model of Jaipur Rugs Foundation, *IUP Journal of Corporate Governance*, pp. 52–58.

Allen, James (2016). Jaipur rugs founders mentality in action video.aspx. Retrieved from http://www.bain.com.

Allen, James (2015). Jaipur rugs selling a family's blessing. Retrieved from https://www.foundersmentality.com.

Allen, James (2015). When weavers disagree. Retrieved from https://www.foundersmentality.com.

Biehl, M., Prater, E., & Realff, M. J., (2007). Assessing performance and uncertainty in developing carpet reverse logistics systems, *Computers & Operations Research*, Volume 34, Issue 2, pp. 443–463.

Bogoert, S.J. (1975), Developing Entrepreneurs and Entrepreneurship in Typical Backward or Primitive Areas: A case study of Ronchi District in Chhotanagpur, Bihar. Seminar on Entrepreneurship, New Delhi, (pp. 62–75).

Chakrabarty, S., & Grote, U., (2009). Child Labor in Carpet Weaving: Impact of Social Labeling in India and Nepal, *World Development*, Volume 37, Issue 10, pp. 1683–1693.

Chandler, G.N., & Hanks, S.H. (1993). Measuring the performance of emerging businesses: A validation study. *Journal of Business Venturing* 8:391–408.

Chaudhary, N.K. (July, 2016). Personal interview with Thakurata Kamalika Guha (Sr. Executive Corporate Communication).

Cheng, P. (n.d.). NK Chaudhary. Retrieved from http://www.impactmania.com.

Daft, R., Sormunen, J., & Parks, D. (1988). Chief Executive Scanning, Environmental Characteristics, and Company Performance: an Empirical Study, *Strategic Management Journal* 9: 123–139.

Das, P.K., Shukla, K.P., & Öry, F.G., (1992). An occupational health programme for adults and children in the carpet weaving industry, Mirzapur, India: A case study in the informal sector, *Social Science & Medicine*, Volume 35, Issue 10, pp. 1293–1302.

Davig, W., & Brown, S. (1992). Incremental Decision Making in Small Manufacturing Firms, *Journal of Small Business Management* 30 (2): 53–60.

Goel, A., & Tyagi, I., (2016), Status of Handloom Industry in Uttarakhand, ITIHAS, *The Journal of Indian Management*, Vol. 6 Issue 4, p35–40.

Gulrajani, M. (1994). SPECIAL ISSUE: Child Labour within the Globalizing Economy, *Labour, Capital and Society*, Vol. 27, No. 2, pp. 192–214.

Heilbrunn, S. (2008). Factors influencing entrepreneurial intensity in communities. *Journal of Enterprising Communities: People and Places in the Global Economy, 2*(1), 37–51.

Iyer, L., Khanna, T., & Varshney, A. (2013). Caste and Entrepreneurship in India. *Economic & Political Weekly,* 48 (6), 52–60.

Kalita , D. (2014), Socio-Economic Status of Women in Home-Based Industries (HBIs) in Sonitpur District, Assam, *Northeast Journal of Contemporary Research*, Vol. 1 No. 1, pp.99–108.

Kaushik, M., (1994) Entrepreneurial Competencies & Gender wise Variation, Women in Management Champion of Change, University Press Ltd. Dhaka, Bangladesh.

Lin, R., & Chan, C., (2007). Effectiveness of workstation design on reducing musculoskeletal risk factors and symptoms among semiconductor fabrication room workers, *International Journal of Industrial Ergonomics*, Volume 37, Issue 1, pp. 35–42.

Mohanty, S., & Sahu, A. (2015). Tribal Entrepreneurship: A study on Tribal Cooperative Marketing Development Federation of India. *Gyanpratha,* 7 (1), 20–24.

Morris, M.H., Sexton, D., & Lewis, P. (1994). Reconceptualizing Entrepreneurship: An Input-Output Perspective. SAM *Advanced Management Journal*, 21–31.

Motamedzade, M, Choobineh, A., Mououdi, M., & Arghami, S. (2007). Ergonomic design of carpet weaving hand tools, *International Journal of Industrial Ergonomics*, Volume 37, Issue 7, pp. 581–587.

Prahlad, CK (2010). Jaipur Rugs: Connecting Rural India to Global Markets. The William Davidson Institute.

Radjabi, A. (1983), Carpets, hand-woven. In: Encyclopedia of occupational health and safety. 3rd ed. Geneva, Switzerland: International Labour Office. 416p.

Sharma, A., Verma, R., & Joshi, M.C. (2016). Sports Goods Foundation of India: A Case Study of a Solution Based NGO, Prabhandhan, *Indian Journal of Management*, Volume 9, Issue 4.

Shukla, A., Kumar, S., & Öry, F.G. (1991). Occupational health and the environment in an urban slum in India, *Social Science & Medicine*, Volume 33, Issue 5, pp. 597–603.

Srivastava, N., & Syngkon, R.A. (2007). Marketing Management and Entrepreneurship Development in a Tribal Dominated Economy: A Case Study of Small Scale Industries in Esat Khasi Hills District of Meghalaya. *The Icfai Journal of Entrepreneurship Development,* 4 (4), 28–47.

Wilson, F. (1996). Ten Roads that Lead to Success in Carpet Manufacturing, *Textile World* (May): 28–30.

Relevant Videos

India's Culture and Cuisine
https://www.youtube.com/watch?v=7thQHD81glA

An introduction to Indian business culture
https://www.youtube.com/watch?v=VV7oVfT65dl

How to Follow Proper Business Etiquette in India
https://www.youtube.com/watch?v=u4dmfmerw0c

India Carpet Expo - 2017, New Delhi, 27-30 March 2017
https://www.youtube.com/watch?v=DyPzJySDc74

Indian carpet making demonstration - New Delhi, India (Aug. 9, 2013)
https://www.youtube.com/watch?v=Sg3BUIFB6Z8

Chapter Four

GLOBAL BUSINESS PLAN

DR. SHINGLE GOES INTERNATIONAL: A ROOFER'S DREAM

Dianne H.B. Welsh
The University of North Carolina at Greensboro

Learning Objectives

1. *Analyze* how new products are identified in a market.
2. *Understand* the importance of product engineering in new product development.
3. *Evaluate* intellectual property issues.
4. *Evaluate* the marketability of the product worldwide.
5. *Analyze* what distribution channels may be utilized for this new product.
6. *Evaluate* how safety improvement could be marketed.

Key Words

Innovation   Roofing Industry
New Product Development

Abstract

Developing a new product is no small task. In Cincinnati, Ohio, PJS's CEO Jake Smith faces the many issues that arise from new product development in a worldwide marketplace. PJS is a consolidation of three separate business entities, which Jake Smith founded. He is a consummate entrepreneur. The case involves an entrepreneurship student who is being mentored by the founding entrepreneur when she has an idea for a new product that could have worldwide appeal and benefits for those in the roofing industry, making their job easier and safer.

 Dilemma

Jake Smith met Erin Rogers, an entrepreneurship student, when Jake agreed to act as a business mentor to Erin for one of his entrepreneurship classes. Erin and Jake made multiple visits to roofing sites that Jake managed. While observing the shingle installation process, Erin became aware of the need for a better way of handling new shingles prior to their installation. To install a new roof, first the old shingles are removed and felt paper is stapled to the roof deck. Then the new shingles are delivered to the roof and the shingles must be taken from their thick paper encasing. The shingles can either be placed in a pile next to the roofer who actually nails the shingles to the roof, or a second roofer can hand the nailing roofer the shingles.

Both methods of obtaining shingles for the nailing roofer are areas of concern. The first process, setting the bundle of shingles next to the nailing roofer, presents several different challenges. The placement of shingles on a steeply pitched roof may prove to be hazardous. A high-sloping roof often causes a roofer to install roof jacks (typically thick-gauged steel brackets that hold planks in position) in order to keep the bundle of shingles in place. To install roof jacks, the roofer must first install a third or fifth coarse of shingles. He or she then lifts up the previously installed shingles and slides the roof jack up under the course. Then the roofer nails the roof jack to the deck. The installation of roof jacks can be dangerous and time-consuming.

A roof that does not require roof jacks to keep the shingles from falling may also prove dangerous. Depending on the slope of the roof, the shingles may still have the possibility of sliding out of the nailer's reach, causing other roofers to trip. The sliding shingles may also increase installation time, because the nailer has to retrieve fallen shingles.

The second process, the handing of shingles to the nailing roofer, increases the level of risk and cost to management. The increase of risk comes from having an excess number of workers on the roof. On an average-sized roof, individuals have a limited work area.

Management incurs the cost of an extra worker's time as well as the time it takes to manage another employee. The costs associated with the extra worker also include extra safety equipment for the additional worker, benefits costs, and possible legal issues that may arise.

Erin explained to Jake that she saw an opportunity to make the roofing process safer, lessen the need for two workers, and provide a promotional opportunity for shingle manufacturers.

His new product, Dr. Shingle, is an innovative approach to keeping shingles from slipping down the roof. Dr. Shingle also eliminates the need for a second worker to hold the extra shingles. Fewer people on the roof decrease the chance of injury. Shingle manufacturers could use Dr. Shingle in their marketing by personalizing the product with their company's name and giving it out with their shingles to demonstrate their concern for roofers' safety. It could have worldwide applicability.

Dr. Shingle is an "L"-shaped bracket. The long part of the "L" is 36 inches. On the back of the long side is a piece of non-slip foam rubber. The short side of the "L" is eight inches. The back of the long side is laid on the roof; the shingles lie flat on this side with their bottom edges against the short side.

Safety is important in any construction job. Dr. Shingle will not only improve safety but will also decrease labor costs. One thing to consider, however, is that many roofing operations are strongly unionized. Even though the union supports the increase in safety, it may be concerned about potential job losses.

Increased productivity could offset some of the adverse impact on labor. If roofers are compensated based on the area roofed per day, this increased productivity may result in higher wages per roofer.

A helpful and innovative product is only a small part of capitalizing on a business opportunity. The product must also reach the market (which involves targeting the audience, proving the product's usability and benefits to this audience, finding a distribution channel, and branding the product).

Market research showed that there were 150,000 roofers in the United States in 1998. Tests by actual roofers showed the product was valuable. Their comments included "Dr. Shingle allows me to work alone," and "That product really helps me save time and money."

Finding a distribution channel could be more difficult. Dr. Shingle could be sold in stores or sold to shingle distributors (to be used as a promotional item when certain amounts of shingles are purchased).

Discussion Questions

1. How does one identify a new-product opportunity? Does Dr. Shingle seem to be a viable product to introduce? Why or why not?
2. How can the market be identified for Dr. Shingle? Could Dr. Shingle have a significant impact on the roofing industry? What are the challenges of introducing a product of this caliber into a mature and traditional industry?
3. What determines whether or not a patent will be pursued? If this is the first product of its kind, should a patent be considered immediately? Are there any drawbacks to seeking a patent/provisional patent?
4. Based on the chapter discussion of positive attributes for successful products, what positive attributes does Dr. Shingle possess?
5. Based on the chapter discussion of fatal flaws of new products, what potentially fatal flaws (if any) does Dr. Shingle possess? What are they and how can they be overcome?

Case Update

Dr. Shingle's story has a sad ending. Two prototypes worked extremely well. The product name was changed to Shingle Shelf. Erin Rogers contacted the owner and CEO of one of the largest contractor suppliers in the country, ABC Supply. As she described Shingle Shelf to him, he said, "That sounds very similar to Bear's Grip." Upon checking out Bear's Grip, the company found that Bear's Grip is almost identical to Shingle Shelf. The company making Bear's Grip claimed a patent, which was not verified, but the product was. Even though the Bear's Grip manufacturer was small, it was enough to stop PJS and Erin Rogers from pursuing the product further.

Even though a considerable amount of research was conducted, it was not until PJS had the conversation with the CEO of ABC Supply, who knew the business better than PJS did, that they obtained information about the other product already in the market.

The author would like to thank Adam Selsby, Luke Dautovic, Chris Garwood, and Josh Ferrara, John Carroll University, Cleveland, Ohio, for their assistance in preparation of this case study.

References

Cowley, S. (2017, October 1). Starbucks closes online store to focus on in-person experience. *The New York Times*.

Saltzman, R. (2012, May 1). Improper shingle nailing. *Structure Tech*.

Freedonia Group. (2015). Roofing—demand and sales forecasts, market share, market size, market leaders. *Freedonia*.

Hicks, A. (2013, June 24). Should roofers use nail guns or hand nail shingles? *Angie List*.

Industries, IKO. (2017). 3 trends in the roofing industry you need to know. *IKO*. Retrieved from https://www.iko.com/na/residential/building-professional/3-roofing-industry-trends-you-need-to-know/

Relevant Videos

Roof Top Safety Anchor
https://www.youtube.com/watch?v=Q_zxiiCgreY

HUGS Guardrail system
https://www.youtube.com/watch?v=zZZfUpja0BA

Steep Assist
https://www.youtube.com/watch?v=7pVJs7GmqtM

Counterweight Non-Penetrating Roof Anchor
https://www.youtube.com/watch?v=6R2VyRJBF4Q

Leading Edge Work: Prevention Video (v-Tool): Falls in Construction
https://www.youtube.com/watch?v=G991LcaZQd8

Chapter Five

BUSINESS OPPORTUNITIES FOR GLOBAL ENTREPRENEURSHIP

GROWING GLOBAL PAINS AT GROWTH CYCLE STRATEGIES, INC.

Dianne H.B. Welsh
The University of North Carolina at Greensboro

Learning Objectives

1. *Analyze* how to achieve market penetration for a small business with limited resources.
2. *Evaluate* how to determine the target market for a company.
3. *Understand* the challenges of market penetration for a small company.
4. *Evaluate* the most effective sales methods that are available for the company.
5. *Evaluate* the most effective growth strategies for a small business in the marketing area.

Key Words

Growth   Small Business
Marketing Issues

Abstract

This case discusses a small, growing marketing consulting firm that works primarily with product managers to build strategy skills. Growth Cycle Strategies targets industrial and high-tech firms with sales volumes of at least $25 million annually. Firms with lower revenue levels will not typically employ product managers. To continue to expand, the company must expand its company base from 30 clients. The firm has established goals to complete 24 training seminars and 12 consulting jobs per year. The dilemma for the company is how to best strategically grow the entrepreneurial client companies while keeping its culture and client base. Should they target entrepreneurial companies that have gone global?

 **Dilemma**

Growth Cycle Strategies is a firm that helps maximize the role of product managers for other firms through two means. First, the firm trains product managers to perform their roles as strategists. Second, the firm consults with those who manage product managers to help them understand how to realize a better return on their investment from their employees. A variety of industries are realizing that training product managers is crucial to success.

In over three years of business together, Jack Elliot and Joe Brooks have built a base of approximately 30 clients. Growth Cycle Strategies has earned a high level of customer satisfaction in its consulting and training engagements. The partners' experience in the area of product development, and their ability to share their knowledge effectively with the product managers of their clients, make their service unique and valuable.

The backgrounds of the partners of Growth Cycle Strategies combine knowledge of technical detail with sales ability; however, both have confided that sales were the least favorite part of their job.

The company target is industrial and high-tech firms with sales volumes of $25 million or more annually. Firms with lower revenue levels will not typically employ product managers. Growth Cycle Strategies targets industrial firms rather than consumer goods firms because this is the area where its partners' expertise lies.

Decision makers within the target market tend to vary widely. That is, the firm has worked with marketing managers, directors of product management, vice presidents of sales, and presidents of companies.

For the company to continue to succeed, Growth Cycle Strategies must continue to grow its client base. The firm currently conducts one training seminar per month and completes one consulting project every two to three months. The firm has established goals to complete 24 training seminars and 12 consulting jobs per year.

Jack and Joe handle the marketing efforts of the company, which takes about one third of their time. Growth Cycle Strategies has a website that gets about 1,000 hits per month (without being linked to other sites). The firm tried a direct-mail campaign last April and had a response rate of 1.5 percent, which was good for direct mail; however, the quality of the leads was poor. Often the individual responding was not the appropriate decision maker within the company. Now the focus is on building a referral network via existing satisfied clients. A $100 gift certificate to Amazon.com for any referral that generates business has resulted in a number of new accounts. When the firm connects with a prospective client's decision maker (regarding that company's training budget), "we have no problem selling (our service)," says Jack.

As Growth Cycle Strategies continues to grow, Jack and Joe will have less time to devote to marketing and will need to concentrate on servicing their clients. Jack and Joe acknowledge that it may be time to add someone to the company in some capacity. In order to serve the client well and maintain Growth Cycle Strategies' high level of customer satisfaction, they considered hiring a person with a product development background whom they could train to handle a portion of their responsibilities, including sales/marketing and consulting/training. The dilemma of Growth Cycle Strategies is how to grow the company effectively.

The author would like to thank students Kelli Newman, Michelle Laramee, and John McMullen for their assistance in preparation of this case study.

Discussion Questions

1. What is the current target market and what research needs to be undertaken regarding this target market? Should a global market be included? How does the company go about attracting these firms?
2. Why isn't the firm reaching the targeted volume of sales now?
3. Is the current marketing strategy sufficient to increase the volume of sales? Why or why not?
4. What are ways of maximizing the current client base?
5. What are the advantages and disadvantages of hiring an additional sales person or direct sales force?
6. Can the company grow and maintain its current staffing structure?
7. What would you recommend the company do to achieve its goal of growing the business?

Relevant Videos

7 Small Business Marketing Strategies
Top small business marketing strategies:
https://www.youtube.com/watch?v=674OfDJwlAl

Inbound marketing Houston . B2B Marketing . Houston SEO . Industrial Marketing:
https://www.youtube.com/watch?v=tvTX6XyKAmo

B2B marketing in a digital world:
https://www.youtube.com/watch?v=-nTkBhsUlRQ

Small business growth:
https://www.youtube.com/watch?v=Q0rUKthhTVM

How to Attract Customers to Your Small Business | SB Startup 1.0:
https://www.youtube.com/watch?v=6rQ-U6zDNDE

Flextronics: Foreign Direct Investment Decisions in Central Europe

Pavel Štrach

Institute of Management and Marketing, Škoda Auto University, Mladá Boleslav (Czech Republic)

André M. Everett

Department of Management, University of Otago, Dunedin (New Zealand)

Learning Objectives

1. *Examine* multiple factors that influence the decision of a business on where to locate its operations, particularly the role of government incentives.
2. *Discuss* the potential conflicts of interest that may arise between a business and the location it chooses to start up or expand operations.
3. *Assess* the implications of the decision by a business to relocate away from (or disestablish or diminish) operations in a particular location, from the perspectives of both the business and a variety of other stakeholders.
4. *Evaluate* the impact of social responsibility on entrepreneurial decisions.
5. *Debate* the merits and drawbacks of government incentives in attempting to attract foreign investment or to boost local entrepreneurship.

Key Words

Community Impacts

Corporate Social Responsibility

Divestment

Eastern Europe

Foreign Direct Investment (FDI)

Government Investment Incentives

Short Summary

This case describes the investment, establishment, and divestment of a major electronics manufacturer in the Czech Republic and its impacts on local government policies and popular perceptions.

Abstract

As one of the world's largest original equipment manufacturers (OEM) of electronics, Flextronics has won numerous awards for quality and is a key supplier to many famous brand names. Among its manufacturing operations in over 30 countries, one example stands out as more interesting and intricate than the rest. This case describes Flextronics' investment in and subsequent divestment from a major factory in Brno, Czech Republic, with a focus on government incentives and community involvement, contrasting attitudes and perceptions of the parties involved. Entrepreneurship decisions are undertaken by the national and local governments, a major foreign multinational enterprise, and local firms, with changes in the situation leading to questions about the viability of early decisions and what should replace the firm after it departs.

Reprinted by permission of Pavel Štrach and André M. Everett.

The events described here took place primarily between 2000 and 2002, when Flextronics developed their production site in the Czech Republic. Awareness of both the contextual background predating the case, and subsequent consequences and options, is important to understanding the long-term aspects of commitment (by all parties) to entrepreneurial ventures, particularly when they involve volatile foreign direct investment.

◎ Czech Republic

The geographic center of Europe is not located in Germany or Austria, but in the small country called Czech Republic, which premiered on world maps in 1993 after the dissolution of the former Czechoslovakia. In November 1989, Czechoslovakia experienced the so-called Velvet Revolution that initiated democratic development and a graceful exit from under the direct influence of the former Soviet Union. The Czech Republic borders on Germany, Poland, Austria, and the Slovak Republic—half its neighbors were in the European Union at the time of the case, but the Czech Republic was not. Ten million Czechs reside on 78,860 km², speak Czech (a Slavic language similar to Polish or Slovak), are the biggest per capita beer consumers in the world, and honor their history and traditions. The capital Prague is the natural centre of the country, with 1.2 million inhabitants. The Czech Republic is a member of the United Nations, North Atlantic Treaty Organization (NATO), and Organization for Economic Cooperation and Development (OECD), among many other international associations. Economically, at the time of the key events of this case, the country was under transition from a centrally planned economy into a market model. Privatization of some key industrial giants had already been accomplished. Development of selected economic indicators leading up to the investment is documented in Table 5.1.

The Czech Republic is strategically located on the border between the classical West and the emerging East European markets. The extensive transport infrastructure and geographical position highlight the country's role as a crossroads

TABLE 5.1 **Economic Indicators of the Czech Republic**

	1997	1998	1999	2000
GDP per capita (USD, PPP)	13,200	13,300	13,700	13,800
Budget balance (% GDP)	−1.4	−1.4	−2.4	−3.4
Long-term interest rates (%)	10.53	12.12	7.57	6.77
Trade balance (% GDP)	−9.2	−4.6	−3.5	−6.1
Average inflation rate (%)	8.5	10.7	2.1	3.9
Unemployment rate (end of period, %)	5.23	7.48	9.37	8.78
Average monthly gross wage (USD)	NA	361	366	350
Average exchange rate CZK/USD	31.71	32.27	34.60	38.59
Average exchange rate CZK/EUR	35.80	36.16	36.68	35.61

Source: CzechInvest (2003):4

of major European transit corridors. For example, there are more railway lines per square kilometer than in any other country except Luxembourg, and the motorway network is the densest in Central and Eastern Europe.

Investment Incentives

CzechInvest was founded in 1992 by, and reported to, the Ministry of Industry and Trade of the Czech Republic. The major goal of this governmental agency was to attract new investors. The organization drove its business through several domestic and seven international representative offices—two in the U.S.A., and one each in Belgium, Germany, France, Great Britain, and Japan. One of the major concerns of CzechInvest was that foreign investors preferred to place their new facilities in neighboring transition economies, especially in Hungary, where investment incentives were introduced in 1993.

The first incentives package, setting the minimum investment threshold at USD 25 million, was approved by the Czech government in April 1998 (Decree No. 298/98). In December 1998, the minimum investment level was reduced to USD 10 million (Decree No. 844/98). In February 2000, the Czech Parliament approved a new Act on Investment Incentives, effective May 2000, which replaced the above decrees and reduced the minimum investment amount to CZK 175 million (approximately USD 5 million) for specified geographic areas experiencing high unemployment.

The Czech scheme consists of public support incentives typical in OECD countries. Tax relief on corporate tax for 10 years was granted to newly established companies, while partial relief from corporate tax for 5 years was offered to existing legal entities. Job-creation grants varied across industries and regions according to government strategy, which was strongly influenced by unemployment levels. In 2000, the national unemployment rate reached 8.8%, a rather moderate figure for the region. Grants for re-training staff and for further education of potential employees were offered for up to five years of a new investor's operation. The final point of the incentive scheme was provision of low-cost land. Overall, the subsidy for start-up business activities could last up to ten years and cover up to 50% of investment costs.

The City of Brno

Brno is the second largest city in the Czech Republic, with 380 thousand inhabitants, and is located in the southeast of the country, near Austria and Slovakia. The city constitutes the center of the province of Moravia, one of the historic lands of the Czech people. The earliest known settlement in the area of Brno, by Homo Erectus, has been dated to earlier than 400,000 BC. The town's key architectural feature, its medieval castle, traces its origins to 1021 AD. Two rivers, the Svratka and Svitava, flow through the town.

Masaryk University, with more than 20,000 students, the second largest in the country, was founded in 1919, and its nine faculties comprise a wide range of areas including law, medicine, science, arts, education, economics, informatics, social studies, and sport education. More relevant to the investment and entrepreneurial focus of this case is the Brno University of Technology, with 15,000 students in civil engineering, mechanical engineering, electrical engineering and communication, business and management, fine arts, chemistry, and information technology. The Brno University of Technology was established in 1899 by a decree of Austro-Hungarian Emperor Franz Joseph I. The capability of Czech engineers is believed to be a crucial factor for attracting foreign investors. To complete the picture, there are several other smaller tertiary education institutions—Mendel University of Agriculture and Forestry (6,000 students), Veterinary and Pharmaceutical University (2,000), Janacek Academy of Musical Arts (500), and Brno Military Academy (1,000).

At the time of this case, focused around the year 2000, there were 25 banks in the city, including branches of foreign banking houses. More than 500 advocates (lawyers) and 11 legal advisory firms operated in the area at that time. All the necessary services were available to Western standards. Although the local international airport dispatched 110,000 passengers in 2000, it was more common to land at the much larger and better-connected Prague or Vienna airports, each about 2 hours drive from Brno. The city lies on the highway between Prague and Bratislava (capital of the Slovak Republic). Brno has many leisure facilities, ranging from its own opera house to large sport grounds. A dozen important museums can be found in the city, along with twelve theatres. The Tugendhat Villa, designed by the architect Mies van der Rohe, is a unique example of the "international" style of modern architecture from the 1920s, designated by UNESCO as a world cultural heritage site. The city annually hosts a large international fireworks competition at the end of May/beginning of June.

Brno's long industrial history produced local capabilities that are especially favorable toward machinery and electronics. At the end of the 1990s, the city decided to attract new businesses and enlarge its existing industrial districts. Two potential locations, called Industrial Zone Černovická Terasa and Czech Technology Park, were established. In 1999, the Industrial Zone Černovická Terasa was ready to accommodate its first investors, for whom it was hoped the unemployment figure in the Brno region (9.4% at that time) would appear rather attractive. The whole area was the property of the City of Brno, which bought out 50 hectares from private owners for 260 million Czech Koruna. In total 179 hectares of flat terrain were available for new greenfield investment sites. The locality had good access to major highways, a rail line, and the airport. For the total tender, including the technical network on the land, the city treasury paid roughly half a billion Czech Koruna, expecting to recoup this investment within 10 years.

Company Background

Flextronics was founded in 1969 in Newark, California. Entrepreneur Joe McKenzie and his wife provided manufacturing services to electronic companies in Silicon Valley. In 1980 Flextronics was bought by a group of private investors, who transformed the company into a contract manufacturer, assembling for instance Hayes Modems or early servers for Sun Microsystems. By the late 1980s the company had grown to 200 million USD annual revenues.

A Singapore manufacturing facility was set up in 1981; the company went public in 1987, and in 1990 returned to private ownership through a leveraged buyout, and shifted its operational headquarters to Singapore, although the corporate office remained in San Jose. (In 1994 it went public a second time, and remained public throughout the time of this case.) Major clients included Microsoft, Hewlett Packard, IBM, Ericsson, Cisco, and Philips. The company positioned itself in low labor-cost territories with an emphasis on minimal time delays and transit costs during production. In 1998 revenues reached 1 billion USD; a year later, 2 billion; and the following year 4.3 billion. Globally, the company employed more than 36,000 mostly blue-collar workers. In 2000, the firm was just about to launch production of the game console Xbox. In April that year, Flextronics completed the acquisition of the DII group, adding 50,000 workers in a variety of assembly operations. Multek, the semiconductor design division of DII, was the pearl in this deal. At the end of 2000, Flextronics ran more than 100 facilities in 28 countries.

Building the Czech Plant

In 1998, Flextronics established a factory in the former facilities of the Tesla Brno company, where they employed 1,100 people. In May 2000, a delegation from the city with the Lord Mayor of Brno Petr Duchoň traveled to the larger premises of Flextronics in Nyiregyháza, Hungary, to witness deep co-operation between a city and Flextronics in progress. Members of the delegation were impressed by the responsible and mutually beneficial relationship between the local community and the company.

The day when Flextronics officially announced construction of a new plant in Brno was about to come. The foundation stone was laid on 28 June 2000; in it, U.S. Ambassador to the Czech Republic John Shattuck embedded a metal casket with newspapers of the day, factory construction plans, and Czech and American coins. At the accompanying press conference, Flextronics made public the development of a new industrial park located at Černovická Terasa, proposing an investment of up to 20 million USD and employment for 3,000 workers. The city representatives, company senior managers, and the U.S. ambassador faced the cameras and revealed enthusiastic plans about prosperous local communities and a new partnership of local and global know-how. Flextronics believed the final investment could reach up to 100 million USD during the following 5 years.

After negotiations with CzechInvest, Flextronics was awarded government subsidies for creating new jobs, and a tax allowance, totaling 100 million Czech Koruna (3.5 million USD). The contract between the company and the government stated that Flextronics would invest no less than 10 million USD within the following three years. More than 40% of the overall investment had to be spent for machinery and technology. Another commitment comprised training a minimum of 225 people.

Furthermore, the City of Brno provided 7 hectares of land for the symbolic price of 1 Czech Koruna, and rented additional properties free of charge, providing 45 hectares of land in the industrial zone. Official valuation carried out by the competition authority (Czech Office for the Protection of Competition) reported that the 7 hectares would be priced at 291 million Czech Koruna (8 million USD) and the annual letting fee for the additional land would be 29 million Czech Koruna (800,000 USD). In return, the contract between Flextronics and the City of Brno guaranteed creation of 3,000 job opportunities by 2005 and maintaining of such employment levels until 2010.

The construction of an 18,500 m² hall started immediately in July 2000 and was finished at the end of October 2000. Production started ceremonially on November 6, 2000. Continuous operation required that each worker undertake three 12-hour shifts per week. An average employee had a high school education, while 10% had a university degree (echoing the percent of the total population with that level of qualification). 5% of staff attended free English classes offered by the company. Flextronics' annual report for the fiscal year ended March 2001 comments: "We also anticipate incurring significant capital expenditures and operating lease commitments in order to support our anticipated expansions of our . . . regional manufacturing facilities in the Czech Republic" (Flextronics, 2001:30). Due to high demand, the company added temporary jobs, and the total employment peaked in 2001 with 2,500 workers. In April 2001, Flextronics offered two-years scholarships for up to 15 prospective students at Brno tertiary education institutions.

A new 17,000 m² hall was built within 105 days and started producing electronic components in December 2001. Total investments exceeded 400 million Czech Koruna. Everything seemed to be a big success. In March 2002, Flextronics actively participated in the big national job fair held at six major technical universities throughout the country, trying to recruit the best university graduates. Production lines ran at full capacity. The company had been regularly reported to be among the most benevolent employers in the region.

Take Off

The annual report for fiscal year 2002 contains a scant four pages—including the front cover consisting of a single photograph, and the back cover featuring only contact details. The introductory paragraph of the CEO's Letter to Our Shareholders notified them that:

> The 2002 fiscal year was one that saw many changes at Flextronics. It will come as no surprise to our shareholders that the year was a tough one, for our company, our industry, and especially for our customers. . . . Margins came under pressure, and we were forced to engage in major cutbacks. (Flextronics, 2002:2)

From the beginning of 2002, Brno's factory started to continually reduce its staff. When the Labour Office registered 200 to 300 new applicants—former Flextronics' workers—for unemployment benefits, warning lights began to flash. In the middle of May 2002, it was made public that a part of the Hungarian activities would be shifted to China, as a joint decision of Microsoft and Flextronics. Hungarian Internet-based daily eVilággazdaság indicated that relocated production of Xbox game consoles would cut some 1,200 jobs in Hungary. A few days later, Flextronics made public its decision to cut 550 jobs in the Czech plant by the end of August. The reason—global recession in the industry.

In a shock announcement, Flextronics' managing director for European operations Jutta Devenish announced on July 11, 2002 that the Brno plant would be entirely closed. One thousand employees lost their jobs virtually in the blink of an eye. The shutdown was declared to be a part of European consolidation. Activities were believed to be transferred to Hungary and mostly to China. This decision by the American-Singaporean company immediately received a high degree of publicity in the Czech media. The first foreign investor to be awarded government incentives was leaving the country. Headlines asked: Did Flextronics meet all the requirements stated in the contracts with the Czech government and with the City of Brno? Did they provide as many jobs and for as long a time as promised?

Flextronics' managing director for the Czech Republic and Hungary Hugh Kelly specified that the workers would be laid off in December. In Brno, the research laboratory with some 34 staff would continue in operation. It was the biggest single dismissal of workers in the history of Brno. The city fell into shadow.

A few days later, the Czech Ministry of Industry and Trade released its preliminary findings. Deputy Minister Václav Petříček proposed that Flextronics had fulfilled all the obligations arising from the memorandum. Ministerial officials were on the way to carry out a detailed investigation on the premises. City representatives contributed to the media discussion with the press release: Market rent for the land would be 55 million Czech Koruna. The city would consider legal action to make Flextronics pay appropriate compensation.

In August, the City of Brno renounced the contract on the 7 hectares of land purchased by Flextronics to prevent the possible sale of that land by the company. On September 26, 2002 the Czech Office for the Protection of Competition initiated its official investigation of Flextronics International Ltd. on suspicion of not fulfilling the condition for public support. Legal machinery took the helm. The situation became even more difficult when the public learned in November that Flextronics had negotiated in the Ukraine to establish new foreign direct investment there in exchange for government incentives.

Final Bill

In December 2002, the name of the company attracted the attention of European media once more. The Multek division of Flextronics International Ltd. decided to close factories in Irvine (California) and in Kumla (Sweden) to further reduce operational costs. Multek sites supplying the European market remained located in Böblingen (Germany) and Doumen (China). Restructuring costs were estimated at less than 100 million USD. On the day of the announcement, the company's shares rose 4 cents to 10.08 USD.

In the beginning of 2003, the City of Brno and Flextronics finally agreed on mutual compensation. Flextronics accepted an obligation to pay 38 million Czech Koruna to the City of Brno. The company retained title to the land under the production site. The City of Brno gained the company parking, entrance building, access roads, and infrastructure.

The company's proxy statement for fiscal year 2003 revealed expected results: Cumulative shareholder return dropped by half within one year (see Table 5.2).

In April 2003, the former production site of Flextronics found its new use. The American giant Honeywell signed a contract with Flextronics, renting the facilities for seven years. Honeywell established a new manufacturing and R&D center for the aerospace industry and for automated fire and security systems for buildings. Honeywell bought the land under the factory and announced a project for further site development. The company was already known in the country for its research and development facilities, located in Prague since 1993. The Prague technological laboratory was the first such R&D facility established by the company outside the U.S.A. Honeywell moved some of its manufacturing lines to Brno from West European locations, allowing "Go-East-mania" to reveal its friendly side. The mutual deed of release between Flextronics and the City of Brno made it possible for the Czech competition authority to officially cease its investigation on 6 May 2003.

Foreign Direct Investment in the Czech Republic Since 2003

Since 2003, the investment roadmap has changed significantly, both in the Czech Republic and worldwide. The Czech Republic entered the European Union in 2004, together with Hungary, Poland, Slovakia, and Slovenia; the Baltic states of Estonia, Latvia, and Lithuania; and the Mediterranean islands of Malta and Cyprus, followed by Bulgaria and Romania in 2007. Accession to the European Union created opportunities for free movement of goods across national borders but within one common market. However, it also resulted in the economic conditions of newcomers gradually converging with those in Western Europe. With rising labor costs, the new member countries have lost their appeal to host low-skilled and low-technology manufacturing sites, which have been shifting eastwards again (to Central Asian countries such as Kazakhstan).

TABLE 5.2 Comparison of 5-Year Cumulative Return (Million USD)

	1998	1999	2000	2001	2002	2003
Flextronics International Ltd.	100.00	236.18	652.39	277.86	338.06	161.53
S&P 500	100.00	118.46	139.72	109.43	109.69	82.53
Peer Group	100.00	219.52	426.86	215.46	154.44	67.76

The table compares the cumulative total shareholder return on ordinary shares, the Standard & Poor's 500 Stock Index, and a peer group that includes Benchmark Electronics, Inc., Celestica, Inc., Jabil Circuit, Inc., Sanmina-SCI Corporation, and Solectron Corporation. Data as of March 31.

Source: Flextronics (2003):18

Entry to the European Union also meant that investment incentives have been decreasing and governments became more cautious about awarding large incentives to insecure investment projects. Similarly, there has been a lesson drawn from the less-than-successful Flextronics example. Since 2003, there was no further divestment by any company until the global economic slowdown hit world markets in 2008.

Hitachi began constructing its factory for plasma televisions in the industrial park Triangle located 60 km northwest of Prague near the city of Žatec in 2006. Investment incentives granted by the central government reached 252 million Czech Koruna—160 million for creating new jobs, 23 million for staff training, and 69 million worth of land. The company's investment peaked at 1.733 billion Czech Koruna, with a projected total of more than 2,500 jobs. However, the company was forced to announce closure of the factory in March 2009 due to deteriorating demand. The company declared it would pay back all of the investment incentives and meet all its obligations to the Czech government. However, all 800 employees lost their means of earning a living.

Another casualty of the global crisis was a smaller plant in Brno's industrial zone Černovická Terasa. Ohmori Technos—a Japanese parts supplier for air conditioning units—pulled out of the country in April 2009. Their investment of 440 million Czech Koruna was not entirely lost, as most of their plant and some 100 employees transferred to Daikin (an air conditioning units producer with facilities nearby). Within weeks, Ohmori repaid all the investment incentives it had received, in excess of 200 million Czech Koruna.

Since the era of Flextronics, the city of Brno shifted its focus and successfully attracted more (but smaller and younger) entrepreneurial firms from all over the world to its industrial zone. Companies producing plastics, precision machinery, and telecommunication technologies have been operating from the zone, employing in total over 2,000 staff. The former Lord Mayor of Brno, Petr Duchoň, served as a parliamentarian in the European Parliament between 2004 and 2009, running unsuccessfully for the Czech Senate in the meantime. Brno emerged as the economic centre for that part of the country, gaining a reputation as a welcoming home for innovators, entrepreneurs, and smaller investors.

Flextronics continues to grow and thrive, investing in multiple locations around the world. Its 2010 Annual Report states that "Our facilities include large industrial parks, ranging in size from approximately 400,000 to 6.0 million square feet, in Brazil, China, Hungary, India, Malaysia, Mexico, and Poland. We also have regional manufacturing operations, generally ranging in size from under 100,000 to approximately 1.0 million square feet, in Austria, Brazil, Canada, China, Czech Republic, Denmark, Finland, France, Germany, Hungary, India, Indonesia, Ireland, Israel, Italy, Japan, Korea, Malaysia, Mexico, Netherlands, Norway, Poland, Romania, Singapore, Slovakia, Sweden, Taiwan, Ukraine, United Kingdom, and the United States. We also have smaller design and engineering centers and product introduction centers at a number of locations in the world's major electronics markets" (Flextronics, 2010:24).

Discussion Questions

1. Why do businesses such as Flextronics move "East"? Summarize the key arguments. Consider the role of labor costs for wealth creation in the "West" and the implications this has for the location decisions of entrepreneurs in various types of industry and for different business activities.
2. What are the ethical concerns about the decision to shut down Flextronics' plant in Brno? Are those different from the legal obligations of the firm? Define the stakeholders involved in the decision, and their perspectives on the situation.
3. Discuss the importance of government incentives for entrepreneurs. Are there any grant schemes or programs available for entrepreneurs in your country, or specifically in your region? In which sectors or areas? (Why is your government focusing on these particular sectors or areas?)
4. Why do smaller entrepreneurs receive relatively smaller subsidies? Is such a policy wrong? (Why or why not?)

References

Čipálková, J. (2001) Černovická terasa. *BVV Magazín 1*, 29.

CzechInvest. (2000). Flextronics vybuduje průmyslový park. *CzechInvest Newsletter 1*. Retrieved from http://www.czechinvest.cz/ci/ci_cz.nsf/(NewslettersW)/C9903DDD66472E0AC12569D0002CC13A?OpenDocument

CzechInvest. (2001). Flextronics postavil v rekordním čase novou halu. *CzechInvest Newsletter 2* Retrieved from http://www.czechinvest.cz/ci/ci_cz.nsf/(NewslettersW)/EC41171DA741E220C12569D0002B6C5C?OpenDocument

CzechInvest (2003) Investment climate in the Czech Republic: Your complete investment guide. *Czechinvest*. Retrieved from http://www.czechinvest.cz/ci/ci_an.nsf/Publikace?OpenPage

Flextronics (2001) Annual Report. *Flextronics*. Retrieved from http://www.flextronics.com/Investors/annualReportSEC.asp

Flextronics (2002) Annual Report. *Flextronics*. Retrieved from http://www.flextronics.com/Investors/annualReportSEC.asp

Flextronics (2003) Proxy statement. *Flextronics*. Retrieved from http://www.flextronics.com/Investors/annualReportSEC.asp

Holý, T. (2009). Hitachi zavře u Žatce továrnu na televizory. *MAFRA*. Retrieved from http://www.novinky.cz/ekonomika/165009-hitachi-zavre-u-zatce-tovarnu-na-televizory.html

IDNES (2002). Investoři z Čech mizí, ale ne masově. *MAFRA*. Retrieved from http://ekonomika.idnes.cz/ekonomika.asp?r=ekonomika&c=A021121_221559_ekonomika_was&l=1

IDNES (2002). Divize Flextronics International Ltd. uzavírá některé podniky. *MAFRA*. Retrieved from http://akcie.idnes.cz/ekoinv.asp?r=ekoinv&c=A021209_091400_ekoinv_4442

IDNES (2002). Flextronics asi nebude státu vracet pobídky. *MAFRA*. Retrieved from http://ekonomika.idnes.cz/ekoakcie.asp?r=ekoakcie&c=A020714_212316_ekoakcie_pol&l=1&t=A020714_212316_ekoakcie_pol&r2=ekoakcie)

IDNES (2002). Většina lidí opustí Flextronics v prosinci. *MAFRA*. Retrieved from http://ekonomika.idnes.cz/ekoakcie.asp?r=ekoakcie&c=A020711_160153_ekoakcie_KLU&l=1

IDNES (2002). Flextronics International uzavře brněnský závod, propustí 1000 zaměstnanců. *MAFRA*. Retrieved from http://akcie.idnes.cz/ekoinv.asp?r=ekoinv&c=A020711_162800_ekoinv_1604

IDNES (2002). Veletrhy pracovních příležitostí v roce 2002. *MAFRA*. Retrieved from http://zamestnani.idnes.cz/zamestnani.asp?r=zamestnani&c=2002M062Z01C

IDNES (2003). Honeywell si v Brně plácl s Flextronic-sem. *MAFRA*. Retrieved from http://ekonomika.idnes.cz/ekoakcie.asp?r=ekoakcie&c=A030325_183527_ekoakcie_ven&l=1&t=A030325_183527_ekoakcie_ven&r2=ekoakcie

iHNed.cz (2002). Volkswagen Group rozvíjí výrobu na Ukrajině. *Economia*. Retrieved from http://ihned.cz/mail/0/11796370

iHNed.cz (2002). Společnost Flextronics International tvrdí, že dohodu neporušila. *Economia*. Retrieved from http://ihned.cz/mail/0/11339260

iHNed.cz (2002). Flextronics propouští, přestože sliboval opak. *Economia*. Retrieved from http://ihned.cz/mail/0/11049550

iHNed.cz (2009). Japonská Ohmori opustila Brno. *Economia*. Retrieved from http://proc-ne.ihned.cz/c1-36659680-japonska-ohmori-opustila-brno

Kanellos, M. (2015). Flextronics: A quiet giant in solar. *Green Tech*. Retrieved from https://www.forbes.com/sites/michaelkanellos/2015/09/08/flextronics-a-quiet-giant-in-solar/#31dd38017ceb

King, R. (2015). Flextronics will manage global supply chain with new real-time software. *The Wall Street Journal*. Retrieved from https://www.wsj.com/articles/flextronics-will-manage-global-supply-chain-with-new-real-time-software-1436311241

Simon, B. (2004). TECHNOLOGY; Flextronics Will Acquire Nortel's Equipment Plants. *The New York Times*. Retrieved from http://www.nytimes.com/2004/06/30/business/technology-flextronics-will-acquire-nortel-s-equipment-plants.html?rref=collection%2Ftimestopic%2FFlextronics%20International%20Ltd.&action=click&contentCollection=business&region=stream&module=stream_unit&version=latest&contentPlacement=4&pgtype=collection

Tiezzi, J. (2016). Flextronics: Strong growth projected to 2020. *Seeking Alpha*. Retrieved from https://seekingalpha.com/article/3975432-flextronics-strong-growth-projected-2020

Relevant Videos

The UK: The Number 1 Destination for Inward Investment (FDI) in Europe:
https://www.youtube.com/watch?v=R0UT6TGstEI

Conference: "The best FDI practices in Central and South Eastern Europe", June 5th, 2017:
https://www.youtube.com/watch?v=q2iUljSDpRI

Tutorial 1 - How to influence the EU decision-making process:
https://www.youtube.com/watch?v=ySXaFsu9BD4

Tutorial 2 - The Common Fisheries Policy:
https://www.youtube.com/watch?v=oT5hkgsTQVg

CSR Europe: Stimulating an Entrepreneurial Mindset and Promoting Entrepreneurship Education:
https://www.youtube.com/watch?v=4HnwK6SSoFA

IngPro Ltd: Grow in Central Europe:
https://www.youtube.com/watch?v=8du4TShByLk

Part Two

Specialized Topics

Chapter Six

EXPORTING

UNAGRO CORPORATION: NOTHING IS IMPOSSIBLE![1]

Flavia Barbery and Janet L. Rovenpor, Manhattan College

Learning Objectives

1. *Compare* the alternatives facing a general manager who must decide whether or not to sell two factories, sell one factory in order to save the second factory, or implement a third, innovative solution.
2. *Identify* the internal factors (e.g., company values, talented managers) and external factors (e.g., support from parent company, the imposition of new quality standards by the EU) that led to the successful restructuring of a company.
3. *Appreciate* how popular management techniques, such as the Balanced Scorecard and Goal Setting, can be implemented in companies in developing nations who employ workers from indigenous populations.
4. *Describe* the forces that enable innovation to occur within a large, diversified company.
5. *Explain* the importance of "strategic fit." All the parts of an organization—its strategy, corporate entrepreneurship goals, organizational culture, human resources, technology, and governance structure—need to be aligned in order to maximize potential and achieve goals.
6. *Understand* what is meant by "intrapreneurship" and how it is related to innovation.
7. *Realize* how exporting can be an important strategy for the international development of an entrepreneurial business.

Key Words

Amazonas SA	Exporting
Bolivia	Manutata SA
Brazil nuts	

Abstract

Union Agroindustrial de Cañeros SA (UNAGRO) was a large diversified company based in Santa Cruz, Bolivia. It operated a number of plants dedicated to the processing of sugar cane, Brazil nuts, grain, pork, and wood. This case study focuses on the restructuring of one of UNAGRO's plants, Manutata, that was respon-

Contributed by Flavia Barbery and Janet L. Rovenpor. Copyright © Kendall Hunt Publishing Company.

[1] We wish to thank the following individuals for their generous time and assistance: Mr. Clover Paz, General Manager of UNAGRO; Mr. Napoleon Montaño, Manager of Human Resources of UNAGRO; Mr. Marcelo Paz, General Manager of Manutata; Mr. Alejahdro Paz, Manager of Production of Manutata; Jose Padilla, Commercial Manager of Manutata; Karen Toledo, Quality Manager of Manutata; Pricila Mariaca, General Accountant of Manutata; Lucia Cordano, Manager of Human Resources of Manutata; and Rosendo Barbery, Executive Vice President of Business Development of UNAGRO. Without their input, this case study would not have been possible.

sible for processing and exporting Brazil nuts. In order to keep the plant open, Clover Paz, the general manager, implemented a new human resource management system and a new nut processing technology. Improvements in the quality of the product enabled Manutata to become a leading Bolivian exporter of Brazil nuts.

A Critical Decision

Union Agroindustrial de Cañeros SA (UNAGRO) was founded in 1972 by a group of farmers in Santa Cruz, Bolivia. With Roberto Barbery at the helm as the company's visionary leader, the farmers planned to build and operate a plant dedicated to sugar and sugar alcohol production. The startup of UNAGRO was a unique undertaking. Barbery was able to convince 1,200 peasants to pool their resources and invest in the company. England's Lloyds Bank Limited provided the rest of the financing, which was guaranteed by the Bolivian government. Barbery's primary concern was to establish a just and fair working relationship between owners of sugar cane factories and farmers. A few government-owned factories in Santa Cruz had been criticized for exploiting the farmers who supplied the raw sugar cane.

UNAGRO opened its first sugar and sugar alcohol refinery in 1977. From the beginning, the plant's managers showed concern for its employees, many of whom were also shareholders. They refused to follow a common industry practice in which laborers in the sugar cane fields were required to stay awake for 24 hours until a truck came to pick up the cut sugar cane if they wanted to receive fair wages. The company offered employees medical insurance. Its shareholders were able to lift themselves out of poverty and send their children to good schools so that they could enter professional occupations.

Roberto Barbery was UNAGRO's first president, a position he held until 1994. Under his guidance, UNAGRO became a large agricultural firm supplying products to customers on a national and international scale. In 1985, it merged with Kholvy SA and Jihussa Agropecuaria Y De Servicios SA. In 1989, UNAGRO opened Amazonas SA and in 1995, it acquired Manutata SA. Both plants were dedicated to the harvesting, processing and exporting of Brazil nuts. UNAGRO soon diversified into the cultivation of grain, the processing of pork, and the production of wood (see Figure 6.1).

UNAGRO had a democratic governance structure. Shareholders were invited to a yearly meeting to review the company's performance. Every two years, elections were held in which a slate of candidates (and their alternates in case the officials were not able to fulfill their responsibilities) was presented to shareholders for voting. The shareholders selected 10 representatives and 10 alternates to serve on UNAGRO's board of directors. In turn, the board of directors elected the president, vice president, and treasurer.

The Asian financial crisis in 1997 affected the Bolivian economy. The country's banks tightened their lending practices and denied UNAGRO's request for a loan. The timing could not have been worse. UNAGRO was still paying down debt it had incurred to finance the acquisition of Manutata and to purchase new equipment for a major plant renovation at Amazonas.

UNAGRO Corporation

UNAGRO S.A. (1974)	KHOLVY S.A. (1985)	JIHUSSA AGROPEC-UARIA Y DE SERVICOS S.A. (1985)	AMAZONAS S.A. (1989)	CHANE S.A. (1993)	MANUTATA S.A. (1995)	MACONS LTDA. (1998)	UPON SOFTWARE S.A. (2003)	SAMCO S.A. (2006)	G&B Enterprise Import and Export S.A. (2008)
A sugar factory that produces high quality sugar and alcohol. It also produces energy for its own factory; the rest is sold to an electricity company, CRE (Cooperative Rural of Electrification).	A retailer that provides massive product in a national scale.	Responsible for grain cultivation and pork processing.	A factory that harvests, transports, processes, and exports Brazil nuts. It is run by the same managers as Manutata and uses the same processing technologies.	The company specialized in the cultivation, harvest, and transport of sugar cane as well as grains.	A factory that harvests, transports, processes, and exports Brazil nuts. The processing system was designed by employees. The facility is 100% environmentally friendly.	In charge of the collection, sawing, drying, and commercialization of wood.	Specialized in production and commercialization of computer programs as well as providing companies with computer consultant services.	A new business concept that provides security services and covers fires, theft, and medical emergencies through the digital monitoring of businesses and residences.	A company that produces and commercializes snacks and chocolates with Brazil nuts.

FIGURE 6.1 UNAGRO Corporation's Businesses

Luis Barbery, the chief executive of UNAGRO in 1997, scheduled an emergency meeting with Clover Paz, the general manager of Manutata and Amazonas, to discuss the company's financial difficulties. Because UNAGRO's ability to raise capital had been curtailed, it would no longer be able to provide the same level of funding that Manutata and Amazonas had enjoyed in the past.

At the meeting, Luis Barbery mentioned that decision-making at all UNAGRO companies would be decentralized. In the particular case of Amazonas and Manutata, Clover Paz would assume responsibility for deciding on a future course of action. Clover had three options: 1) sell the two factories, 2) sell one factory and use the funds raised from the sale to invest in the second factory, and 3) develop an alternative solution.

Paz made the difficult decision to close Amazonas and to focus his efforts on restructuring Manutata. He vowed that he would "do things differently." Paz was eager to implement some new ideas about management that he had been working on. Before the financial crisis in Bolivia, he had taken courses at INCAE University in Costa Rica. He was introduced briefly to such management techniques as the Balanced Scorecard and Goal Setting. The course inspired him to study these topics in greater detail on his own. On behalf of Manutata, Paz took out a loan for $25,000 at an interest rate of 6 percent from a private lender. He was now ready to get to work.

A Brief History of Manutata

In 1988, Roberto Barbery, the founder of UNAGRO, hired Clover Paz, a 23-year-old mechanical engineer. Paz's first assignment was to implement a new irrigation system for the company. His second assignment was to travel to Riberalta to study the feasibility of expanding UNAGRO's businesses into prospecting for gold deposits. The city of Riberalta was situated at the intersection of two rivers, the Beni and the Madre de Dios, in the northeastern region of Bolivia. The rivers were a rich source of minerals. Early explorers even believed that El Dorado, the legendary City of Gold, could be found nearby.

Barbery accompanied Paz on the visit. He had seen Paz's potential and viewed this as a way to develop the young engineer's management skills. At a local hotel where the gentlemen were staying, the talk of the townspeople was not about precious metals but about hard-shelled fruits. The Brazil nut grew on trees from the Lecythidaceau family found in the region's pristine forests. The nut was rich in magnesium, thiamine, and selenium. It could be pressed into oils. Added to fresh butter, cream, and vanilla, the Brazil nut became an important ingredient in a popular Ben and Jerry's ice cream flavor called, "Rainforest Crunch."

Barbery and Paz recognized that UNAGRO had an opportunity to diversify into the harvesting and processing of Brazil nuts. A case for Brazil nuts could be made easily in front of other executives back in Santa Cruz. UNAGRO's expertise was in agricultural products; it had little knowledge of the gold exploration and mining industry. Moreover, a feasibility study on the exportation of Brazil nuts showed that the industry was headed towards profitability. In 1989, UNAGRO opened its first plant, Amazonas SA, to harvest and process Brazil nuts.

Seeing an increase in demand in the market for Brazil nuts, UNAGRO acquired a second plant, Manutata SA, in 1995.

The word, Manutata, in the indigenous dialect spoken in the region, meant "father of the rivers." The phrase had significance for the company's employees. A "river" was associated with "water" which was necessary for all life. Manutata gave employees "water" from two rivers. It acted like a "father." Manutata played a supportive and nurturing role in the lives of its employees. Employees, who were trying to escape from poverty, viewed their wages as a way to improve their standard of living.

Manutata's Mission, Vision, and Values

Clover Paz became the general manager of Manutata in 1998. With the assistance of other senior managers, he created a new mission and vision for the company. Manutata's mission was "to become a leader in the Brazil nuts' industry, marketing the nuts as an ecologically nutritive and rejuvenating product throughout the world." It was dedicated to bringing pride and recognition to the region, Riberalta, and to the country, Bolivia. The company's vision was "to provide its clients with a high-quality product, delivered through the outstanding efforts of a motivated workforce that generated economic growth, which would enable Manutata to become an international market leader."

Human capital was Manutata's most important asset. In an interview, Clover Paz stated, "Companies do not triumph, people triumph; working together means winning together. The way to achieve success is helping others to achieve success." All employees were treated equally. The only difference was that every employee had a different function. In an effort to erase distinctions between line and staff, employees were encouraged to look into each other's faces when speaking as opposed to looking down at the floor, a habit consistent with Bolivian culture. Employees invented nicknames, such as "Inge," to address Manutata's general manager. Employees were even allowed to enter their manager's office and interrupt meetings if they had an important concern that needed immediate attention. Sometimes, the manager made the employee part of the meeting.

Employees were put in charge of the physical space in which they occupied in the factory. They were expected to keep it meticulously clean. There were strict rules and procedures that needed to be followed. Employees were tested every month on their knowledge of processing and marketing Brazil nuts. Leaders of the work teams rotated every month in order to give all members a chance to develop their skills and meet with senior managers to discuss their team's successes and failures.

Employees were not penalized for mistakes but were expected to use them as opportunity to identify and eliminate the causes for the mistakes, thereby making the company stronger.

As Clover Paz said, "There are no bad troops, there are bad officials. Every person wants to be successful and if they do not contribute it is because the organizational culture does not let them contribute."

To support the new mission and goals, Paz put in place a new organizational structure (see Figures 6.2 and 6.3).

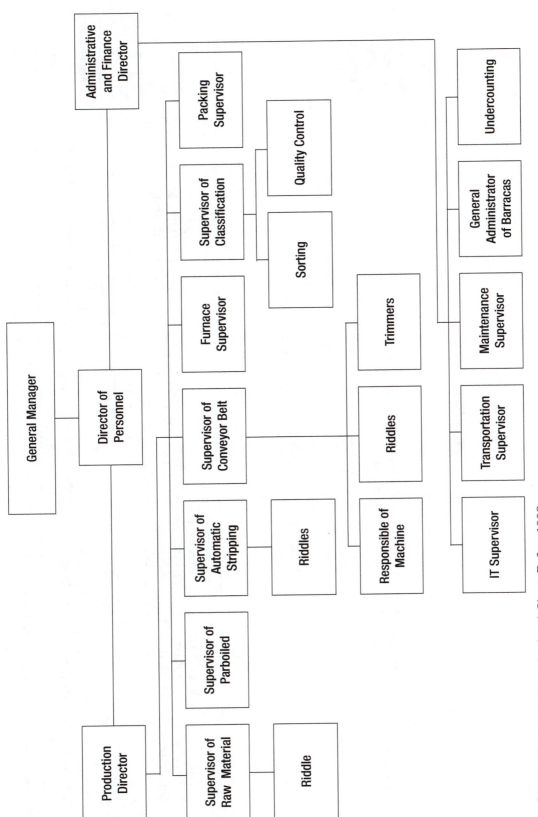

FIGURE 6.2 Manutata's Organizational Chart: Before 1998

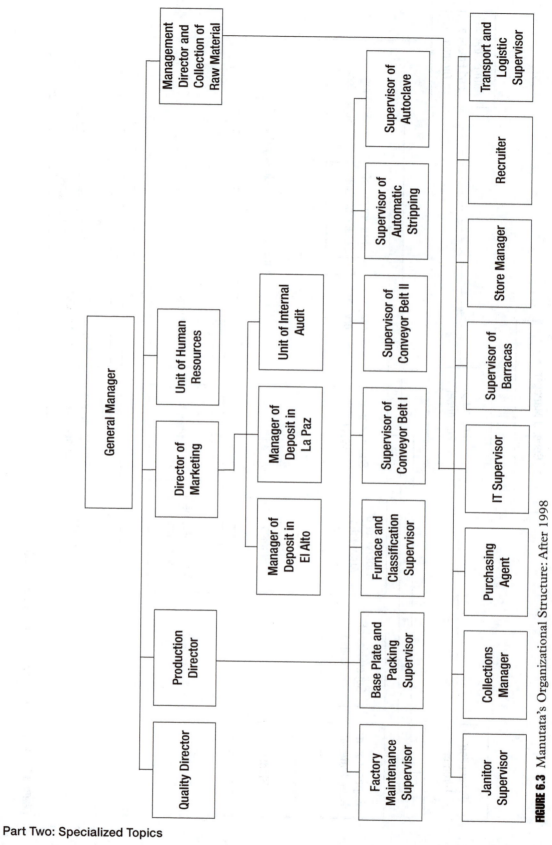

FIGURE 6.3 Manutata's Organizational Structure: After 1998

Human Resource Management

In 1998, Manutata did not have a Human Resources Department. A director of personnel was responsible for all administrative functions, including payroll, employee contracts, and labor relations. Napoleon Montaño, a psychologist, was hired and charged with developing a Human Resource Management Department. He established formal policies regarding the selection, hiring, training, and orientation of new employees. He implemented a new motivation system in which monetary and non-monetary rewards for excellent performance were made available to employees.

Montaño reflected on why the new motivational program at Manutata was so successful. He said, "Between 80–90 percent of companies fail to implement sound incentive systems. Many companies in Bolivia had a head start on us but they did not realize how important it is to get employees to embrace the new techniques. Employees must be included in strategic planning, and learn about how the balanced scorecard will help them achieve their own personal goals. They need to clearly understand what is expected of them. The only way to do this is to make sure objectives are measureable and understandable. Employees must have the objectives in the foremost of their minds every day when they are at work. This is critical for the launch of a new incentive system."

Goal Setting and the Use of Incentives

Manutata's incentive program was divided into two parts: Macro or general objectives referred to the company as a whole; micro or individual objectives were associated with an employee's position within the company. Both were interrelated and of equal importance. When every employee achieved his or her micro objectives, the company, as a whole, would achieve its macro objectives.

Macro objectives consisted of reducing costs, increasing sales, and improving productivity. They were consistent with the company's mission but could change over time. The way to reach the objectives was through the development of strategies. The objectives were to be clear and understood by all employees. The starting point for an objective was higher or equal to the one reached so far.

Micro objectives related to an employee's position, knowledge, and hygiene. Employees were trained to become their own internal auditors. They understood the steps required to deliver a high quality product. Every month, objectives were set. Often, the macro objective was to increase production. A related micro objective for an individual employee might have been to ensure that humidity in the plant ranged from 13–16 percent. Another related micro objective might have been to keep misclassifications of nuts by quality at the end of the conveyor belt run to under 2 percent.

Incentives were proportional to the level of achievement of the objectives. They were based on individual and team performance. A percentage of wages was added to an employee's pay at the end of the month. The extra earnings could double an employee's pay for the month. Employees who reached their objectives, and who were considered among the best employees at Manutata, won a year-end trip to Santa Cruz, Cobija, Rurrenabaque, or some other place in Bolivia.

To support the achievement of the macro and micro objectives, Manutata held two different types of monthly meetings. In one meeting, managers gave employees feedback on their performance that month. Human resource specialists, with the help of sector heads, created plans for improvement for those employees that did not perform as well as expected. Employees worked in self-directed teams, and the leaders were responsible for coordinating the completion of tasks.

Another monthly meeting usually took place outside the factory where employees could be in touch with nature. Employees from each sector had the opportunity to inform the audience of recent achievements, needs, and opportunities. Employees, not their managers, gave presentations and ran the work sessions. This gave employees an opportunity to develop their management skills. Sometimes, to prepare for the meetings, employees were given training ahead of time in the art of public speaking. Managers and area managers were people who listened, not people who directed. Employees showcased quality tools (e.g., Pareto Analysis) that they knew their sector had put to good use. Everyone in the meetings learned something new and participants helped each other find solutions to problems. At the end of the meetings, participants enjoyed a barbeque, and played sports.

The rollout of the new incentive system was not always smooth. One of the managers realized that employees did not seem to understand the objectives that were given to them. The reason was that several employees could not read or write. The managers learned that because employees could not fill out the forms required to become eligible for a monetary reward, they lost out on extra incentives. Instead of firing the employees, the manager decided that the company would teach them basic skills. In 2004, an "Alphabetization" program located in a nearby learning center was started to teach employees to read and write. Employees received their full pay even when they were in class. Manutata paid all required course fees. By 2010, at least 10 students had graduated from the school.

Many of Manutata's employees came from an indigenous population. They were not initially equipped with a basic understanding of workplace conventions. Employees took soap home from the factory restrooms thinking that it was like picking fruit from a tree. They jumped over the shoe-cleaning equipment because they did not know what it was used for and they wore their uniforms at home as well as at work. Managers at Manutata took it upon themselves to provide basic skills training to its employees. Alongside the new incentive system, a series of comprehensive training and educational programs were launched. Some employees were deaf. Courses in sign language were given so that other employees could communicate with their deaf coworkers. Additional courses in home economics (to help families save for future needs) and family planning (to prevent unwanted pregnancies and drug abuse; to understand and manage different stages in a child's development) were also offered.

Once employees understood and got accustomed to the new incentive system, they began to earn a lot of extra money. Their purchasing power increased, and many bought household items and motorcycles. Several employees expressed an interest in working on Sundays. They often tried to offer their coworkers free meals in return for their Sunday shift at the factory. If they had the choice, they would work from Sunday to Sunday. Managers felt that a focus on money and possessions was not healthy. Employees should seek an appropriate work/life balance. They were encouraged to exercise on a regular basis, spend time with their families, seek out cultural activities, and develop their spiritual sides. Manutata launched athletic, cultural and family programs.

Once a year, production at Manutata was halted. Employees took a scenic 5-kilometer walk in the Amazon. The message of the march was to demonstrate that the company was not just concerned with making profits. Managers were willing to give up output in order for employees to get some exercise and appreciate the beauty of their natural surroundings.

Training and Quality of Life Programs

On-the-job training was made a priority at Manutata. The company provided 2,400 hours of training per year. Employees took courses in quality management tools (e.g., the cascade system, cause and effect, and cobweb). They could also choose courses that taught them how to become a leader or how to manage their relationships with coworkers and acquaintances in social situations.

Each employee was provided with a food safety manual filled with simple explanations and diagrams describing the quality certification system (i.e., HACCP), the steps in the processing of Brazil nuts, and the requirements for maintaining a clean work environment. The manual even pointed out the proper way to wash hands before and after work. A company-provided uniform had to be worn correctly before entering the factory and removed at the end of the workday. Policies promoting excellent hygiene were to be meticulously followed by highly qualified employees. All employees, not just those who worked in the plant, were required to know the manual perfectly.

Managerial employees were also trained constantly. If funding was available, they took classes abroad like the senior management program or the human resources program taken at the INCAE University. After finishing a class abroad, employees were supposed to come back and teach the most important skills that had been learned to the group.

Not everything at Manutata was hard work. There was time to relax and have fun as well. Sport and recreational activities were held during the year. These included: internal soccer tournaments, volleyball championships, and marathons. UNAGRO's Olympic games for Manutata's employees and also for employees at the other companies were the most popular. The games were held in Santa Cruz City. It was possible for employees to meet one another in person for the first time even though they had communicated with one another on the phone for business purposes.

Manutata celebrated special days like Mother's Day, Father's Day, Labor Day, and the company's anniversary. The children of Manutata employees also had their own celebrations where they got presents and played games. They visited the factory and learned about the jobs their parents held. They joined the company's cinema club. Once a month, employees who had their birthdays that month were recognized.

The Processing of Brazil Nuts

The original Manutata plant relied on a manual peeling process for the nuts. The process was time-consuming and inefficient. As soon as the plant was acquired by UNAGRO, managers went to work to implement a new technology first developed by Amazonas. The extensive factory renovations increased productivity and the quality of the product, making its exportation to other countries possible (see Figures 6.4 and 6.5).

Here is how Manutata's processing system worked. In the first phase, state forest owners or "barracas" gathered the Brazil nuts that had fallen to the ground in the Amazon. They were packed in bags of 60 kilograms and transported on barges that moved along the river or on trucks that traveled on roads down to Manutata's factory. As soon as the bags arrived, they were weighed. The Brazil nuts were then dried in rotating cylindrical machines and placed in special containers for preservation.

In the second phase, the shelled nuts were spread out on conveyor belts for classification by size. An autoclave thermal system, which applied steam pressure to the shelled nuts, started the third phase of processing. The pressure needed to be adjusted for small batches, depending on the size of the nuts in each batch. This phase was critical in order to prevent the proliferation of pathogens. The use of high temperature and the subsequent injection of cold water facilitated the separation of the seed from its shell.

Courtesy of UNAGRO

FIGURE 6.4 Classification of Brazil Nuts According to Quality

FIGURE 6.5 Brazil Nuts Pass through Ultraviolet Light to Ascertain Aflatoxin Levels

The fourth phase involved the final peeling and classification of the nuts. Specially designed mechanical equipment broke the shell via impact. A strong air stream, circulating inside a cyclone, enabled the separation of the fruit from its shell. The unshelled nuts traveled along sterile conveyor belts and were classified according to their quality by highly trained employees (See Figure 6.6). Unshelled first-class Brazil nuts were whole, healthy, and of uniform color. Unshelled second-class nuts were healthy but chipped, cracked, or slightly discolored. Unshelled third-class nuts were healthy but broken. Unshelled fourth-class nuts were broken into pieces and had black dots or ulcers; they were discarded.

The fifth phase consisted of the thermal dehydration process, which reduced the humidity within first, second, and third quality Brazil nuts from 25 percent to between 2.2 percent and 3.2 percent. Dehydration times depended on the humidity of the nuts before they entered the dehydration chamber.

The last phase was called final classification and packaging. The nuts were subjected to rigorous inspection by specialized personnel in a sterile environment. They were weighed using a precision electronic scale and packed in flat polyester bags that had been treated with aluminum and polyethylene to ensure the preservation of the product. Each 44-pound bag was placed inside a cardboard box and readied for export from Bolivia to the rest of the world.

The final product could be consumed for up to two years after processing. Manutata made good use of waste materials that accumulated during processing. The discarded shells became fuel used to produce steam.

First Quality: whole Brazil nuts, with uniform color, healthy, without physical damage

Extra Large	90 Units per pound
Large	90–110 Units per pound
Medium	110–130 Units per pound
Small	140–160 Units per pound
Midget	160–180 Units per pound
Tiny	180–220 Units per pound
Super Tiny	220 Units per pound

Second Quality: lightly chipped Brazil nuts that presented small stripes, breakage, physical defects on the surface or not of characteristic color.

No size classification (no more than 1/10 of the original size).

Third Quality: Size ranges

Broken Normal	Broken Brazil nuts, healthy without any specific size
Broken Especial	Manually cut Brazil nuts in (50% broken)
Broken 5	Manually cut Brazil nuts in (70% broken)
Broken 6	Manually cut Brazil nuts in (85% broken)

Fourth Quality:

Chia	Brazil nuts or pieces of Brazil nuts that presented black dots or ulcers and were discarded.

Note: a unit is equal to one seed

FIGURE 6.6 Classification of Brazil Nuts

In 2002, Manutata introduced Hazardous Analysis and Critical Control Points (HACCP standards). These standards were developed by the Food and Drug Administration and the U.S Department of Agriculture to identify potential food safety hazards. In 2007, Manutata was granted HACCP certification. It also obtained Kosher and Organic certifications.

Productivity and Export Statistics

Besides improving the way in which Brazil nuts were processed, Manutata also significantly expanded the market. It exported nuts to the U.S., Holland, England, Italy, Germany, South Africa, Qatar, Russia, Greece, Spain, Canada, Norway, Colombia, Australia, Poland, Israel, Belgium, and the United Arab Emirates. In recognition of its achievements, the Bolivian Chamber of Commerce granted an award to Manutata in 2008.

Manutata's restructuring in 1998 was so successful that Clover Paz was able to reopen Amazonas approximately one year later. Figure 6.7 shows that the total exports of Brazil nuts (in metric tons) attributed to Manutata and Amazonas combined increased from 1,050.37 in 1999 to 3,989.22 in 2009. Clover Paz noted that operating costs decreased from 46 cents per pound to 39 cents per pound over the same time period, despite the rise in wages and company contributions to the incentive program. Because of its new management system and equipment overhaul, Manutata was able to extract greater quantities of first-class nuts from the raw materials, which resulted in higher profits. Employees were

	1999	2000	2001	2002	2003	2004
Total Exports in Boxes of 44 lbs. (in thousands)	52,518	59,985	84,492	92,192	129,871	167,345
Operating Costs US$/lb. (in cents)	46	43	42	41	41	40
Total Exports in Metric Tons	1,050.37	1,199.70	1,689.85	1,843.85	2,597.42	3,346.90

	2005	2006	2007	2008	2009
Total Exports in Boxes of 44 lbs. (in thousands)	162,755	139,465	151,029	242,683	199,461
Operating Costs US$/lb. (in cents)	40	43	40	39	39
Total Exports in Metric Tons	3,255.10	2,789.30	3,020.58	4,853.66	3,989.22

Note: 2008 was a banner year for Brazil nuts due to their abundance and high yield. Manutata/Amazonas were also able to purchase raw materials from Brazil and Peru.

Source: Company documents

FIGURE 6.7 Export Statistics for Manutata and Amazonas

better trained, made fewer errors, and had access to automated processes. Costs were kept low by generating power for the steam using the discarded hard shells of the Brazil nuts.

Social Responsibility at Manutata

Managers believed that Riberalta residents, not just Manutata employees and UNAGRO shareholders, should benefit from the company's profitability. Manutata sponsored sports teams, such as the first division soccer team of Riberalta and men's and women's volleyball teams. It supported an alcohol rehabilitation center, a nursing home, and an association for the deaf. At the end of the harvesting season, Manutata donated medicine not used by the forest workers to a local hospital. It also gave funds to pave roads and build schools.

The Market for Brazil Nuts

In the mid to late 1990s, the international edible nut market consisted of Brazil nuts, groundnuts, cashew nuts, desiccated coconut, hazelnuts, almonds, walnuts, macadamia nuts, and pistachios. This industry generated approximately $2.5 billion in revenues, of which the Brazil nuts accounted for just 2 percent. Groundnuts and hazelnuts accounted for 50 percent of the market. The world supply of Brazil nuts varied between 17,000–20,200 tons of shelled kernels per year. The countries that exported this product were Brazil, Peru, and Bolivia (Bojanic, 2001).

The Brazil nut had many attractive features compared to other NTFPs (non-timber forest production). The Brazil nut benefited from a high value per unit of weight, low perishability, strong international demand, and the ability to generate a considerable amount of employment (employing nearly half of the work force in the Riberalta region). In addition, the extraction of the fruits within the nuts did not have a negative environmental impact on the forests (Zuidema as cited in Bojanic, 2001).

Although the supply of Brazil nuts fluctuated with good and poor harvesting seasons in the forests, demand was relatively stable, with a slight tendency to increase. Almost all Brazil nuts were destined for international markets; domestic consumption was low, ranging from 3 percent to 5 percent of shipments (Bojanic, 2001). European countries, mainly Great Britain, Germany, and the Netherlands, imported 50 percent of the production, 40 percent was transported to the Unites States, and the remaining 10 percent went to Australia, South Africa, Russia, Qatar, Canada, Israel, United Arab Emirates, and some Latin American countries.

Brazil nut producers were affected by a 1998 European Union (EU) requirement that lowered the levels of aflatoxin permissible in the nuts from 20 parts per billion to 4 parts per billion (Rienstra, 2004). Aflatoxin was a carcinogenic chemical produced by molds that grew on protein-rich foods. To meet the challenge, producers were required to upgrade their equipment (e.g., replace contamination-prone wooden benches with plastic or metal counters); institute strict quality-control procedures (e.g., employees should wear facemasks and hairnets); release child laborers from employment (many factory workers were women who brought their children to help); and train production personnel to keep logs and use European standards when determining whether or not a nut was edible (Coslovsky, 2007).

The EU requirement created turmoil in the Brazil nut industry and changed the competitive landscape. Before the requirement, Brazil was the leading exporter of Brazil nuts; after the requirement, Bolivia assumed the leadership position (see Figure 6.8). Bolivia eventually gained control of 80 percent of the market for Brazil nuts (Rienstra, 2004). Bolivian firms were successful because they decided to cooperate with one another and share knowledge regarding production methods. They supported a business association, headed by a professional food engineer that ran a central testing lab, brought in foreign experts on aflatoxin, and provided training to local processors in HACCP certification (Coslovsky, 2007).

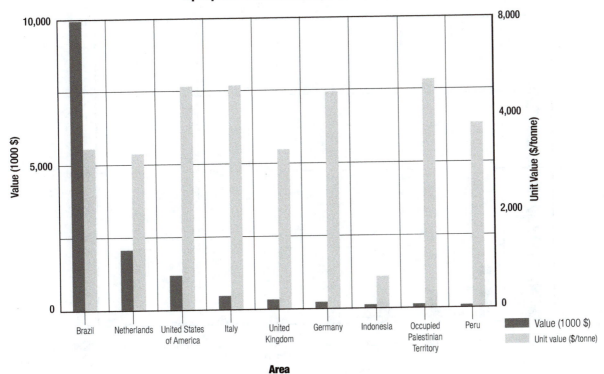

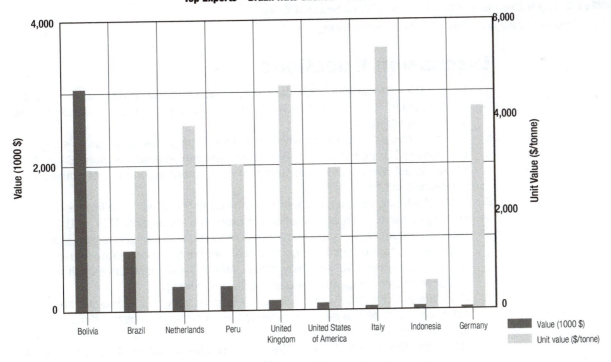

FIGURE 6.8 Top 9 Exporters of Shelled Brazil Nuts, Selected Years

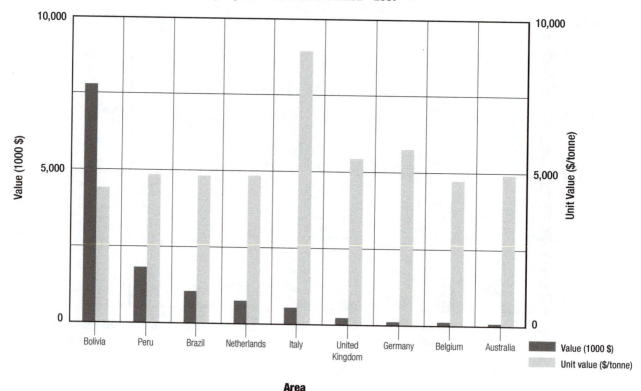

FIGURE 6.8 Top 9 Exporters of Shelled Brazil Nuts, Selected Years

Source: Food and Agriculture Organization (http://faostat.fao.org)

Discussion Questions

1. Do you think Clover Paz made the right decision to close Amazonas and invest in Manutata in 1997 when UNAGRO's request for a bank loan was denied? What were Paz's alternatives?

2. An "intrapreneur" is a person who creates something new inside an existing company rather than through the route of establishing a new venture (Baron & Shane, 2008). What were the factors that allowed entrepreneurial activities to flourish within Manutata?

3. Yeoh and Jeong (as cited in Chang, 2000) stated that innovation involves seeking creative or unusual solutions to problems and needs. This includes product innovation, development of new markets, and new processes and technologies for performing organizational functions in a corporate entrepreneurial environment. To what extent did UNAGRO and Manutata exhibit the characteristics of innovativeness and entrepreneurship?

4. Compare and contrast Manutata's organizational structure before and after 1998. Do you think the new structure was an improvement over the old structure? Why or why not?

5. What were the reasons for why Manutata was able to successfully export Brazil nuts to other countries? Why were Manutata's exporting activities important to the Bolivian economy?

References

Administration, Trade International (2017). Bolivia - Business Customs. *Export.gov.* Retrieved November 6,2017, from https://www.export.gov/article?id=Bolivia-Business-Customs Baron, RA, & Shane, SA (2008). *Entrepreneurship: A process perspective*. Thompson South-Western.

Baron, R.A., &, Shane, S.A. (2008). Entrepreneurship: A process perspective. Mason, OH: Thompson South-Western.

Bojanic, AJ (2001). Balance is beautiful: Assessing sustainable development in the rain forests of the Bolivian Amazonia. PROMAB Scientific Series 3. Retrieved from http://www.fao.org/3/a-af851b.pdf

Bridges, T. (2006, December 18). Latin America finds the green in organic: American farmers can thank health-conscious US consumers for a booming export business. Knight Ridder Tribune Business News, p. 1. Retrieved from http://agecon.centers.ufl.edu/documents/2006/FarmerDec18.pdf

Chang, J. (2000). Model of corporate entrepreneurship: Intrapreneurship and exopreneurship. International Journal of Entrepreneurship, 12(4), 69-104.

Coslovsky, S.V. (2007). Economic development without pre-requisites: How Bolivian firms displaced Brazilian competitors and dominated the global brazil-nut business. Boston, MA: Department of Urban Studies and Planning, Massachusetts Institute of Technology.

International Trade Administration. (2017). Bolivia - business customs. Retrieved from https://www.export.gov/article?id=Bolivia-Business-Customs

Rienstra, D. (2004). Can a nut save the rainforest? International Trade Forum, 10 (4), 97-101.

TMF Group. (2016). Top 10 challenges of doing business in Bolivia. Retrieved from https://www.tmf-group.com/en/news-insights/business-culture/top-challenges-bolivia/

UNAGRO Corporation. (2017). MANUTATA SA. UNAGRO S.A. Retrieved from http://www.corp-unagro.com/empresa/manutata-s-a/

UNAGRO Corporation (2017). *UNAGRO S.A.* UNAGRO S.A. Retrieved November 6,2017, from https://translate.google.com/translate?hl=en&sl=es&u=http://www.corp-unagro.com/&prev=search

Williams, D.A. (2010, March). Export initiation in small locally-owned firms from emerging economies: The role of personal factors. Journal of Developmental Entrepreneurship, 15(1), 101-119.

Relevant Videos

What Is Intrapreneurship?
https://www.youtube.com/watch?v=dzd6AXM6JY4

UNAGRO AVP July 11 RELEASE 4:
https://www.youtube.com/watch?v=TFhQpyyQQfg

UNAGRO AVP:
https://www.youtube.com/watch?v=QOMIF_ueO7E

Bolivia: Economy Has Improved Significantly During Morales' Administration:
https://www.youtube.com/watch?v=bgOKeuXsaBk

Bolivia's Economic Growth:
https://www.youtube.com/watch?v=WWwdKKEGxkE

Condor Trekking Bolivia - Social Enterprise Tourism - Five Point Five:
https://www.youtube.com/watch?v=iKu6FjWWlkM

TESY: Exporting in an Uncertain Environment

Mark Potts, J.D.
Saginaw Valley State University

Learning Objectives

1. *Discuss* the credit risk facing firms who export.
2. *Analyze* mechanisms to manage the currency risk associated with exporting.
3. *Discuss* the political risk facing firms who export.
4. *Evaluate* how to select the appropriate distribution channel for export.
5. *Discuss* whether a company should enter a foreign market directly or indirectly.

Key Words

Direct exporting
Pegged
Credit risk

Economic risk
Political risk

Abstract

TESY is a successful Bulgarian company that has recently transitioned from being a distributor of space heaters to a local producer and distributor. To grow the business, TESY must export. However, management faces decisions on how to manage credit, political, and foreign exchange risks. They must also decide to which markets they will export and what distribution channel to choose.

 ## The Dilemma

TESY, a successful Bulgarian startup company, looks to grow beyond its domestic market. TESY successfully transitioned from being a distributor of foreign space heaters to a local producer and distributor. The company is working to obtain the international quality certificate ISO 9001/2000 for the production of space heaters. However, TESY is quickly outgrowing its domestic market. TESY management knows that if they can produce in Bulgaria and sell abroad, their profit margins will be better than that of their competitors. Due to technical specifications, only European markets are on the table. However, TESY management has its concerns.

A large export business means much of the company's cash flow will be tied up in "accounts receivable" abroad. TESY management is worried about foreign exchange fluctuations and about collecting payment in foreign countries. If the company is unable to collect in 30 or 90 days, the value of the Bulgarian Lev (the Bulgarian currency) may fluctuate greatly against foreign currencies. This could lead to significant losses. TESY is also aware of political risks in some export market countries as Central and Eastern Europe transform after the fall of the Soviet Union. As part of their export strategy, TESY management must decide to which markets they will export, and what distribution channel to choose. What markets and channels should TESY consider? How should it manage its risk?

Company Background

TESY is a brand name of Ficosota Syntez. Ficosota Syntez was founded while Bulgaria began its transition from a command to a free market economy. In addition to space heaters, Ficosota Syntez produces detergents, home products, and personal care products. By this time, TESY has become a successful distributor of Italy's De'Longhi space heaters in the Bulgarian market. The company acquired a Bulgarian factory, built during communist rule, that produced heating appliances. TESY has begun work toward obtaining the international quality certification ISO 9001/2000. TESY prides itself in the ergonomic design of its products, quality control, and commitment to research and development.

TESY personnel have experience with markets in Russia, the other former Soviet Republics, and countries in Central and Eastern Europe. Growing up in communist Bulgaria, these were the languages management learned, countries to which they were allowed to travel, and their country's trading partners. The markets in Central and Eastern Europe are also similar to the domestic Bulgaria market; they are not fully developed and lack the sophistication of more developed markets. While TESY management has limited knowledge and experience of Western European markets, they have a competitive advantage in production costs as compared to their Western European competitors. Asian firms use a currency pegged to the dollar and are not competing in the European market. The cost and quality of their products do not make them competitive. TESY is not considering other markets, since different technical specifications are required.

Within Central and Eastern Europe, TESY also has a competitive advantage in transportation costs. For example, road transport from Shumen, Bulgaria, to Bucharest, Romania, is 187 km (116 miles). De'Longhi, based out of Treviso, Italy, would face a distance of 1,549 km (963 miles) from Treviso to Bucharest. However, the Central and Eastern European strategy brings political risk because of its weak legal systems and its location in a region that is undergoing economic and political transition. Western Europe presents much less political risk, but management is concerned about the legal fees associated with collecting accounts receivable.

TESY must decide on its distribution channel. One option is indirect exporting. Using a third party to coordinate entry on TESY's behalf would limit the company's risk. TESY may also seek to use an export management company or find a retail chain willing to sell its products abroad. However, TESY knows selling wholesale to a retail chain would mean a lower profit margin than would selling directly to consumers. Accordingly, TESY is also considering establishing subsidiaries abroad to sell its products directly. If the company does this, it will need staff with country-specific language skills and time to build a reputation. Obtaining brand awareness abroad is a further challenge.

Due to European Union (EU) product and safety standards, TESY believes that if it can meet the standards of one EU country, it will have the capability to meet the standards in all EU markets. It is widely believed that EU standards exceed non-EU regulatory standards. Since EU standards are higher than those in the rest of Europe, TESY will likely be able to export easily to Central and Eastern Europe. These countries are also looking to harmonize their standards with EU regulation in anticipation of their accession to the European Union.

Regional and Economic Context

After growth in recent years, Bulgaria is experiencing economic turmoil. This is largely due to government inaction on structural reforms and privatization. The severe depreciation of the national currency has led to extreme inflation. This has led the Bulgarian government to seek loans from the International Monetary Fund and peg its currency (the Bulgarian Lev). International observers question the Bulgarian government's political will to make tough choices regarding interest rates and spending in order to preserve the currency's integrity. The Bulgarian public is uncertain about the government's policies and worry about their falling standard of living.

In this time of uncertainty, many have chosen to heat using space heaters. Europe largely relies on natural gas from Russia for heating. It is widely believed that Russia uses the price and supply of its gas for political purposes. TESY's space heaters are electric. The cost of heating with an electric space heater can often be cheaper than using natural gas based sources. Furthermore, consumers value the fact that heat is not dependent upon the supply of foreign gas, but rather upon the domestic production of electricity. The cost and certainty of using space heaters makes them an attractive method of home and work place heating. The market for space heaters is strong throughout Europe, but especially in Central and Eastern Europe.

TABLE 6.1 **Market Analysis Summary by Ranking: 1 (highest) to 5 (lowest)**

COUNTRY	MARKET SIZE	QUALITY EXPECTATIONS	POTENTIAL GROSS MARGIN*	TRANSPORTATION ADVANTAGE
Ireland	5	2	3	5
Germany	2	1	1	3
Spain	3	3	2	4
Romania	4	4	5	1
Russia	1	5	4	2

*Potential gross margin equals sales revenue at the competitive local price, less the cost of goods and transportation. It does not include the reduction in revenues associated with different types of distribution channels.

Bulgarian Economic Data

TABLE 6.2

Currency Fluctuation in Current Year and Prior 3 Years*

	T–3	T–2	T–1	CURRENT YEAR (T)
Bulgarian Lev vs. Euro Target	.0116	.0115	.0010	.0009
Bulgarian Lev vs. Russian Ruble	38.7599	3.8602	.0060	.0135
Bulgarian Lev vs. U.S. Dollar	.0077	.0007	.0006	.0005

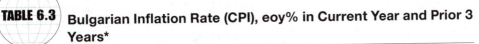

TABLE 6.3 **Bulgarian Inflation Rate (CPI), eoy% in Current Year and Prior 3 Years***

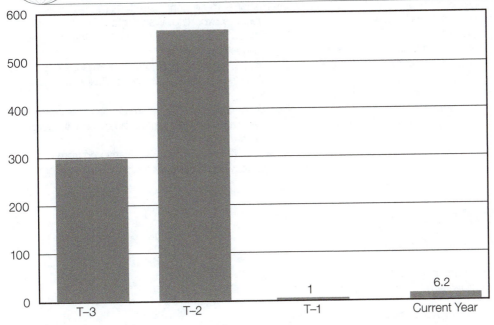

*Data taken from Oleynik's (2004) "Bulgaria Business Intelligence Report" and OANDA—Forex Trading and Exchange Rates Services

Discussion Questions

1. What are the credit risks facing TESY and how should the company manage those risks?
2. What are the foreign-exchange risks facing TESY and how should the company manage those risks?
3. What are the political risks facing TESY and how should the company manage those risks?
4. How does TESY decide where to export?
5. Should TESY decide to export directly or indirectly?

References

Anticalc. (2017) Energy Efficiency of Electric Water Heaters. *TESY*. Retrieved from http://www.tesy.com/public/files/advertisings/106/en-US/print.pdf

Brown, R.L. and Gitterman, A.S. (2008). *A short course in international business plans*, Novato, CA: World Trade Press.

Carraher, S. and Welsh, H.B. (2008). *Global Entrepreneurship*, Dubuque: Kendall Hunt.

Crampton, R.J. (2010). *A Concise History of Bulgaria*, Cambridge, UK: Cambridge University Press

Foley, J.F. (2004). *The Global Entrepreneur: Taking your business international*, 2nd ed., New York: Jamric Press International.

Ganev, V.I. (2007). *Preying on the State: The Transformation of Bulgaria after 1989*, Ithaca, NY: Cornell University Press.

Hall, R.R. (1998). *Trade Secrets: The export answer book for small to medium sized exporters*, Lansing, MI: Michigan Economic Development Corporation.

Heinze, Aleksej (2014) 10 things that US businesses need to be aware of when developing business in Europe. *Passport to Trade*. Retrieved from http://businessculture.org/blog/2014/05/29/differences-between-america-and-europe/

Hinkelman, E.G. (2008). *Dictionary of International Trade*, 8th ed., Petaluma, CA: World Trade Press.

Hinkelman, E.G. (2003). A *Short Course in International Payments*, 2nd ed., Novato, CA: World Trade Press.

International Trade Administration (2008). *A basic guide to exporting*, Washington, D.C.: United States Department of Commerce: International Trade Administration.

Oleynik, I.S. (Ed.) (2004). *Business Intelligence Report*, Washington, D.C.: International Business Publications.

Passport, Trade. (2017) Western Europe. *Passport Trade*. Retrieved from http://businessculture.org/western-europe/

X. Studio. (2017) TESY. *TESY*. Retrieved from http://en.tesy.com/products/electric-water-heaters

Relevant Videos

https://www.youtube.com/watch?v=uXT4qv9YhZY

10 reasons to set up your company in Bulgaria:
https://www.youtube.com/watch?v=2k5jQvVh9Fg

Did you know? - Bulgaria - Bulgarian Business Culture video:
https://www.youtube.com/watch?v=tGXP7YraUJQ

Imports, Exports, and Exchange Rates: Crash Course Economics #15:
https://www.youtube.com/watch?v=geoe-6NBy10

Chapter Seven

GLOBAL ECONOMICS AND FINANCE

OWENS SAWMILL: A FAMILY BUSINESS FACING A SOCIAL RESPONSIBILITY DILEMMA

Dianne H.B. Welsh, The University of North Carolina at Greensboro
David Rawlings

Learning Objectives

1. *Explain* the importance of Human Resource Management and how a family business should align its Human Resource strategy with is overall business strategy.
2. *Discuss* the basic concepts and functional areas, including training, compensation and benefits, safety, and performance management as it relates to the case.
3. *Assess* the legal and social responsibility implications of this family business case.
4. *Analyze* the current issues facing the Owens' as it relates to their business' profitability.
5. *Describe* the current human resource trends in the workplace and the projection of future developments as it relates to the Owens' ability to compete in the lumber industry.
6. *Identify* the environmental and safety issues, including government regulations and sustainability, on small business viability.
7. *Identify* the effect of technology innovations on small business viability in the short- and long-term, particularly in regard to the lumber industry.
8. *Evaluate* how the strength of Human Resources at all levels affects the ability for a business to compete in the worldwide marketplace.
9. *Discriminate* between Human Resource Management from the perspective of an employee.

Key Words

Ethics   Social Responsibility
Family Business

Abstract

This is a real case involving a Small to Medium Sized Enterprise (SME) that produces southern hardwood finished lumber. The family business faces a social responsibility dilemma in terms of displaced workers and limited job opportunities in the surrounding labor market if they purchase a new saw that would modernize production, improve profitability, and eliminate 50 percent of their labor costs. The most logical employment for these workers would be a cutter, loader, or hauler of logs, which have been determined to be some of the most dangerous jobs in the United States. This case requires students to examine the decision-making process of a small family business in small, cohesive community, and the ramifications of these decisions, as well as issues concerning technology and production improvements, displaced workers, social responsibilities, and the rights and responsibilities of employers and employees.

⊙ The Dilemma

A small, family-owned sawmill is seeking to improve profitability. Scott and Beth Owens have the opportunity to purchase a new saw that is capable of cutting as much wood in one shift as the current saw can cut in two shifts. Additionally, as employees become more proficient with its use, productivity will drastically improve. They must quickly decide whether to purchase a new saw or continue using the old saw, because they have a short window of opportunity to sell the old saw, which will bring additional revenue. Normally, this type of saw is difficult to sell. Capital investments are difficult to recoup in this industry because the investment costs must be spread out over far fewer units of production than other types of sawmills ("Economic Choice," 2003).

The purchase of the new sawmill would allow Owens Sawmill to reach or exceed its usual two-shift production in only one shift. Therefore, the second shift will be eliminated. The most likely opportunities for those who work on the second shift will be out in the field as a cutter, loader, and hauler of logs. This job has been determined by safety officials to be the most dangerous job in the United States. The fatality rate for this position is the highest of any position, twenty-six times greater than the national average (Christie, 2003). While the Owens' are legally obligated to provide a safe environment for their employees, do they have a social responsibility?

Personal Background

Owens Sawmill is currently owned by its founders, Scott and Beth Owens of Arlington, Kentucky. Both Scott and Beth are very involved in the day-to-day operations and share making decisions. The two owners make up the entire upper management of Owens Sawmill.

Scott was born in Spokane, Washington, where his mother raised the family while his father, Tom Owens, worked in Alaska. Scott played on his high school basketball team and graduated in 1980, at the age of 17. After graduation, he joined his dad in Ketchikan, Alaska. His father was on one of the first teams that went into the Alaskan wilderness to initiate the construction of the road systems. Scott's job was to drill and blast rock to clear land for road construction. Scott's job was seasonal, so he returned to Washington State when operations shut down during the winter months, where he attended community college for one quarter and decided it wasn't for him.

By 1982, his father had moved to Kentucky and Scott joined him to operate a farm. He soon met his future wife, Beth in the same town. Beth was the only girl in a family with three boys. Beth's family owns a horse farm that specializes in quarter horses. She attended community college and completed an associate's degree while working part-time at a local hospital and volunteering at Hospice. Scott soon realized that agricultural employment did not pay well, so he returned to Alaska in 1983 to work on road construction. When he returned to Kentucky that winter, he had saved enough money to build a home for him and his wife. In 1988, Scott's father started logging, so Scott bought a truck and a loader and was cutting, loading, and hauling the logs to the mills with his Dad. Scott soon realized that there was more profit to be made by cutting the logs into lumber himself rather than just delivering the logs to another lumber mill. Owens Sawmill was born.

Scott and Beth received a government loan in 1989 for $30,000 at 5 percent interest with the requirement that he hire four employees. They also borrowed $30,000 from a local bank and purchased a mill and land in Arlington, Kentucky where they erected a building where the business still operates. Scott ran the daily logging operations, while Beth performed the bookkeeping and administrative functions. After six months, they realized that not enough lumber was being cut to pay their expenses. Therefore, a second shift was implemented and four additional employees were hired so they could double production without increasing their fixed costs, such as insurance and loan payments. As production increased, the company paid off their loans and became profitable. In 1992, they formed an S Corp. for tax purposes and to reduce their personal liability.

The Owens have expanded their operation over time by purchasing large tracts of forest land. Scott deploys his cutting crew to the tracts of land where there is demand for a specific type of wood. His crew cuts, loads, and transports the logs to the mill. Most of the same employees also work in the sawmill producing the finished lumber, which is then sold. The average tenure of the Owens Sawmill employees is 10 years, ranging from 5 to 17 years. The Owens are contemplating starting a family and they would like to hire at least part-time help to assist Beth with the bookkeeping and office management duties. Beth enjoys her interaction with the employees and their families, and considers this part of her life's purpose. Scott is 43 years old and Beth is 35 years old. Their current savings totals around $50,000 and they have under $5000 in their retirement accounts.

Industry Background

The National Hardwood Lumber Association releases a weekly *Hardwood Market Report* that separates hardwood lumber into three price categories: Northern Hardwoods, Southern Hardwoods, and Appalachian Hardwoods. The Kentucky area has Southern Hardwood. A red oak log that is 12 feet long and has a small-end circumference of 24 inches will have a total of 300 feet of usable lumber. A sawmill will purchase this log for about $0.70 per foot, which makes it worth about $210. From this $210, the money is split evenly between the landowner and the logger. This same 300' log will result in about 420' of lumber, due to the scaling methods used. The lumber will then be separated into grades that determine the prices paid for the lumber.

It is estimated that the new technologically advanced saw would increase productivity by 25%, which would result in approximately $30,000 more profit per year. The core of the employee base would remain intact if the technologically advanced saw were purchased. The job loss will be minimal; ranging from four to six displaced employees. The highest performing employees with the best accident records and the longest tenure would be retained. The laid-off employees may be offered employment in the future if Owens Sawmill keeps to its strategic long-term expansion plan.

Discussion Questions

1. What factors will affect Scott and Beth Owens' decision about the new saw?
2. What, if any, are the Owens' responsibilities concerning the hazardous jobs at the Sawmill?
3. Should potential unemployment time for permanent employees during the installation of the new saw be a concern to Owens Sawmill?
4. Should the Sawmill consider expanding operations into areas that are safer for employees? If so, what are some potential entrepreneurial opportunities?
5. What decision-making process should Scott and Beth Owens use when making their decision(s)?
6. What decision should Scott and Beth Owens make?

References

Byfield, M. (1997). Farmers line up for their slug of pulp mulch. *Alberta Report, 24*, 18-19.

Career Planner. (2017). Sawmill Worker. *Career Planner*. Retrieved from https://dot-job- descriptions. careerplanner.com/SAWMILL-WORKER.cfm

Christie, L. (2003). America's most dangerous jobs: The top 10 most dangerous jobs in America. [online]. Retrieved October 13. 2003, from http://www. money.cnn.com/2003/10/13/pf/dangerousjobs/ index.html

Dogan, C.A. (1998). Simulation modeling and analysis of a hardwood sawmill. *Simulation and Practice Model*, 5, 387-403.

Economic choice for hardwood sawmill operations. (2001). [online]. Retrieved September 28, 2001, from http://www.cfr.msstate.edu/fwrc/forestp/echo.html

Egan, A. (1998). Danger trees in Central Appalachian forests of the United States: An assessment of their frequency of occurrence. *Journal of Safety Research, 29,* 77–85.

Freedman, D. (1998). Sawmill thrives with mulch division. *Bicycle 39*, 74–75.

Kuratko, D. & Hodgetts, R. (Eds.) (2004). *Entrepreneurship*. Columbus, OH: Thomson South-Western.

Loyalty contract: Employee commitment and competitive advantage. (2003). [online]. Retrieved September 28, 2003, from http://www.ups.com/europe/ch/news/ speech/gerloyalty.html

Malaysian National News. Negligence the cause of most fatal cases in timber industry. (2003, February). *Malaysian National News Agency*, p. 1.

Malaysian National News. Safety training for timber workers vital, says Backbencher. (2001, October). *Malaysian National News Agency*, p. 1.

Negligence the cause of most fatal cases in timber industry. (2003, February). Malaysian National News Agency, p. 1.

Safety training for timber workers vital, says Backbencher. (2001, October). Malaysian National News Agency, p. 1.

Sawmills. (2004). [online]. Retrieved September 28, 2004, from http://www.fnr.purdue.edu/inwood/ sawmill.html

Stebbins, S., Comen, E., & Stockdale, C. (2018, January 8). Workplace fatalities: 25 most dangerous jobs in America. *USA Today*. Retrieved from https://www. usatoday.com/story/money/careers/2018/01/09/ workplace-fatalities-25-most-dangerous-jobs-america/1002500001/

Struttmann, T. (2001). Fatal injuries caused by logs rolling off trucks: Kentucky, 1994–1998. *American Journal of Industrial Medicine, 39*, 203–208.

Tooch, D.E. (1992). *Successful sawmill management*. New York: Northeastern Loggers Association.

United States Department of Labor. (2012, January). Injury and illness prevention programs white paper. *OSHA*. Retrieved from https://www.osha.gov/dsg/ InjuryIllnessPreventionProgramsWhitePaper.html

United States Environmental Protection Agency. (2016, July 1). Background document: General air quality permit for new or modified minor source sawmill facilities in Indian country. *United States Environmental Protection Agency.* Retrieved from https://www.epa.gov/sites/production/files/2016-09/ documents/sawmill_facilities_background_ document_version_1.0_0.pdf

Web Editor. (2017, June 13). Logging and sawmill jobs go high-tech. *Timber Harvesting & Wood Operations*. Retrieved from http://www.timberharvesting. com/logging-sawmill-jobs-go-high-tech/

Relevant Videos

Socially Responsible Family business:
https://www.youtube.com/watch?v=vC2fzJLOXp4

From Opportunity to Responsibility. Family Businesses and the Challenge of Sustainability:
https://www.youtube.com/watch?v=GP2axTM8tVg

Human Resource Management:
https://www.youtube.com/watch?v=9ZLbSk1Te68

Putting the human back into human resources | Mary Schaefer | TEDxWilmington:
https://www.youtube.com/watch?v=0Mq2TiJmqCl

Small Businesses Find Success in Innovation Technology:
https://www.youtube.com/watch?v=Rzf2_eLeG6Y

Logs to Lumber - An aerial journey through the sawmill:
https://www.youtube.com/watch?v=NvbgwdTGoyo

Chapter Eight

CROSS-CULTURAL CUSTOMS AND COMMUNICATION STYLES

AL-BAHAR & JACOROSSI ENGINEERING & CONTRACTING COMPANY: A STUDY OF THE EFFECT OF KUWAITI AND ITALIAN CULTURE ON HUMAN RESOURCE MANAGEMENT AFTER THE IRAQI INVASION

Dianne H. B. Welsh, The University of North Carolina at Greensboro
Abdulrahman Al-Bahar

Learning Objectives

1. *Analyze* the implications of cultural differences on human resources.
2. *Analyze* the impact on human resources and companies after war.
3. *Analyze* how family businesses are different based on country and cultures.
4. *Analyze* how family businesses can have a positive impact on human resource issues.
5. *Determine* decision-making capabilities of companies during conflict.

Key Words

Cultural Differences

Family Business

Human Resources

Joint Ventures

Abstract

This case encompasses cross-cultural, human resources, and crisis management issues that a joint venture dealt with after their employees experienced an invasion in a war zone. The Al-Bahar & Jacorossi Engineering & Contracting Company was formed in 1993 and is a privately held shareholding company. The Al-Bahar family of Kuwait owns 51 percent of the stock, and Jacorossi Imprese of Italy owns 49 percent of the stock. The company mainly contracts out maintenance of work pertaining to mechanical, electrical, instrumentation, fire, pumps, pipes, and high-voltage signs. This joint stock company was formed for the purpose of contracting engineering activities in the oil sector, power sector and industrial infrastructure by combining the experience and expertise of these two companies. Global entrepreneurship issues are discussed.

 ## Background

Kuwait is a tiny country that is located in the northeast corner of the Arabian Gulf. It is bordered by Saudi Arabia and Iraq. The total population of Kuwait in 2006 was 2,765,300, with 1,653,700 men and 1,111,600 women. Based on an annual population growth rate between 2000–2005 of 3.73 percent, the population is predicted to grow to 3,201,546 by 2010 (United Nations, 2006). A large percentage of the population is non-Kuwaitis. The main language is Arabic, although English is widely used in business.

Kuwait covers an area of 17,818 sq km, most of which is flat desert. There are only two notable areas of high ground in the country, Mina Al Zor and Muttla Ridge, and the Ahmadi Range. Kuwait coastal waters cover 2,200 square miles, and the coastline stretches 290 km.

According to the 1985 census, 59.5 percent of Kuwaiti men and 13.8 percent of Kuwaiti women were employed in the work force. In 1993, only 20.1 percent of the work force was made up of Kuwaiti men, although the number of women working has remained about the same. The government employed 90 percent of the Kuwaiti work force in 1993. About 91.7 percent of non-Kuwaiti men and 42.7 percent of non-Kuwaiti women were part of the labor force. According to the most recent compilation of data by the Institute of Banking Studies (2007), the total Kuwaiti and non-Kuwaiti labor force is 1,962,955. Kuwaiti men comprise 10.1 percent of the total labor force, while Kuwaiti women make up 7.25 percent. About 83.6 percent are employed by the government. Of the total labor force in 2006, non-Kuwaitis make up 1,621,770 or 82.62 percent. Non-Kuwaiti males are 79.86 percent and non-Kuwaiti women are 20.14 percent of the total non-Kuwaiti labor force. Many foreign workers come from countries such as Pakistan, India, and the Philippines for the main purpose of finding employment.

> *"Wages are considered the most important distribution channel for effecting social justice in the State of Kuwait, since 90 percent of the Kuwaiti labor force, both men and women, worked in the administrative positions in the state and public sectors till the end of 1994"* (Kuwaiti Ministry of Planning, 1995, p.14).

Many women have continued to be employed primarily as teachers, doctors, nurses, and secretaries. Many have gone into other professions as well. Families have developed their own private businesses. Through government programs or family assistance, many Kuwaitis have developed profitable businesses in the last 20 years.

Kuwait is interesting because it is a combination of a welfare state, private enterprise, and a state-run economy. The government controls the oil production and resources of Kuwait. This is the source of the great wealth that has come to the country. However, with this wealth, the government has helped many privately owned businesses become prosperous, it has brought many opportunities to private business, and it has allowed a great increase in the standard of living for all people living in Kuwait.

> *"The philosophy of modernization and building a contemporary state developed into a philosophy that aims at promoting the citizens' standard of living due to the increase in oil revenues and the local developments"* (Kuwaiti Ministry of Planning, 1995, p. 31).

One of the most important policies of the Kuwaiti government is the continuous advancement in programs of education, culture, information, social care, and religious service that is tied to maintaining the unity of the family.

Kuwait is classified among the group of richest countries in the world. The gross domestic product (GDP) per capita was estimated at $23,100, up from $16,420 in 2004 (U.S. Central Intelligence Agency, 2007). This increase is due primarily to high oil prices that have helped build Kuwait's budget and trade surpluses and consequently, have had a positive effect on the average Kuwaitis' standard of living. Although there are many very wealthy families in Kuwait, there are no very poor families as compared to other parts of the world. The government provides all families with a nice home, and a garage. These homes have three bedrooms or more. All education is paid for by the Kuwaiti government, which includes a free college education. Non-Kuwaitis can also receive free education if they maintain a high grade-point average in high school. Because of this, there is a strong middle class. However, there is a higher ratio of millionaires as compared to other countries.

Employment Security

The Kuwaiti laws governing labor are valid whether or not you have a written contract. Some of the main points of the law are as follows. A contract between employer and employee can be verbal, but it is preferable to have it in writing. It must be written in Arabic. The normal working week is 48 hours, usually six days at eight hours per day. Overtime is paid at a rate of time and a half of the normal rate, with two times the normal rate on holidays. In addition to official holidays, all workers are entitled to 14 days of vacation after one year of employment. The normal work days for public sector workers are Saturday through Wednesday; Thursday and Friday are days off. For the private sector, the work week is Saturday through Wednesday, with a half day on Thursdays. The banking sector employees work Sunday through Thursday.

There is no set minimum wage. Female employees must receive equal pay. Trade unions are allowed, but only one can be formed per establishment and only one for each profession will be recognized. Because all expatriates must be sponsored by a Kuwaiti national or company, theoretically, there should be no unemployment. All unemployed Kuwaitis must register at the Ministry of Social Affairs and Labor, where employment assistance is available. A person who intends to be employed in Kuwait must have a work permit and a No Objection Certificate (NOC). The first is issued by the Ministry of Social Affairs and Labor, and at that time, the Ministry of the Interior must be applied to for the NOC and entry permit. In order to obtain a residence permit, the sponsor must complete a form issued by the Ministry of the Interior. The persons then are fingerprinted and undergo a medical check. Once residence procedures are completed, the person must then register for a civil identification card, which should be carried at all times.

Joint Stock Companies

These are known as Kuwaiti Private Shareholding Companies (KSC). It is necessary to obtain a decree from the Ministry of Commerce authorizing the incorporation of a KSC. The shareholders are issued with negotiable shares of equal value, and their liability is limited to the nominal value of their shareholding. Public subscription is permitted, but 51 percent of the share capital must be Kuwaiti-owned. The accounts of a Joint Stock Company must be independently audited. Copies of the company's accounts must be filed with the official commercial register.

Al-Bahar & Jacorossi Engineering & Contracting Company (KSC)

The Al-Bahar & Jacorossi Engineering & Contracting Company was formed in 1993, and is a privately held shareholding company. The Al-Bahar family owns 51 percent of the stock, and Jacorossi Imprese of Italy owns 49 percent of the stock. The Chairman of the joint venture is Fahad Al-Bahar. The Vice President is Adel Al-Bahar. Fahad Al-Bahar is Adel Al-Bahar's uncle. A foreign company can own no more that 49 percent of the stock in a Kuwaiti operation. The company mainly contracts out maintenance of work pertaining to mechanical, electrical, instrumentation, fire, pumps, pipes, and high voltage signs. This joint stock company was formed for the purpose of contracting engineering activities in the oil sector, power sector, and industrial infrastructure, by combining the experience and expertise of these two companies.

Fahad Al-Bahar & Sons Trading Company has been in existence in Kuwait since 1988 as a general trading and contracting company. It is familiar with all the local government laws, procedures, and systems. This knowledge is essential for any company operating in Kuwait. The company also has experience in the importing and exporting of industrial and consumer goods.

The Jacorossi Imprese Company (formerly known as Petrochemical International Instrument Company) has been in existence in Italy since 1953 as an engineering and contracting company. It deals primarily with service construction and maintenance work in the following industries: oil, power, and petrochemicals. Its field is mainly in mechanical, electrical, instrumentation, and telecommunications works. The company has vast experience completing infrastructure projects in Italy, as well as countries in Northern Europe, South America, the Middle East, and North Africa. Additionally, the company has done a great deal of business in the Middle Eastern countries of Saudi Arabia, Oman, United Arab Emirates, Iran, Iraq, and Bahrain. In the 1980s, the company wanted to establish a presence in Kuwait to expand their operations in the Persian Gulf. Kuwait had become a major force in the oil industry, and it is a very profitable market. PIICO started their Kuwait operations under the umbrella of the Al-Bahar International Group, who was acting as their agent. The company is still known as the PIICO Company.

While fulfilling a maintenance contract with the Mina Al Ahmadi Refinery, the Iraqi Invasion occurred. The Al-Bahar—PIICO Company suffered great losses due to the war. All the equipment and vehicles of the association were stolen by the Iraqis. The employee camp for the project was destroyed, including the central kitchen equipment, air-conditioning equipment, and furniture. It was valued at 1.5 million. The Al-Bahar-PIICO Association faced this ordeal with courage and a sense of responsibility to its employees. In August 1990, shifts of 20 people were working twelve hours a day and were paid by the Association without a guaranteed payment from the oil company that owns Mina. The stockholders agreed to keep everyone employed. The Al-Bahar-PIICO company met in London. A liaison office was established in Bombay to prepare for a quick return after the country was liberated. Eventually, all 103 employees were moved to sites immediately after the liberation and returned to their duties.

Due to the destruction caused to the infrastructure during the Iraqi War, there was a great need for skilled labor for reconstruction. PIICO had just changed their name to Jacorossi Imprese. The Al-Bahar Company decided to form a joint engineering and contracting company. Not only were the services of the joint venture greatly in demand, but also forming a joint venture would offer the company advantages that it was unable to obtain when Al-Bahar was acting as Jacorossi's agent. The joint venture would legally be a local company, and the company could receive support of up to 10 percent from the government.

Under Kuwaiti law, the government will supplement the financial contract of a Kuwaiti company by up to 10 percent of the cost during contract negotiations. For example, several companies, including foreign companies, might be bidding on a contract. If a foreign company underbids the Kuwaiti company by as much as 10 percent, the Kuwaiti government will supplement the ten percent bid and the Kuwaiti company will get the contract. On the other hand, if the Kuwaiti company bid 15 percent higher than the foreign interest company, the foreign company would be awarded the contract because it is more than a 10 percent differential.

The Al-Bahar and Jacorossi Imprese Companies realized that they had been losing several bids because Al-Bahar was only acting as an agent and the bids for contracts were not seen as local bids. By forming a joint venture, the Al-Bahar Jacorossi Imprese Company would be able to win more government contracts. Also, the company would not have to pay the 4 percent import tax required on any materials coming into the country. This would save the company millions.

Some of the projects that have been successfully completed or are in the process of being completed are:

1. Maintenance and repair of electrical installation in Shuaiba Power Station, owned by the Ministry of Electricity and Water;

2. Maintenance and repair of electrical installations in an oil field, owned by the Kuwait Oil Company;

3. Construction of mechanical, piping, and electrical installations of the Ethylene Glycol Project, owned by the Equate Petrochemical Company;

4. Operation and maintenance of the control room in Kuwait International Airport for Directorate General of Civil Aviation;

5. Revamping and modernization of an oil refinery at the Mina Al Ahmadi plant, owned by the Kuwait National Petroleum Company;

6. Construction of a new control room, with computerized and electronic controls, owned by the Kuwait National Petroleum Company; and

7. Design, engineering, construction, and commission of mechanical, electrical, and instrumentation installations for water treatment plants at the Az Zour and West Doha power and water stations, owned by the Ministry of Electricity and Power.

The company employs around 1,400 personnel. Employees range from laborers and technicians to highly qualified engineers with master's degrees. The company serves oil-related industries, as well as utilities. The company has ongoing contracts with the Kuwait National Petroleum Company to revamp the Mina Al Ahmadi Refinery, the Kuwait Oil Company for electrical maintenance at different locations, the Ministry of Water and Electricity for water treatment, and a number of petrochemical industries for piping works.

Starting an international company outside of a parent country is full of challenges. There are many obstacles to overcome. One major obstacle is relocating key personnel. One of the biggest problems faced by Italian employees who moved to Kuwait to work was trying to adapt to the very different climate and culture. Most expatriates confirm that it takes a minimum of six-months to adjust. The summer months are extremely hot and dry, reaching 120 degrees F., and those Kuwaitis who can travel outside the country during that time do so. For individuals who are not used to this heat, adjusting to traveling and being outside is difficult. That is why Kuwaiti companies often have hours in the summer time where the workers go home for several hours during the afternoon, which is the hottest time of the day, and then return to work around 6:00 p.m. and work until 8:00 p.m. in the evening, when the temperatures are a bit cooler.

Of course, customs are very different in Kuwait, which is especially evident in religious traditions. For example, the Italian workers have a hard time being in Kuwait during Christmas. Most Kuwaiti citizens do not celebrate Christmas because the country is predominantly Islamic. There are usually no company holiday parties at Christmas, although in the last few years, the Al-Bahar/Jacorossi Company has held a Christmas party for the Italian workers. But there are still no community celebrations.

Another adjustment that has to be made is during the month of Ramadan, which is the Islamic traditional thirty-day period of fasting and increased religious observance. During this time, Muslims often keep shorter hours and leave for prayer breaks. Kuwaiti companies accommodate the observance of holy rituals. However, other workers, such as the Italians, who are predominantly Roman Catholic, are not working shorter hours. This could lead to some conflict in the workplace. However, Al-Bahar/Jacorossi has prepared the foreign workers, explaining the importance of the holiday and why accommodations are made for the Muslim employees.

Kuwait has become much more open, with men and women gathering together for dinners and meetings. Before the 1960s, men and women were traditionally separated. However, for social gatherings such as parties, it is still common that men and women socialize separately, but this, of course, is not required. However, Italian men and women are used to celebrating together. This has made for interesting situations in the work place when social events occur. It is difficult to simulate both cultures.

English is the second language for most Kuwaitis and Italians, so language is not a major barrier; however, minor differences in usage sometimes occur. There are many cultural similarities between the Italians and Kuwaitis. Some of the common characteristics are that both are quick decision makers. They both talk loudly with lots of hand gestures. Many Kuwaitis believe it is easier to do business with the Americans because they are more straightforward in their business dealings. Both Italians and Arabs do not talk in a straightforward manner, and so it takes longer to close a deal. Americans are more flexible. Americans would rather get business out of the way and then socialize. The British stop to have their afternoon tea, and usually are much more rigid concerning their schedules.

The Case Study

Mr. Adel Al-Sulaiman sat at his desk in the corporate offices of Al-Bahar & Jacorossi Engineering Company, looking out the window. It was three months after Kuwait had been liberated from the Iraqi soldiers, and although this had been a great relief for his people, there were still many obstacles to overcome. He was enjoying looking outside because the skies had begun to clear. It had been a while since Kuwaitis could enjoy any clear sky due to the burning oil fields left behind by Saddam Hussein's soldiers. For the first few weeks, it was difficult to tolerate being outside for very long, due to the gases and smoke that filled their environment. With assistance from all over the world, Kuwait was getting back on its feet much more quickly than anyone expected.

Mr. Al-Sulaiman was the director of human resources for the Al-Bahar Company. The Jacorossi Engineering Company had a separate director, although they generally worked together to develop human resource policies. As he sat in his office, he began to contemplate the major challenges that lay ahead. He thought about their employees, and the trauma of the last several months they had endured. Most families lost everything of value that could be carried away by Iraqi soldiers. They lost their automobiles, office equipment, computers, and family mementos. Still, most Kuwaitis felt lucky if their family members were safe, although most knew those who had disappeared or were killed during the invasion. Mr. Al-Sulaiman knew that they would need extra moral support and assistance from the company.

Mr. Al-Sulaiman also knew that the returning Italian employees would have fears and challenges as well. Many of the Italians also had lost important personal possessions. They had been forced to leave the country right after the invasion, and they did not have time to take much with them. They were apprehensive about the current security conditions of the country. Saddam Hussein was still in power, and this was enough to create fear and anxiety.

Because of the high anxiety and the losses suffered by their employees, it was Mr. Al-Sulaiman's job to create assistance programs to help their employees readjust to normal life. However, no one in his country had ever faced this sort of situation. He worried about whether he would be using the right approach. He worried that the company might not be doing enough. A meeting was set up with the owners and the top management to introduce his ideas.

The company was very concerned about two issues. First, they were concerned about the well-being of their employees. The company has a strong sense of community and loyalty to every employee. Management understood the pain of loss, and they wanted to help in any way they could. They also understood that the regular pressures of life, the demands of a job, and that (for the Italian employees) living in a new culture was very stressful. Add the anxiety, fear and loss brought by a hostile invasion, and this compounds problems of employees being able to do their jobs well. The company wanted to find ways to help employees relieve some of their stress and feel more secure in their environment again.

Mr. Al-Sulaiman had three programs in mind to help with these problems. First, he would get approval to have an assistance program for any employee who needed help with their financial and housing needs. If the employee had lost their automobiles, their furniture, and other personal belongings, there were several programs in Kuwait where people could receive financial assistance. This assistance was particularly important for the Italian employees who did not have family and community support systems. The company would submit the names of employees, list their needs, and be the spokesperson for the employees to the outside agencies.

The company also wanted to help employees deal with the psychological problems they might be facing. Again, the Kuwaiti employees had outside resources from their families and religious affiliations, while the Italian employees would need extra support from the company. However, the company still felt it was important for all employees to be able to communicate about the invasion and their personal reactions. Mr. Al-Sulaiman suggested holding several company meetings to address the issues of employees. First, they would discuss the kinds of problems that were common in the situation, and then they would give information regarding sources of assistance and the commitment of the company to provide support.

Finally, a program would be created that would help individual employees if they needed extra counseling. Mr. Al-Sulaiman would personally contact and set this up with agencies in the community that could help employees cope with their psychological problems. The costs of any counseling would be paid for by the company.

Discussion Questions

1. What kind of training could the Italians receive before coming to Kuwait that would help them be better prepared for cultural differences?
2. What are the obligations of the company in this situation?
3. What more could the company do to support its employees?
4. Do you agree with Mr. Al-Sulaiman that management should not become too personally involved with personal problems of employees? Why or why not?
5. The company created an Employee Assistance Program (EAP). What are the benefits of this kind of program?
6. What are some other employee issues where an EAP might be appropriate?
7. Is the Al-Bahar/Jacorossi Engineering Company doing enough for the Italian employees? Kuwaiti employees? Why or why not? Are there any other suggestions you could make?

References

Dann, C. (2016). 2016 Engineering and construction industry trends. *Strategy &*. Retrieved from https://www.strategyand.pwc.com/trends/2016-engineering-and-construction-industry-trends

Global Entrepreneurship Institute. (2017). Special issues for the entrepreneur. *Global Entrepreneurship Institute*. Retrieved from https://news.gcase.org/special-issues-for-the-entrepreneur/

Industrial Info. Resources. (2017). Electric power industry. *Industrial Info. Resources*. Retrieved https://www.industrialinfo.com/database/power/

Investopedia. (2018). Joint Stock Company. *Investopedia*. Retrieved from https://www.investopedia.com/terms/j/jointstockcompany.asp

Kuwait Institute of Banking Studies (2007). *Finance and economy related data about Kuwait and GCC*. Retrieved November 20, 2007, from http://www.kibs.edu.kw/eikgcc.html.

Kuwait Ministry of Planning. (1995). *Kuwait, A country report*. Kuwait City, Kuwait: Kuwaiti Government Printing Office.

Kuwait Ministry of Planning. (1996). *Kuwait and social development*. Kuwait City, Kuwait: Kuwaiti Government Printing Office.

Mathis R.L., & Jackson, J. H. (2006). *Human resource management* (11th ed.). Mason, OH: Thomson Learning.

Sobolewski, M., Kent, A., & Berg den Van, J. (2017). 2017 Engineering and construction trends. *Strategy &*. Retrieved from https://www.strategyand.pwc.com/trend/2017-engineering-and-construction-trends

United Nations, Dept. of Economic of Economic and Social Affairs. (2006, August). World population prospects: ROM edition-comprehensive dataset. Retrieved February 28, 2007, from http://unstats.un.org/unsd/demographic/products/dyb/default.htm

U.S. Central Intelligence Agency (2007, Nov. 15). *The world fact book: Kuwait*. Washington, DC: US Government Printing Office. Retrieved November 27, 2007, from https://www.cia.gov/library/publications/the-world-factbook/geos/ku.html

Relevant Videos

HR Cultural Diversity:
https://www.youtube.com/watch?v=JujMw_Z0ne8

The Importance of Home Business in Kuwait:
https://www.youtube.com/watch?v=10EJ_QDsCWc

How To Start Your Business in Kuwait?
https://www.youtube.com/watch?v=xS2SPsGz3wl

Did you know? - Italy - Italian Business Culture video:
https://www.youtube.com/watch?v=6BR99GzrVDo

Business culture in Italy:
https://www.youtube.com/watch?v=LBHZ6mZnGv0

Invasion of Kuwait – Explained:
https://www.youtube.com/watch?v=dphDS6OS1lc

BADRIYA'S SHORT CAREER IN SAUDI ARABIA

Dianne H.B. Welsh, The University of North Carolina at Greensboro
Mohammed Al-Boluhad, Eastern Washington University

Learning Objectives

1. *Identify* a clear case of a hiring decision based on gender.
2. *Respond* to the actions of the company.
3. *Analyze* the effect of government regulations and its impact on this case.
4. *Analyze* the responsibilities of employees and the employers.
5. *Analyze* the effects of tradition, religion and culture on the law.
6. *Determine* if these regulations should be adjusted, and if so, how.

Key Words

Gender

Government Regulations

Hiring Decisions

Saudi Arabia

Abstract

This case describes a hiring decision based on gender in Saudi Arabia. It requires students to consider relevant issues in determining an appropriate managerial response. These issues include government policies, legal compliance, gender issues, employee commitment and job satisfaction, employer and employee rights and responsibilities, and tradition, religion, and culture.

Badriya's Short Career in Saudi Arabia

Badriya Al-Khaleed was a young woman from Saudi Arabia when she came to America. She was married, and her husband was working at the Saudi Arabian Embassy in Washington, D.C. At the time, they had no children. She was accepted for admission to Georgetown University's Computer Science program. She first took a year of intense English language courses. After a year of these courses, she began attending Georgetown. Her husband was very supportive. She was highly successful in her course work, and enjoyed working with the high technology systems available in the United States.

Badriya graduated with honors in 1985 with her undergraduate degree and completed a master's degree in Computer Science in 1987. Badriya's chosen area of study was quite unusual for a woman from Saudi Arabia. The traditional areas of study for women are literature and the social sciences. Majors in psychology or the medical professions are also common. The university system is also very different in Saudi Arabia. The only university where men and women can attend together is at King Saud Medical University. The rest of the universities are separated by gender and offer mostly traditional programs. While education is highly regarded for men and women, women are usually not encouraged to go beyond a bachelor's degree. Not surprisingly, when Badriya came to America, she experienced culture shock by attending classes with men and participating fully. She also learned that employment opportunities that are available for women in the United States as compared to Saudi Arabia were measurably different.

In 1990, Badriya and her husband returned to Saudi Arabia. Her husband worked for the government. Badriya wanted to find a good job to utilize her skills and education. She was immediately hired by King Saud University to teach computer programming. She did not really like teaching. She wanted to work for a company as a computer analyst, programmer, or consultant.

After teaching for a few years, she read about a job opening at a petrochemical company as a computer analyst and program designer. She applied for the job. However, Saudi Arabian law forbids women to work for public companies. She thought there a high probability that she would not get the job, but she applied anyway. She was hoping that they might make an exception because of her extraordinary qualifications. She wanted to make a significant contribution to this company's success. She was told she was by far the most qualified applicant, but the company hired a man anyway.

Badriya was upset and frustrated. She wrote a letter to the editor of the largest newspaper. She asked the government to make its regulations more flexible and wanted to know why the government would not allow women with such education and experience to work and contribute to the country. No reply appeared in print.

She still is at King Saud University, where she now is the Chair of the Computer Science Department. She has gained managerial experience in addition to her technical skills and education. Yet, she continues to be overlooked simply because she is a woman.

Background

The Religion of Islam:

> "Al-Qur'an, the revealed book of Islam, declares that man and woman proceed from the same stock, they are the members of the same species, they are born of the same parents. Man and woman are spouses of each other, companions and helpmates. Besides restoring her human dignity, Islam bestowed on the woman innumerable rights in every field of human life." (Ashraf, xii)

Ibn Hazm said, "Woman is entitled to possess houses, gardens, and estates, engage in business, guarantee other parties; give away whole or part of her dower to whom she wants without objection from the part of her father or husband" (Bahnassawi, 17). Muslim women are not obliged to change their names to their husband's after marriage. A woman's obedience is not to a man but to Allah and the Prophet.

Islam grants both men and women equal rights to refute the legitimacy and constitutionality of laws, regulations, and orders. Islam gives women the right to assent in marriage. No marriage is considered valid if the woman does not give her consent.

Islam grants women equality. Women stand at par with men on almost every plane of similarity: spiritual, moral, and intellectual. In true Islam, "Muslim women are equal to men in all aspects of Islam except in one: "As mothers, women are superior to men by as much as a ratio of three to one" (Siddique, 135). In Faith, spirituality, prayer, fasting, zakat, hajj, or jihad, women are the equals of men. Muslim women are encouraged to acquire education and knowledge; and be courageous in objecting to men's opinions if they are incorrect. The Prophet Mohammed said, "The acquisition of knowledge is incumbent upon every Muslim man and every Muslim woman." Because Islam makes no differentiation between either of the two sexes, it considers them both intellectually equal. "Women are the twin-halves of men" (Bahnassawi, 62).

In general, these are some of the rights given to women through the Islamic religion. However, this does not mean that Islamic women always enjoy these rights. Part of the problem arises in Muslim families where there is no distinction is made between actual Islamic principles and how they are implemented. Additionally, many tribal legacies have been included in family cultures that do not reflect Islamic beliefs. Muslim men today often ignore the fact that the Islamic religion grants women equal rights and independent identities.

Epilogue

Badriya is still teaching at King Saud University and is Chair of the Computer Science Department. She has two children and a full family life. However, she feels she has not achieved her highest career potential.

Discussion Questions

1. How will Badriya's job satisfaction and commitment be affected by not getting the private sector job and having to continue to teach?
2. Could the administrators at King Saud University do anything in the workplace to improve Badriya's job satisfaction and commitment?
3. What factors might affect the company's decision in this case?
4. What could the Saudi Arabian government do to try to improve their regulations regarding employment of women?
5. Do you think the Saudi Arabian employment laws are fair?

References

Beiter, K. (2016, November 12). A changing Middle East: New Jobs for women in Saudi Arabia. *The Jerusalem Post*. Retrieved from http://www.jpost.com/Middle-East/A-changing-middle-east-New-jobs-for-women-in-Saudi-Arabia-472395

Clyde & Co. (2016, June 20). Employment & labour law in Saudi Arabia. *Lexology*. Retrieved from https://www.lexology.com/library/detail.aspx?g=6ba28ace-2bcf-49a7-9cba-98b08a8ff5a6

D'Cunha, S.D. (2017, October 3). To this Saudi startup, allowing women to drive is a game changer. Retrieved from https://www.forbes.com/sites/suparnadutt/2017/10/03/to-this-saudi-startup-allowing-women-to-drive-is-a-game-changer/#7bfb0b08442f

Gray, A. (2017, October 18). The Middle East's biggest ride-hailing firm is hiring women drivers in Saudi Arabia. *World Economic Forum*. Retrieved from https://www.weforum.org/agenda/2017/10/the-middle-easts-biggest-ride-hailing-firm-is-hiring-women-drivers-in-saudi-arabia/

Human Rights Watch. (2016, July 16). Boxed in: Women and Saudi Arabia's male guardianship system. *Human Rights Watch*. Retrieved from https://www.hrw.org/report/2016/07/16/boxed/women-and-saudi-arabias-male-guardianship-system

Relevant Videos

Women Driving Ban Lifted: What Is Happening In Saudi Arabia?
https://www.youtube.com/watch?v=HogwoOSNgl0

10 Tips on Arab Culture for Successful Business in the Middle East:
https://www.youtube.com/watch?v=U9XoD9V9Bvg

Do's and Don'ts: Doing Business with Arab Business People:
https://www.youtube.com/watch?v=UIA9X67IC7c

Saudi Arabia: Government and Religion:
https://www.youtube.com/watch?v=KC6gzsV6cU8

Providing Students with a Worldview: A Competency-Based System for International Entrepreneurship, Education, and Development

THE HIT AND RUN EXPATRIATE EMPLOYEES

Dianne H.B. Welsh, The University of North Carolina at Greensboro
Ibrahim Al-Fahim, Al-Fahim General Trading Company

Learning Objectives

1. *Explain* the importance of human resource policies and procedures within a firm, including government compliance.
2. *Discuss* the basic definition of an expatriate and how human resource policies and procedures are impacted.
3. *Assess* the ethical responsibility implications of the main players in this case.
4. *Analyze* the current legal issues facing Mr. Kamal, the owner of the Zag Company, in relation to Saudi Arabian law.
5. *Describe* how workforce employee commitment and job satisfaction could be affected by this situation among expatriates and non-expatriate employees.
6. *Identify* employer and employee rights and responsibilities.
7. *Discuss* the impact of this situation on the personal relationship between the two companies.
8. *Determine* what responsibilities the owner of Zag has to the company, the government, the general manager, and the other employees of Salam Wholesalers.

Key Words

Expatriate Employees   Saudi Arabia
Government Regulation

Abstract

This case describes an expatriate employee in Saudi Arabia. It requires students to consider relevant issues in determining an appropriate managerial response. These issues include government policy regarding compliance with the law, expatriates, employee commitment and job satisfaction, employer and employee rights and responsibilities, and personal relationships between companies.

The Hit and Run Expatriate Employees

Salam Wholesalers is a trading company that handles consumer personal goods, such as sunglasses, cosmetics, colognes, and various sundries. Saudi Arabian law dictates that when an expatriate leaves a firm for any reason, the person cannot work for another firm unless they have written permission from their former employer. The person is prohibited from working for another Saudi Arabian firm for three years. It is permissible to resign and return to their home country. Two salesmen, Badr and Jalil, got a better job offer and they decided to leave Salam Wholesalers. These two employees were from

Egypt. They did not tell the government they were changing employment nor did they request written permission.

Subsequently, their former general manager, Mr. Hadad, found out that they were working for a competitor. They had defrauded Salam Wholesalers, and had broken Saudi Arabian law. Therefore, they would be sent back to Egypt. Mr. Kamal, the owner of the Zag Company, enjoyed a good relationship with the owner of Salam Wholesalers. This was despite the fact that they were direct competitors. After the the Zag Company found out that Mr. Hadad took action against former employees, Mr. Kamal called Mr. Hashim. He asked him to give them written permission to work for their company. They were excellent salesmen and Mr. Kamal did not want to lose them.

Salam Wholesalers has invested a great deal of time and money to train the salesmen. In addition, they had incurred relocation expenses as well as other expenses. Salam Wholesalers had trained them well by providing them with on-the-job training and experience. Within six months from their point-of-hire, Badr and Jalil found a better opportunity and left. It is important to understand that Saudi Arabian companies traditionally do not pay expatriate employees as well as natural-born citizens. Oftentimes, once expatriate employees acquire on-the-job experience, they want to change jobs because they can earn more money at another firm.

When the Zag Company found out that Mr. Hadad, the general manager, had taken legal action and informed the government, Mr. Kamal tried to convince Mr. Hashim to reverse the actions of his general manager. The owner of Salam Wholesalers felt he needed to support his general manager. He did not want these two expatriate employees to break the law and have other employees see that they could get away with it. Mr. Hashim had a major dilemma to solve.

Note: Fictional names have been used in this case.

Epilogue

Mr. Hashim, the owner of Salam Wholesalers, told Mr. Kamal, the owner of the Zag Company, that if there was anything else he could do for him, he would. However, he could not comply with his wishes in this instance. Normally, the general manager would have been involved in the decision-making. The Saudi Arabian government deported the two salesmen back to Egypt.

Discussion Questions

1. How would Mr. Hadad's commitment and job satisfaction level be affected if the owner reverses Mr. Hadad's actions?
2. How would job satisfaction be affected if the owner of Salam Wholesalers complies with the wishes of the owner of the Zag Company?
3. What factors might affect the commitment level of these two employees?
4. What could the Saudi Arabian government do to try to prevent expatriate employees from wanting to leave the company that originally hires them? Is there anything the firm could do?
5. Do you think the Saudi Arabian three-year law is fair?

References

Abdulwahab A., Cosgrove P., Mohamed G., & Hassan A. (2017, January 19). The personal and workplace characteristics of uninsured expatriate males in Saudi Arabia. *BMC Health Services Research*. Retrieved from https://doi.org/10.1186/s12913-017-1985-x

David D., Steven, W.C. (2017) Expat pay and compensation: fair or not fair? *The CASE Journal*, 13(2),168-186.

Franco, N.C., Severke, F., Sverke M., Dick, R.V., & Monzani, L. (2017). *Does it matter whether I am a happy and committed worker? The role of identification, commitment and job satisfaction for employee behaviour*. An Introduction to Work and Organizational Psychology: An International Perspective.

Harter, J.K., Schmidt, F.L., & Hayes, T.L. (2018). Business-unit-level relationship between employee satisfaction, employee engagement, and business outcomes: A meta-analysis. *Journal of Applied Psychology*, 87(2), 268-27.

Muhammad, H.R., & Muhammad, S.M., (2017). Impact of human resource (HR) practices on organizational performance: Moderating role of Islamic principles. *International Journal of Islamic and Middle Eastern Finance and Management*, 10(2).

Relevant Videos

The Impact of Saudization Policy on HR Practices in Retail Sector in Saudi Arabia: https://www.youtube.com/watch?v=XLV6JYPfZvM

What is EXPATRIATE? What does EXPATRIATE mean? EXPATRIATE meaning, definition & explanation: https://www.youtube.com/watch?v=aLvzWni2Tz0

Dependent's Fee on Expatriate Workers in Saudi Arabia: https://www.youtube.com/watch?v=WtTCz2Y3HtA

Chapter Ten

Global Franchising and Other Forms of Entrepreneurship

FRANCHISE RELATIONS IN THE GULF REGION: THE CASE OF THE ELEGANT SHOPLIFTER

Dianne H.B. Welsh, The University of North Carolina at Greensboro
Peter V. Raven, Seattle University
Faisel Al-Bisher, Al-Bisher Mercedes Benz

Learning Objectives

1. *Evaluate* the cultural norms and legal issues involved in breaking the law in Kuwait.
2. *Evaluate* the ethical issues in the case.
3. *Analyze* the best method for law enforcement to work with women in a predominately Islamic country.
4. *Analyze* the rights and responsibilities of the company taking into account local law and cultural and religious rights.
5. *Evaluate* the best method to utilize trained security in a predominately Islamic country.

Key Words

Automobile Dealership	Kuwait
Culture	Shoplifting

Abstract

The following case concerns a spare parts shoplifter in a Mercedes Benz retail franchise. The reader must determine the suitable managerial and sales person's actions, while considering legal implications, security, and cultural and gender issues. The influences of culture, nationality, and religion in the Gulf Region and how these influences affect management are discussed.

 Introduction

Before entering the Middle East, franchisors and their headquarters staff must first understand the differences between their culture and the countries in this area. While there is a natural tendency to generalize the overall culture of this region, there exist unique differences from country to country. It is important for the franchise to examine these differences, as it will affect the relationships between the franchisor and franchisee, as well as consumer behavior and attitudes that ultimately affect the success of the franchise. The franchisor may have to adjust their systems, products, and human resource policies to reflect these mores.

The Gulf Region

Culture. Residents of the Gulf Region are not strangers to contradiction and conflict. Idiosyncrasies, both ancient and modern, have shaped this region. Since the discovery of oil in the Gulf Region in the 1970s, the region has been in transition. The subsequent increases in revenue have resulted in drastic changes and significant industrialization within these countries (Abbasi & Hollman, 1993; Ali, 1990; Ali & Al-Shakhis, 1986). Contact with Western countries and corporations improved the standard of living in the Gulf Region through better education, improved health care, greater mobility, and increased communication (Ali, 1990; Ali & Al-Shakhis, 1986). Western thought often conflicts with Arab culture and religion. Industrialization, while welcome, complicates the duties of managers who strive to achieve modern results while maintaining their traditional values. This duality is not new to the people of the Gulf Region. Contradiction is an inherent part of Islamic culture. For centuries, Muslims have upheld religious ideals that conflict with political routine (Ali, 1990, 1993).

Nationality. In addition to religion, nationality probably has the next most significant effect on the Gulf Region. Saudi Arabians tend to be more conformist and have high structure needs compared to other Gulf Region residents. Predominately authoritarian management is the norm in organizations in Saudi Arabia. Kuwaitis are more tribalistic; they are submissive to authority and tradition. In addition, the Kuwaiti people have had more exposure to new ideas and Western culture than their counterparts from other Gulf Region nations (Ali, 1988). Kuwaiti organizations were the first to hire managers based on education rather than family connections (Yasin & Stahl, 1990). The Iraqi and Qatari hold more existential values and lean toward consultative management styles (Ali, 1988, 1989a). A pseudo-consultative management style is dominant in Kuwait. Managers in this region seem to value an appearance of consensus and consultation, but often make decisions without considering the discussions they facilitate (Ali, 1989b). Gulf Region managers under 30 years of age prefer more participatory management techniques regardless of nationality (Ali, 1989b; Yasin & Stahl, 1990).

Management. Islamic culture shapes the region, and therefore the organizations that operate there. Passages in the Quran, the Islamic holy book, specifically address business transactions, from spending habits to financial and management concepts. Different interpretations of the Quran are yet another source of contradiction and are the basis of differences in the culture (Ali, 1990).

Management style is one contradiction that finds roots in differing Muslim sects. Authoritarian management is predominant in large organizations, while consultative methods prevail in other arenas. Some Islamic sects prefer consultative methods of management, which is more consistent with tribalistic traditions (Ali, 1989; Ali & Al-Shakhis, 1986), while others prefer religious interpretations that promote authoritarian styles and encourage absolute authority of rulers (Ali, 1990). Early colonial possession of the region also set a precedent of authoritarian management (Abbasi & Hollman, 1993; Ali, 1990). These patterns find additional roots in the fundamental precepts of the Islamic religion, which encourage respect of elder family members and stress a father's authority within a family. Family members usually hold management and other key positions within organizations (Abbasi & Hollman, 1993). Additionally, family members often collect regular pay but are not required to work (Ali, 1990). Tribal-family traditions can further reinforce authoritarian management styles but often support consultative management techniques as well (Ali, 1989, 1990). Tradition dictates that a sheik follows rather than leads tribal-family opinion (Ali, 1993). Furthermore, consultative methods are proven to be more effective with multicultural work forces such as those that predominate in the Gulf Region (Enshassi & Burgess, 1991). However, management style in organizations located in the Gulf Region is in transition. Younger managers who have been educated at Western universities, or those who work primarily with foreign corporations, use participatory management. They tend to encourage decentralization and teamwork. Participatory management is not alien to the Gulf Region, but is more common among managers who work with Western organizations (Ali, 1993).

Tribal-family relations and religion affect other aspects of management. Managers from the Gulf Region tend to disregard rules and procedures as man-made prefects (Ali, 1993). They prefer flexibility, but are by no means risk-takers. Tribal-family norms and values encourage conformity and discourage creativity (Ali, 1990, 1993). Stability is highly valued in Islamic culture (Ali, 1990). Managers from the Gulf Region are rarely innovative; they prefer implementing someone else's plan to developing creative strategy (Ali, 1989, 1990). Other characteristics of Gulf Region managers include a tendency to avoid delegation and an inherent belief that centralization encourages respect (Ali, 1989). Understanding the culture, nationality, and management styles of this region are important for franchisors, as it can affect all aspects of the franchising system, from product offerings and training.

The Country

Kuwait is a country the area of 6,880 square miles, with a population of 1.9 million. Over 1.2 million live in the capital city (Russell, 2000). The neighboring countries are Saudi Arabia to the south and Iraq to the north. The official language is Arabic but English and Persian are very common. The country became independent of England in 1961. The government structure consists of the Emir as the chief executive of government and is assisted by a Prime Minister and 20 men who are members of the royal family who serve on the Council of Ministers. An elected National Assembly makes recommendations and serves as a forum for discussion.

On August 2, 1990, Iraq invaded Kuwait. Seven months later, the war was over due to the United States, the United Kingdom, and other allies supporting the Kuwaiti troops. Today, there are few signs that the country had ever been invaded. The 700-plus oil wells that were torched by Iraqi troops have all been repaired. Almost everything has been rebuilt. For the most part, Kuwait City, the capital, is a picture of wealth (North, 2000). Kuwait has the fourth-largest oil reserves in the world, plus an estimated $45 billion in public savings invested abroad (Lynch, 1999). The people of Kuwait depend heavily on the income from oil. However, of the Persian Gulf states, Kuwait is the best positioned financially. It is commonplace to see Jaguars, Range Rovers, and Mercedes on the road. Upscale shopping malls offer Swiss watches, Italian suits, and other luxuries.

The Case

Al-Bisher, Inc. owns the Mercedes Benz franchise in Kuwait. The two largest dealerships are located in Kuwait City and Shuwaikh, Kuwait. The case in question describes events at the Mercedes spare parts dealership and showroom in Shuwaikh. Shuwaikh is a large port city, approximately 3.2 million square meters, which has just been modernized. Many new buildings have been built in the last few years, and the port has been enlarged greatly. This means that there are many more visitors and business people coming to Kuwait through the port of Shuwaikh. There are about 57,000 people living in this city.

The dealership itself is located in a large building on Al-Fares Street, with five other automobile dealerships located in the same neighborhood. The building is modern, with large glass windows, and is blue and gray. The sales force consists of 14 men, ranging from 25 to 55 years of age, and two managers, Mr. Mahmood and Mr. Fahimi. All salesmen and managers are required to wear gray suits with blue ties, deemed Mercedes colors.

The inventory of the spare parts retail showroom in Shuwaikh had been experiencing shortages of expensive accessories. In light of this, the management had instructed the salesmen to be alert regarding suspicious customers. The specific instructions were if the sales people saw anyone who seemed to be acting strangely, who appeared nervous or asked for unusual requests, then they should be reported to management. In Kuwait, security alarm facilities are usually installed in the jewelry shops, but closed circuit television systems are not typically used in Kuwait, except in banks, as shoplifting and other forms of theft have traditionally been rare. However, after the liberation of Kuwait from the Iraqi forces, shoplifting incidents and even armed robberies are on the increase.

One day Nora, an elegant-looking lady and regular visitor of the spare parts and accessories facility at the Mercedes showroom, visited with her child, aged about 5 years. She asked to look at a number of accessories, including some models of a Becker car stereo, one of the most often sought-after consumer brands. The salesman brought the stereos and displayed them as she had requested. The showroom was unusually busy, and the salesmen were having a difficult time attending to all the customers. Mr. Mahmood, who was the supervisor on duty, was also unavailable because he was managing the showroom. The lady examined the stereo, and then requested the salesman, Mr. Ahmed, to bring out some other parts, which required him to leave the counter for a short period of time. The other salesmen were busy attending to numerous other customers. However, Mr. Mahmood, while completing his routine customer checks, spotted

Nora slipping the car stereo into her large bag. Mr. D'Souza, a salesman, also noticed the incident. He was warned by his manager to be on alert for potential shoplifters.

After selecting some minor spare parts for her stereo, the woman approached the register to pay the bill. Mr. Mahmood followed her to the cash counter to see if she was paying for the stereo and was surprised to note that she did not even mention the item to the clerk.

Mr. Mahmood confronted her, saying he knew she had a stereo in her bag, but she vehemently denied it. When Mr. Mahmood insisted that he check her bag, the woman started shouting at him and told him that he had no right to check a woman's personal bag. At this point, Mr. D'Souza, came and told her that he too had noticed her slipping the stereo into her bag, but Nora, the suspected shoplifter, was adamant and refused to allow her bag to be checked. The security officer hired by Mercedes was also present but was not able to do anything because in Islamic countries, the law does not allow a male to freely talk to a woman or to touch her belongings. This law is respected and followed in Kuwait. Breaking this law is a crime and a person can be arrested. However, the seriousness of the situation caused the cashier, Mr. Fadel, to call the police.

As the commotion grew, the other customers gathered around the area, some taking the woman's side and others just observing the commotion. Some of the customers were yelling that the woman in question was not a thief. Soon, the police arrived on the scene, and after hearing both sides of the story, decided to have the woman's bag checked.

The stereo was found in her bag. Nora strongly defended her innocence. She implied that her child without her knowledge might have put the stereo in her bag. The testimony of Mr. Mahmood and Mr. D'Souza that they had seen the woman slipping the stereo in her bag was sufficient for the police to take her to the police station. Upon interrogation, it was revealed that she had regularly been lifting valuable items, which she took back with her to Pakistan, her home. She could get a very good price for the items in Pakistan. Knowing Islamic religious laws, women are aware they usually cannot be stopped, checked, and held by authorities very easily. It is relatively easy to shoplift at shopping malls and other retail outlets. These shoplifters leave the country when their visa expires with their booty, which will fetch them large amounts of money in their home countries.

The police proceeded to search her house and recovered a variety of expensive items, such as jewelry and small electronic devices like the stereo. They were packed in suitcases, as the woman was going to leave for her country in a couple of days. She was immediately arrested and booked for larceny. She later was found guilty, served her sentence in jail, and was permanently extradited from Kuwait.

Relevant Issues

There are a number of questions that are relevant for the reader to know the answers to that could affect franchising and the relationship between the franchisor and the franchisee. They are embedded throughout the case. The most obvious is the laws governing contact with women. Should the law be changed when the accused is a female? Should a female police officer be used when a woman is accused of a crime in Kuwait? Kuwait is an Islamic country where the culture is very well established and understood. Islamic law is the only governing law, and civil law interfaces with Islamic law. Cultural norms are respected. However, there is a new generation that believes in equal treatment of women. Women, in general, are more educated than in the past. Many possess higher education degrees. A liberation movement is underway. A department in the police force could be established where female police officers could answer calls dealing with women criminal suspects. This would open up new professions for women in Kuwait.

Was there another approach that the staff could have adopted in dealing with the shoplifter? Is there any training that the franchise headquarters provides to the franchisee and their employees? The staff of the showroom, after having seen that the woman was slipping the stereo in her bag, should have responded in a manner that would not have exposed the woman in public. Mr. Mahmood, the supervisor, could have, along with Mr. Ahmed, the salesman, and a female employee of the showroom, taken her to his office and asked her to remove the stereo. This would be a reasonable solution in Kuwait given the social and cultural norms in relation to the religious values of the country. Then the pride of the woman would not have been hurt and she would have given him the stereo. Also, the salesmen have to be trained not to leave expensive items with customers who are unattended. If the dealership were busy, then the customer would have to wait. Perhaps a customer number waiting system could be devised. The showroom could track the number of customers by the hour to determine the busiest times of the day. They could add more sales representatives during these times. Also, the dealership might want to consider the employment of female sales representatives, since the number of female shoppers in Kuwait is rising. Although in this case the franchise does not provide specific training on shoplifting, it might be wise to develop a training video that could address the issue specifically for the Middle East, with the cultural and religious norms. The video could be made available to all franchises to assist in employee training.

A question also arises in the case concerning visas. Three-day visas are granted almost automatically. Many Kuwaitis have close relatives in nearby countries that enjoy visiting. It is estimated that only 40 percent of the population are native Kuwaitis (Russell, 2000). Should the residency laws be changed to allow only eligible foreign employees with a substantial salary level to bring their families, and make the visa requirements more strict to better screen those entering the country? Currently, the authorities allow all working visa holders to bring their families to Kuwait, regardless of financial status. Because of the good financial standing in Kuwait, many foreign workers and their families are hoping to live in Kuwait to raise their standard of living. Many come from poor countries like India, Pakistan, and Bangladesh.

The residency law, which has permitted every foreign employee to bring his family regardless of financial status, is creating social problems, such as robberies, thefts, shoplifting, and many other antisocial activities previously not encountered to much of a degree before—factors which this country was unaware of before. Kuwait enjoys a good economy. Many expatriates are employed in Kuwait because of the high standard of living. Unfortunately, many of the jobs are low paying in a country that is among the ten wealthiest in the world. This creates two social societies, the rich and the poor, which can lead the people to find antisocial ways to survive and to support families here. If the law is amended to allow only people who can afford to shoulder the financial responsibilities of a family, it will decrease the antisocial acts, but could also have other, unintended consequences. For instance, many of these expatriates work in service jobs, such as retail franchise outlets. This could cause a labor shortage and related human resource problems for franchises.

Discussion Questions

1. Should the law be changed when the accused is a female? Should a female police force be used for females accused of crimes in Kuwait?
2. Should the residency laws be changed to allow only eligible foreign employees with a substantial salary level to bring their families? Currently, the authorities allow all working visa holders to bring their families to Kuwait, regardless of financial status. Because of the good financial standing in Kuwait, many foreign workers and their families are hoping to live in Kuwait to raise their standard of living. Many come from poor countries like India.
3. Was there another approach that the staff could have adopted in dealing with the shoplifter?

References

Abbasi, S. & Hollman, K. (1993). Business success in the Middle East. *Management Decisions*, *31*(1), 55–60.

Ahmed, F. (2016, June 11). Criminal laws in Kuwait. *Kuwait Times*. Retrieved from http://news.kuwaittimes.net/website/criminal-laws-kuwait/

Ali, A. (1988). A cross-national perspective of managerial work value systems. *Advances in International Comparative Management*. *3*, 151–169.

Ali, A. (1989a). A comparative study of managerial beliefs about work in the Arab States. *Advances in International Comparative Management*. *4*, 95–112.

Ali, A. & Al-Shakhis, M. (1986, November). The relationship between administrators' attitudes and needs in Saudi Arabia. *Academy of International Business: Southeast Proceedings*, Atlanta, GA.

Ali, A.J. (1989b). Decision style and work satisfaction of Arab executives: A cross-national study. *International Studies of Management and Organization, 19*(2), 22–37.

Ali, A.J. (1990). Decision-making style, individualism, and attitudes toward risk of Arab executives. *International Studies of Management and Organization, 23*(3), 53–73.

Ali, A.J. (1993). Management theory in a transitional society: the Arab's experience. *International Studies of Management and Organization, 20*(3), 7–35.

Enshassi, A. & Burgess, R. (1991, February). Managerial effectiveness and the style of management in the Middle East: An empirical analysis. *Construction Management and Economics, 9*(1), 79–92.

Gibson, Dunn, & Crutcher LLP. (2016). Middle East Private Equity- Franchise Business Targets: Out with the new, in with the old. *Gisbon Dunn*. Retrieved from https://www.gibsondunn.com/middle-east-private-equity-franchise-business-targets-out-with-the-new-in-with-the-old/

Jaworska, A. (2016, April 4). Basic laws and regulations in Kuwait. *Linkedin*. Retrieved from https://www.linkedin.com/pulse/basic-laws-regulations-kuwait-alicja-jaworska

Lynch, D.J. (1999, March 22). Pampered Kuwaitis is for rude awakening? Oil's slide threatens world of hired help, 5-car families. *USA Today*, p. 1B.

Nayef, M. (2017, April 23). Kuwaiti, expat women caught shoplifting from shops in mall. *Arab Times*. Retrieved from http://www.arabtimesonline.com/news/kuwaiti-expat-women-caught-shoplifting-shops-mall/

North, A. (2000, Oct./Nov.). Ten years after Iraq's invasion, Kuwait's prosperity tempered by lingering memories of its trauma. *American Educational Trust*, 32–33, 110.

Russell, M.B. (2000, August). The Middle East and South Asia. *The World Today Series* (34th Ed.). Harpers Ferry, WV: Stryker-Post Publications.

Visit Kuwait. (2017). Basic laws and regulations in Kuwait. *Visit Kuwait*. Retrieved from https://www.visit-kuwait.com/living/laws-regulations.aspx

Yasin, M. & Stahl, M. (1990). An investigation of managerial motivational effectiveness in the Arab culture. *International Studies of Management and Organizations, 20*(3), 69–78.

Relevant Video

What Is Sharia Law:
https://www.youtube.com/watch?v=sjJVO8GASmw

Sharia law debate creates fireworks on Q&A:
https://www.youtube.com/watch?v=Xn6WKOJDzuI

What is Sharia Law and its Principles? | Dr. Jasser Auda:
https://www.youtube.com/watch?v=odmySqc9Qa8

All about Kuwait:
https://www.youtube.com/watch?v=rkwab9vXBUg

TO MARKET, TO MARKET: AN INDEPENDENT LUXURY HOTEL'S BATTLE FOR SURVIVAL

Udo A. Schlentrich and Margaret J. Naumes
University of New Hampshire

Learning Objectives

1. *Evaluate* global entrepreneurial opportunities and threats.
2. *Analyze* the current national and international marketing strategies.
3. *Apply* models from marketing strategy and/or strategic management.
4. *Perform* a competitive analysis of the hotel and its niche position.
5. *Recommend* a course of action.

Key Words

Corporate entrepreneurship
Franchising
Global entrepreneurship

International distribution channels
Marketing
Strategic management

Abstract

The case was developed to give students the opportunity to evaluate global entrepreneurship marketing strategies that an independent luxury hotel could employ in order to achieve maximum market penetration and profitability. In view of the strong competition from international branded hotel chains and the changes that were taking place in the external environment, the management of the Nassauer Hof Hotel felt that new "out of the box" thinking was required in order to ensure the viability of their property. Key issues include increasing occupancy and brand awareness, becoming more effective against the competition of large established hotel chains, and reaching the global marketplace. In addition, the management proposed that the hotel's offerings and services be examined to determine competitiveness and overall guest appeal.

The Dilemma

Karl Nueser[1], 52, Managing Director and Partner of the Nassauer Hof Hotel[2] in Wiesbaden, Germany, had just returned from the hotel's semi-annual marketing strategy review meeting. During the April 2005 meeting, Karl and his executive team had discussed the challenges the hotel was facing in terms of increased competition and reduced occupancy.

---

[1] Karl Nueser quotes and company records reprinted by permission of Nassauer Hof Hotel.
[2] Nassauer Hof Hotel: http://www.nassauer-hof.de

During his 23 years as general manager of the independent five-star hotel, Karl and his team had been able to respond successfully to many economic, political, competitive, and lifestyle changes in the business environment. Now, however, Karl felt uneasy. Although the hotel's restaurants and catering operations were doing well, the property had been steadily losing market share in terms of room occupancy, which had slipped from 58 percent in 2000 to 54 percent in 2005. During the meeting, Karl had reviewed a list of the leading international and European four- and five-star hotel chains with his team.

"Most of the four-star hotel groups already have properties in our region," Karl had commented, "But it's only a matter of time before the five-star chains will also be entering our market—that will be a real challenge for us! In fact, as you know, the Rocco Forte Hotel, which is part of a five-star European chain, is already under construction in Frankfurt."

Although German law did not allow businesses to exchange operating statistics[2], Karl had heard from several of his department heads who had previously worked at competing chain hotels in the area that their occupancy rates were 5–10 percent higher than the Nassauer Hof's. As an independent hotel, it was becoming increasingly difficult to achieve the desired level of occupancy and to reach overseas markets in a cost effective manner. "Rooms are the most important profit center for a hotel," Karl mused. "Is it time for us to consider implementing some radical change?"

During the meeting, Karl and his team had identified several potential strategies: franchise the hotel with a global luxury brand, convert some of the guest rooms into leased apartments, make adjustments to their marketing strategy such as joining an additional international hotel marketing consortia, develop new promotional strategies to reach more of the potential target market segments, and/or develop an entrepreneurial incentive program for the hotel's department heads. What would be the best alternative for the hotel to improve its occupancy and profitability? How could the hotel most effectively attract new markets in order to strengthen the property's viability and compete with the international chains?

Background

The history of Wiesbaden dated from at least 85 CE when the Romans constructed a fortified bridgehead across the Rhine River. The Romans selected the site due to its centrality and the abundance of thermal springs. The Nassauer Hof Hotel was built at the center of the springs in 1813. In 1923, wealthy German industrialist Hugo Stinnes acquired the hotel and expanded its amenities to rival those of the finest hotels of the world. In 1945, WWII bombing raids destroyed the hotel. The only remains of its previous splendor were ruins of the building's external walls.

The Stinnes Group rebuilt the hotel in 1950, taking great care to incorporate the old structure into the new building. The architect's goal was "to create a tasteful synthesis of the past and the future."[3] The hotel was a com-

---

[2] Under German law (Gesetz gegen Wettbewerbsbeschrankungen), companies are not permitted to exchange information such as pricing, business volume, and occupancy. See http://www.bundesrecht.juris.de1/gwb_/html

[3] Press Information: Hotel Nassauer Hof, "View Through a Kaleidoscope of History" p. 3.

mercial success, and the owning group continued to fund further extensions and modernizations.

In 2001, a private real estate investment fund with 50 limited partners, one of whom was Karl, purchased the hotel. Karl and a partner then formed a management company and obtained a 20-year management contract with the real estate investment fund for the hotel. The management company owned the hotel's operating inventory and received a yearly management fee from the investment fund based on revenues and profit.

Hotel Facilities

According to its promotional material, the Nassauer Hof Hotel offered an extensive array of exquisite facilities and services to the discerning upscale guest. Its 139 guest rooms and 30 suites were equipped with state-of-the-art technology and were individually decorated and furnished. The rooftop Spa & Wellness Center provided a scenic view of Wiesbaden. The center's indoor pool was fed by the hotel's own thermal springs. Its extensive fitness, treatment, and massage facilities and the Estée Lauder Beauty Center served 180 local club members in addition to hotel guests. Local membership to the Spa & Wellness Center cost 1,600 Euros per year.[4] See Figure 10.1 for a description of the hotel's facilities.

Guest Rooms:
- 139 guest rooms, 29 suites, 1 Presidential suite
- Every guest room is individually furnished with fax and modem connections
- Marble bathrooms

Spa & Wellness Center:
- Rooftop swimming pool with its own thermal water well
- State-of-the-art Estée Lauder beauty center (10 massage and beauty treatment rooms, sauna and solarium)

Restaurants:
- Gourmet restaurant ("Die Ente") featuring European/Asian "fusion" cuisine (80 inside seats, 40 outside) with its own bar and wine cellar
- Casual elegant bistro restaurant (30 seats)
- All day restaurant ("Orangerie") featuring traditional German and regional specialties (120 inside seats, 60 outside)
- Lobby lounge serving drinks and afternoon tea (25 seats)
- Split level evening cocktail bar with pianist (60 seats)
- 24-hour room service

Other Services:
- Eight conference rooms (10 to 300 persons)
- Around the clock concierge service
- Business Center
- In-house parking (100 cars)
- Security systems (fire and smoke detection, sprinklers, electronic door locks, video surveillance, in-room safes)

Source: Company records

FIGURE 10.1 Hotel Facilities

---

[4] U.S. $2,048 at the May 2005 exchange rate of 1 Euro = $1.28

Departments	*Full Time	Apprentices
Manager's Office	2	
Administration		
Accounting, F & B Control	4	
Purchasing	2	
Marketing	3	
Human Resources	2	
Maintenance	1	
Food & Beverage Department		
Administration	3	
Main kitchen	19	8
Gourmet Restaurant (*Die Ente*)	11	2
Service staff	12	2
Restaurant (*Orangerie*)		
Service staff	14	3
Bar staff	3	
Pianist	1	
Banquet & Room Service	7	5
Rooms Division		
Front Office & Reservations	8	2
Concierge, Bellmen & Doormen	12	
Housekeeping & Laundry	20	
Spa & Wellness Center	18	
TOTAL	**142**	**22**

* Includes managers, supervisors and staff
Source: Company records

FIGURE 10.2 Hotel Nassauer Hof Staffing Guide

The hotel's food and beverage offering was of the highest standard and its restaurants enjoyed a strong local following. The gourmet restaurant, "Die Ente," had received a one-star Guide Michelin[5] rating for the past 26 years and, as a result, had often been written up in the national and international press. The hotel prided itself on the highest level of personal service. There was one maid for every 12 occupied rooms. The hotel had a very low level of staff turnover. All of the concierge and front-office staff were multi-lingual. See Figure 10.2 for a breakdown of the hotel's staff and Figure 10.3 for an executive management organization chart.

Karl was well known and respected within the hospitality and regional community. A number of local and national hotel association boards had elected him to membership. He was a member of several service organizations such as Rotary and served for 12 years on the main board of the Chamber of Commerce in Wiesbaden. Through the hotel, he was involved in sponsoring many charitable and local community events.

---

[5] The Michelin Guide: http://www.viamichelin.com

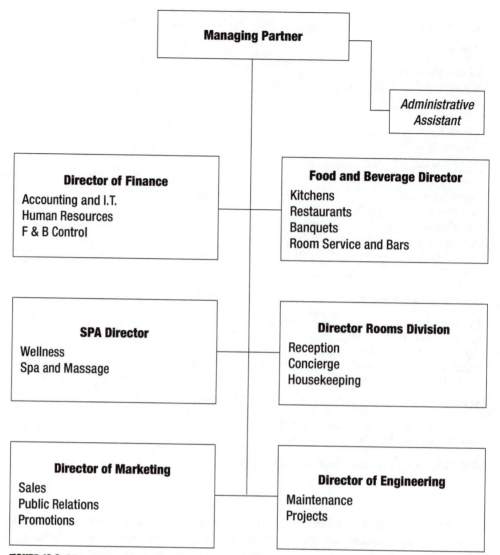

FIGURE 10.3 Hotel Nassauer Hof Executive Management Team Organization Chart

◎ The Wiesbaden Area

The Nassauer Hof Hotel was situated in the center of Wiesbaden, an elegant upscale spa and convention town with international flair. Public parks, the state theater and opera house, and the casino, which was located across the street, enhanced the hotel. The hotel was located on the main shopping avenue, which was lined by beautiful trees and upscale boutiques. Wiesbaden, located in the heart of the Rhine-Main region, one of Europe's largest commercial centers, had a population of 290,000. Fourteen ministries and German federal offices, together with numerous trade associations, made their headquarters in Wiesbaden, the state capital of Hesse. The city also served as a gateway to the famous Rhineland with its historic vineyards and castles.[6]

The picturesque town of Wiesbaden, with its abundance of parks and greenery, was a favorite location for the rich and famous to reside. Wiesbaden was an upscale "bedroom community" of Frankfurt. Villa and apartment residences were among the most expensive in Germany. Wiesbaden was also the home of Europe's renowned "German Diagnostic Clinic,"[7] which was modeled after the famous Mayo Clinic in Rochester, Minnesota. Guests from around the world made use of the preventative checkups the clinic offered.

Wiesbaden was located 45 minutes from Frankfurt, the financial capital of Germany, which housed many of the leading international banks and financial institutions. Visitors came to Frankfurt for exhibitions and conventions at the "Messe," one of Europe's premier convention and exhibition centers, which was well known for its annual book, car, and high tech fairs.

Frankfurt was one of the largest air and rail transportation hubs in Europe.[8] Speed rail connections between the city of Frankfurt and Wiesbaden left on an hourly basis. The trip took 47 minutes each way. Guests arriving at the Frankfurt airport could take a train (the S-Bahn) directly from the airport to Wiesbaden. The express train took 25 minutes.

Wiesbaden and the surrounding area offered many picturesque hikes, quality golf courses, historic sites and world-class museums. The nearby city of Mainz and the Rheingau presented innumerable adventures for wine and culinary lovers. The Rhine River, with its famous villages and castles, featured some of the most well known vineyards in the world, such as Schloss Johannisberg, Schloss Vollrads and Kloster Eberbach. In addition, Wiesbaden and the surrounding towns staged annual cultural festivals that were internationally renowned. Many of these took place in the opera and concert halls located opposite the hotel in Wiesbaden.

The Nassauer Hof's central location and its scenic setting made it the location of choice for upscale business conferences, social events, and a frequent choice of wealthy tourists arriving at the Frankfurt International Airport. See Figure 10.4 for Wiesbaden tourism statistics.

Total Number of Rooms	6,319
Arrivals	437,064
Total Room Nights	967,088
Average Stay	2.2 nights
Bed Occupancy	41.9%
Room Occupancy	53.2%

Source: Hessisches Statistisches Landesamt

FIGURE 10.4 Wiesbaden Tourism Statistics (2004)

---

[6] See http://english.wiesbaden.de/index.php for a map of Wiesbaden and more information about the city.

[7] Deutsche Klinik für Diagnostik (DKD): http://www.rhoen-klinikum-ag.com

[8] See http://frankfurt.de/sis/English.html for a map of Frankfurt and more information about the city, and http://downloads.raileurope.com/map_europe/europe.html for an overview map of Europe

The Marketing Environment

The Nassauer Hof's clientele used to be predominantly German. During the previous 20 years, however, the hotel had experienced a radical shift, from 78 percent German in the 1980s to 52 percent in 2004. The primary reasons for this shift were the increased globalization of the business environment and the influx of Japanese, former Soviet Union, and Middle Eastern visitors to the Rhine-Main region. However, Karl envisioned that, just as these markets had become important to the hotel, markets such as China and India that were virtually non-existent at present could also become important. "But how will we be able to effectively reach these markets?" he wondered.

In 2004, business travelers from Germany and overseas represented 62 percent of the hotel's customer base (see Figure 10.5). Individual business travelers and those attending corporate or association meetings were the major business customers. In addition, the hotel obtained corporate bookings from individuals attending national and international trade fairs and conventions staged either at the nearby Wiesbaden Convention Center or at the large exhibition center in Frankfurt, the Messe.

Independent German hotels used to dominate the Wiesbaden region. The two most prominent of these properties, both luxury hotels, were the Schlosshotel Kronenberg and the Hotel Hessischer Hof. However, during the previous 20 years the competitive environment had changed with many new or re-branded global hotel chains entering the market. See Figure 10.6 for a list of the luxury hotels in the region.

With the growth of the global marketplace, it had become increasingly difficult for an independent hotel to promote its image in far-away countries through traditional distribution channels such as travel agents, toll-free central reservation numbers, and tour and travel operators. Individual guests traveling to Europe from abroad made their decisions in their country of origin, increasingly using the Web as an information-gathering and booking tool. GDS and Web-based reservations systems like Orbitz and Travelocity gave branded hotel chains superior positions on their sites.

In addition to hotels, Global Distribution Systems (GDS), such as Galileo, Sabre, Amadeus, and Worldspan, were linked to car rental and airline companies,

PROFILE		ORIGIN	
Business travel	62%	German	52%
Conference	30%	Other	48%
Individual business	70%	North American	38%
Individual (tourist, spa, culture)	23%	Middle East	12%
		Former Soviet Union	8%
Group	10%	Other Pacific Rim	4%
Diagnostic Clinic	5%	Japanese	5%
		Other EU	28%
		Other	5%

Source: Company records

FIGURE 10.5 Nassauer Hof Guest Profile and Origin (2004)

thereby providing a one-stop reservation network. Other distribution channel intermediaries, such as international tour operators, wholesalers, and corporate travel planners, increasingly preferred to work with one central contact at an established chain in order to plan group bookings that included destinations in many different countries. Similarly, corporations were increasingly negotiating preferred rate agreements with large international hotel chains for all of their company travel.

Promotion

The Nassauer Hof Hotel had a well-established reputation as one of the finest luxury hotels in Europe. This reputation was a result of its high quality of service, outstanding facilities, and the highest level of food and beverage offerings. While there was no single worldwide ranking organization, extensive and very detailed criteria had to be met for a top rating by Mobil (5 Star),[9] Leading Hotels of the World, and others.[10] The Nassauer Hof met all the criteria for a 5 Star luxury hotel rating.

In 2005, the hotel spent 2 percent of its total revenue to support marketing activities, including expenditures for membership in Leading Hotels of the World. Comparable 4–5 star international hotels in Germany typically spent between 3.5–4.0 percent. The Nassauer Hof employed a marketing staff of three

CITY	HOTEL	# OF ROOMS	RACK RATE (EUROS)[1]
Wiesbaden	Radisson Schwarzer Bock*	142	125
	Dorint-Sofitel	298	140
	Crowne Plaza Hotel	233	95
	Ramada Wiesbaden	207	90
Kronberg	Schlosshotel Kronberg	58	145
Mainz	Hilton Mainz City	280	190
	Hyatt Regency Mainz	268	175
Frankfurt	Hotel Frankfurter Hof	321	185
	Hotel Hessischer Hof	185	265
	Arabella Sheraton	378	210
	Hilton Frankfurt	342	270
	Intercontinental Hotel	805	210
	Marriott	508	195
	Maritim	543	240
	Le Meridien Park Hotel*	300	210
	Moevenpick Hotel (to open: 2006)	243	245
	Dorint-Sofitel	155	135
	Villa Kennedy—Forte (to open: 2006)	163	280

*Re-flagged from independent to chain brand
[1]Rack Rate = quoted rate for standard king room
Source: Company marketing sources

FIGURE 10.6 The Regional 4-5 Star Hotel Market (within 16 miles of the Nassauer Hof Hotel)

---

[9] See http://www.mobiltravelguide.com/mtg/index.jsp?menu+mobil_start&bodytid=1031 for a detailed description of the Mobil Travel Guide Lodging Star Definitions

executives who focused on participation in trade fairs and direct sales calls to high-potential accounts in the Frankfurt/Wiesbaden region. In addition, the hotel staged food and beverage marketing promotions in key cities at other international 5-star hotels that were members of Leading Hotels. Travel agents and VIP customers living in the host city attended these promotions. The hotel widely distributed its brochure, which showed public spaces, sample rooms, and glimpses of the nearby attractions, in particular the fountains and plaza across the avenue and in front of the Kurhaus, the location of the gambling casino. The hotel's website, www.nassauer-hof.de, also showed examples of rooms from each category, as well as offering meeting and function room details, in German and English. Room prices had increased with inflation. See Figure 10.7 for occupancy and room rate information and Figure 10.8 for financial statements.

One challenge that the marketing and reservation departments frequently faced was guests and travel agents asking for special rates. Karl's position on price discounts had consistently been that, "Quality has its price—you can't purchase a Porsche for the price of a Volkswagen." The only price reductions that the Nassauer Hof had traditionally given were based on the total number of room nights generated by a travel agency or a company or by individual long-term guests. There was no standard rate, as each discount was negotiated individually, but the range was 10-20 percent depending on seasonality and the volume of business generated. "We are fortunate to have some guests who stay for an extended period of time," Karl commented. "Although this reduces our average rate, these guests increase our occupancy and consume other hotel services."

Creating a mental connection between Frankfurt and Wiesbaden had been a second challenge. International travelers were often not aware that Wiesbaden was located on the outskirts of Frankfurt. An investment banker who had been a guest at the Nassauer Hof for the previous 18 years stated that:

> Wiesbaden and the Nassauer Hof Hotel have to be one of the best kept secrets! It's a jewel of a hotel. I first heard about the hotel from a fellow banking friend who told me to stay at the Nassauer Hof rather than in a commercial hotel at the airport or in busy downtown Frankfurt. The personal service and the almost resort-like setting are well worth the short commute. I not only know Karl and the key staff, but also many of the other guests who stay there regularly. It almost feels like a club.

YEAR	OCCUPANCY	AVERAGE RATE	CURRENCY CONVERSION*
2000	58%	DM 310	1 DM=$0.46
2001	57%	DM 318	1 DM=$0.46
2002	56%	DM 325	1 DM=$0.52
2003	55%	EU 187	1 Euro=$1.23
2004	53%	EU 190	1 Euro=$1.31
2005	54%	EU 192	1 Euro=$1.29

*As of 12/31, except for 2005 which is April 30.
Source: Company records

FIGURE 10.7 Nassauer Hof Hotel Occupancy and Average Room Rate

			2001		2002		2003		2004	
			EURO	%	EURO	%	EURO	%	EURO	%
Room	Sales		5,877.0	100.0	5,370.0	100.0	5,212.5	100.0	5,175.4	100.0
	Payroll		941.0	16.0	855.0	15.9	832.7	16.0	802.3	15.5
	Other expenses		954.0	16.2	750.0	14.0	646.3	12.4	608.5	11.8
	Dept. Profit		**3,982.0**	**67.8**	**3,765.0**	**70.1**	**3,733.5**	**71.6**	**3,564.6**	**72.7**
Food & Beverage	Sales	Food	2,475.9	55.7	2,094.7	56.4	2,010.9	55.7	2,111.5	55.2
		Bevg.	1,493.5	33.6	1,177.3	31.7	1,216.7	33.7	1,212.6	31.7
		Other	475.6	10.7	442.0	11.9	382.7	10.6	501.0	13.1
		Total	**4,445.0**	**100.0**	**3,714.0**	**100.0**	**3,610.3**	**100.0**	**3,825.1**	**100.0**
	Costs	Food	794.8	32.1	676.6	32.3	697.8	34.7	711.6	33.7
		Bevg.	276.3	18.5	213.1	18.1	227.5	18.7	266.8	22.0
		Other	9.0	1.9	7.1	1.6	5.0	1.3	8.0	1.6
		Total	**1,080.1**	**24.3**	**896.8**	**24.1**	**930.3**	**25.8**	**986.4**	**25.8**
	Payroll		2,163.0	48.7	1,874.0	50.5	1,767.4	49.0	1,789.8	48.3
	Other expenses		679.0	15.3	561.0	15.1	452.2	12.5	454.3	12.3
	Dept. Profit		**522.9**	**11.7**	**382.2**	**10.3**	**460.4**	**12.7**	**594.6**	**13.6**
Ente Restaurant	Sales	Food	1,355.0	51.7	1,190.0	49.3	1,019.4	51.7	1,045.6	53.5
		Bevg.	1,135.0	43.3	1,025.0	42.5	780.9	39.6	776.3	39.8
		Other	131.0	5.0	198.0	8.2	171.6	8.7	130.0	6.7
		Total	**2,621.0**	**100.0**	**2,413.0**	**100.0**	**1,971.9**	**100.0**	**1,951.9**	**100.0**
	Costs	Food	453.0	33.4	357.0	30.0	346.2	34.0	340.2	32.5
		Bevg.	338.0	29.8	288.0	28.1	213.9	27.4	197.9	25.5
		Other	8.0	6.1	7.0	3.5	5.3	3.1	9.8	7.5
		Total	**799.0**	**30.5**	**652.0**	**27.0**	**565.4**	**28.7**	**547.9**	**28.1**
	Payroll		1,225.0	46.7	1,119.0	46.4	1,001.0	50.8	975.8	50.0
	Other expenses		348.0	13.3	292.0	12.1	240.7	12.2	286.6	14.7
	Dept. Profit		**249.0**	**9.5**	**350.0**	**14.5**	**164.8**	**8.3**	**141.6**	**7.2**
Telephone	Sales		290.0	100.0	201.0	100.0	252.7	100.0	108.8	100.0
	Payroll		62.0	21.4	60.0	29.9	34.9	13.8	0.0	0.0
	Other expenses		57.0	19.7	48.0	23.8	58.1	23.0	39.0	35.8
	Dept. Profit		**171.0**	**58.9**	**93.0**	**46.3**	**159.7**	**63.2**	**69.8**	**64.2**
Garage	Sales		313.0	100.0	306.0	100.0	256.9	100.0	255.4	100.0
	Payroll		0.0	0.0	0.0	0.0	0.0	0.0	0.0	0.0
	Other expenses		6.0	1.9	4.0	1.3	8.5	3.3	4.9	1.9
	Dept. Profit		**307.0**	**98.1**	**302.0**	**98.7**	**248.4**	**96.7**	**250.5**	**98.1**

FIGURE 10.8 Hotel Nassauer Hof Income Statement (Fiscal year-end: December 31). All values are in 000 Euros.

Promotion for the spa and restaurants was primarily through word of mouth in the local community. The Nassauer Hof co-sponsored local events such as an annual golf tournament at a prestigious local course. The hotel also provided complimentary rooms and hosted receptions in connection with local cultural and civic charity events. The restaurant was part of promotions for the city conducted by the Chamber of Commerce, and took part in the Strassenfest, the yearly street festival attended by thousands of local residents and visitors. "Die Ente's" Michelin guide rating also drew food enthusiasts from a wide region.

		2001		2002		2003		2004	
		EURO	%	EURO	%	EURO	%	EURO	%
Spa	Sales	234.0	100.0	253.0	100.0	261.0	100.0	376.0	100.0
	Payroll	176.0	75.2	178.0	70.4	178.6	68.4	197.0	52.4
	Other expenses	55.0	23.5	63.0	24.9	68.9	26.4	102.1	27.2
	Dept. Profit	**3.0**	**1.3**	**12.0**	**4.7**	**13.5**	**5.2**	**76.9**	**20.4**
Beauty Center	Sales	352.0	100.0	402.0	100.0	353.4	100.0	398.5	100.0
	Payroll	181.0	51.4	182.0	45.3	174.2	49.3	214.4	53.8
	Other expenses	95.0	27.0	86.0	21.4	88.1	24.9	115.7	29.0
	Dept. Profit	**76.0**	**21.6**	**134.0**	**33.3**	**91.1**	**25.8**	**68.4**	**17.2**
Other Income (wines & other)	Sales	86.0	100.0	180.0	100.0	184.3	100.0	171.6	100.0
	Payroll	51.0	59.3	50.0	27.8	33.9	18.4	39.2	22.8
	Other expenses	35.0	40.7	108.0	60.0	90.8	49.3	91.4	53.3
	Dept. Profit	**0.0**	**0.0**	**22.0**	**12.2**	**59.6**	**32.3**	**41.0**	**23.9**
Store rentals	**Dept. Profit**	**271.0**	**1.9**	**270.0**	**2.1**	**278.8**	**2.3**	**221.2**	**1.8**
Admin. & General	Payroll	781.0	5.4	761.0	5.8	737.7	6.0	714.4	5.9
	Other expenses	486.0	3.4	437.0	3.3	429.6	3.5	411.4	3.4
	Total	**1,267.0**	**8.7**	**1,198.0**	**9.1**	**1,167.3**	**9.4**	**1,125.8**	**9.3**
Marketing	Payroll	115.0	0.8	139.0	1.1	93.1	0.8	68.4	0.6
	Other expenses	208.0	1.4	205.0	1.6	149.6	1.2	120.1	1.0
	Total	**323.0**	**2.2**	**344.0**	**2.6**	**242.7**	**2.0**	**188.5**	**1.5**
Energy	**Total**	**376.0**	**2.6**	**363.0**	**2.8**	**435.3**	**3.5**	**457.1**	**3.8**
Repair & Maintenance	Payroll	226.0	1.6	236.0	1.8	199.4	1.6	177.1	1.5
	Other expenses	413.0	2.9	306.0	2.3	298.0	2.4	279.4	2.3
	Total	**639.0**	**4.4**	**542.0**	**4.1**	**497.4**	**4.0**	**456.5**	**3.8**
Total Undistributed Expenses		**2,605.0**	**18.0**	**2,447.0**	**18.7**	**2,342.7**	**18.9**	**2,227.9**	**18.3**
Profit (EBITDA)		**2,976.9**	**20.5**	**2,883.2**	**22.0**	**2,867.1**	**23.2**	**2,800.7**	**22.3**
Total Sales (incl. Store rentals)		14,489.0	100.0	13,109.0	100.0	12,381.8	100.0	12,483.9	100.0
Total Payroll Costs		5,921.0	40.9	5,454.0	41.6	5,052.9	40.8	4,978.4	39.9

Source: Company records

Competition from Hotel Chains

As Karl had noted during the meeting with his executive team, most of the 4-star hotel chains already had properties in the region. He anticipated that many of the 5-star hotel chains would probably also eventually enter the regional market (see Figure 10.9). These chains used several different growth strategies in expanding their market presence: the development of new properties, the conversion of existing properties, and the acquisition of existing brands. Because hotel development was very capital-intensive, hotel chains had primarily expanded their product internationally through management contracts or franchising, as opposed to financing hotel development themselves. With a management contract, a developer/owner would finance and build a hotel, and sign a long-term management agreement for a hotel chain to operate the property. The chain would receive a management fee from the owner based on a percentage of revenue. Most management agreements also provided for an incentive fee based on the achievement of gross operating profit (EBITDA) goals.

With a franchise agreement, on the other hand, the developer/owner would employ its own management team and pay a royalty fee to a hotel chain in exchange for the use of their franchise system. The franchise system provided a formula for successfully operating a hotel or other business by offering an established recognizable brand and a uniform product and service concept. Multi-brand hotel companies that employed franchising as one of their growth strategies, such as Hilton, Marriott, Wyndham, Regent, and Sheraton, received a royalty payment from their franchisees based on a percentage of total sales that varied between 3 and 6 percent, and a marketing contribution that varied between 1.5 and 3.0 percent of room revenue. The franchisor also provided a central reservation system, sales support, and global marketing representation. Hotels operated under a franchise system were typically independently owned and managed. However, not all established international hotel chains would enter into franchise agreements, but would insist on operating control. The Ritz-Carlton, Four Seasons, and Mandarin Oriental chains fell into this category. Typical franchise fees and capital expenditures may be found in Figure 10.10.

INTERNATIONAL MULTI- AND SINGLE-BRANDED HOTEL CHAINS WITH 4- AND 5-STAR PROPERTIES[10]

Hyatt Hotels—217 hotels and resorts
*Marriott Hotels and Resorts—2,700 hotels
*Starwood Hotels and Resorts (Sheraton, Westin and LeMeridien)—780 hotels
*Hilton Hotels—2,388 hotels
Wyndham Hotels and Resorts (Ramada and other brands)—6,300 hotels
*Carlson Hotels Worldwide (Radisson, Regent and other brands)—900 hotels
Four Seasons Hotels and Resorts—71 hotels
Ritz-Carlton—62 hotels
Fairmont – Raffles Hotels and Resorts—87 hotels
Mandarin Oriental—21 hotels

EUROPEAN-BASED 4- AND 5-STAR HOTEL CHAINS

*Accor Hotels (Sofitel and other brands)—4,000 hotels
*InterContinental Hotels Group (Crowne Plaza and other brands)—3,500
*Kempinski Hotels—26 hotels
*Mövenpick Hotels—80 hotels
*Rocco Forte Hotels—15 hotels
Sol-Melia—350 hotels
*Steigenberger Hotels (member of Worldhotels consortium)—77 hotels

*Companies with competitive hotels within 30 miles of the Nassauer Hof Hotel
Source: Company Web sites

FIGURE 10.9 European and International Hotel Chains

SCHEDULE 1: INITIAL FRANCHISE FEE & PROJECTED CAPITAL EXPENDITURE	
Initial franchise license fee	$ 58,000
Computer system	$150,000
Signage	$ 30,000
Printed material and photography	$ 40,000
Guest room FF&E	$550,000
TOTAL:	**$828,000**

SCHEDULE 2: ANNUAL FRANCHISE FEES	
5% of gross room sales	$335,000
2% of food and beverage sales	$147,000
Marketing fund contribution (1% of gross room sales)	$ 67,000
Participation in preferred guest program (1% of gross room sales)	$ 67,000
Central reservation fee	$ 18,000
Annual software updates	$ 10,000
Monthly guest satisfaction reports	$ 6,000
Global Distribution System (GDS) & internet booking fees	$ 35,000
Annual training course fee	$ 12,000
TOTAL:	**$697,000**

Source: Abstracted from 2005 Uniform Franchise Offering Circular (UFOC) of U.S.-based international upscale hotel chains

FIGURE 10.10 Typical Hotel Projected Franchise Fees and Capital Expenditures

Marketing Consortia of Independent Hotels

Independent hotels often joined marketing consortia in order to compete with hotel chains and reach the global marketplace. These consortia generally provided a central reservation network, a membership website and a listing of members' hotels in Global Distribution Systems (GDS) that allowed travel agents to book reservations for hotels, airlines, and rental cars online. In addition, hotel marketing consortia operated sales and marketing offices in the leading capital cities of the world in order to generate business for their member hotels.

The best-known upscale hotel marketing consortia were:

- The Leading Hotels of the World: a prestigious luxury hotel organization representing more than 420 hotels, resorts and spas worldwide (www.lhw. com);
- Preferred Hotels & Resorts: a global brand of independently owned luxury hotels and resorts representing more than 120 hotels (www.lhw.com);
- Worldhotels: an international marketing consortium of 485 hotels representing 70 countries in three quality segments: Deluxe Collection (170 hotels), First Class Collection (230 hotels), and Comfort Collection (85 hotels) (www.worldhotels.com);
- Small Luxury Hotels of the World: a collection of more than 300 independently owned exclusive hotels located in over 50 countries (www.slh.com); and

- Relais & Chateaux: an exclusive international association of 440 small independently owned restaurants and luxury hotels (which must have a gourmet restaurant) (www.relaischateaux.com).

The Leading Hotels of the World

Since the 1950s, the Nassauer Hof Hotel had been a member of The Leading Hotels of the World (Leading)[10]. Leading was founded during the 1920s in order to promote individually owned independent luxury hotels.

Excellence in the art of hotel-keeping is the cornerstone of the Leading Hotels of the World brand. It is our most cherished and protected value. Hotels seeking membership with The Leading Hotels of the World or The Leading Small Hotels of the World must apply for admission, as the organization does not solicit new members. All Leading Hotels must operate in a manner consistent with the standards that are generally understood and accepted within the industry as "five-star" or "superior deluxe."[11]

Membership in Leading gave the Nassauer Hof access to the organization's worldwide reservation centers, which were located in more than 20 offices in the most important cities of North America, Africa, the Middle East, Asia, India, Australia, South America, and Europe. These sales offices generated referrals for its member hotels. In addition, Leading staged periodic trade fairs and participated in the most important travel exhibitions around the world. These exhibitions targeted wholesale travel purchasers (such as travel agents and group wholesalers) or the retail market (the individual customer). According to an article in *Travel & Leisure* (August 2004), 114 of the 500 greatest hotels in the world were members of Leading.

Leading also produced an annual catalogue featuring its member hotels, which these hotels displayed in every guest room. In addition, the organization provided a comprehensive Web page that included information about the member hotels, a reservation link, vacation-planning assistance and special offers. A corporate information link provided information concerning membership in Leading and listed the organization's joint ventures with other brands and travel partners. Leading was also listed in the major global distribution systems (GDS) of the travel industry. Although the Nassauer Hof had no customer loyalty or frequent guest plan of its own, its guests were able to earn benefits through Leading's reward program.

The Nassauer Hof paid a yearly fee of Euros 110,000[12] for membership in Leading and an additional Euro 17 for each reservation generated. In 2004, Leading generated 15 percent of Nassauer Hof's reservations. Although Leading had been doing a good job for the hotel, Karl believed he was losing market share compared to branded chain hotels, especially from overseas markets. "Should we join an additional marketing organization?" Karl wondered.

---

[10] Leading Hotels of the World: http://www.lhw.com/corporateinfo.aspx

[11] "Become a Leading Hotel," Leading Hotels of the World: http://www.lhw.com/corporateinfo.aspx

[12] In Mid-May 2005, 1 euro = $1.28 U.S; 110,000 Euros = $140,800.

ⓞ Selektion Deutscher Luxushotels

The Nassauer Hof, together with five other German luxury hotels, had also created a marketing cooperative, Selektion Deutscher Luxushotels,[13] with the purpose of conducting cross-marketing activities. The other member hotels were located in Hamburg, Bremen, Cologne, Baden-Baden, and Munich (see Figure 10.11). The occupancy at member hotels varied from 50 to 85 percent, with the Mandarin Oriental Hotel in Munich achieving the highest occupancy. Each of the hotels promoted the other five hotels during local and regional sales calls to their own corporate and travel clients. The cooperative developed a high-quality brochure that described the product and service offerings of the six member properties, and maintained a joint website. The members shared jointly in the cost of producing the brochure and maintaining the Web site. The Nassauer Hof's share was 2,500 Euros per year. Karl Nueser stated that, "The cooperative has been extremely effective in leveraging the development of market leads and the cross-referral of clients to the other members."

Guestroom Conversion

Another option for the hotel would be to convert rooms on the top floor into rental apartments or condominiums. The term "condominium hotel" referred to buildings where individuals owned suites and either occupied them or allowed the hotel to rent them.[14] Some hotels rented apartments for occupancy on a long-term basis. Many older hotels had a few guests who lived permanently in the hotel.[15] Apartments in luxury hotels usually commanded a substantial premium due to the amenities and services offered by the hotel and the prestige attached to the hotel brand. Some New York City hotels, such as the Waldorf Astoria and the Loewe's Regent Hotel, rented a number of their suites on a long-term basis.

CITY	NAME OF HOTEL	NUMBER OF ROOMS/SUITES
Baden-Baden	Brenner's Park Hotel & Spa	92
Bremen	Park Hotel Bremen	177
Cologne	Excelsior Hotel Ernst	152
Hamburg	Raffles Hotel Vier Jahreszeiten	156
Munich	Mandarin Oriental Hotel	73
Wiesbaden	Nassauer Hof Hotel	169

Source: Brochures from the listed hotels

FIGURE 10.11 Marketing Cooperative: Selektion Deutscher Luxushotels

---

[13] Selektion Deutscher Luxushotels: www.selektion-deutscher-luxushotels.de

[14] Schlentrich, Udo (2005), "Condominium" in *International Encyclopedia of Hospitality Management*, edited by Abraham Pizam, Elsevier Butterworth Heinemann, Burlington, MA, p. 94.

[15] Eloise, from the popular children's book series by Kay Thompson (first appearing in Eloise, New York: Simon & Schuster, 1955), lived at the Plaza Hotel in New York City.

The executive team thought that some of the hotel's frequent visitors or corporations might be interested in having their own exclusive space that would still receive the hotel's services. However, they felt that there was more of a market to rent apartments than to sell them. No local competitors offered long-term rentals. The team estimated that the 34 existing rooms and suites on the top floor could become 20 upscale one- and two-bedroom apartments. Corporations with out-of-town head offices requiring frequent visits to the greater Frankfurt area would find it convenient and cost-effective to have a permanent suite, which would also function as space for meetings and entertaining. Usually the CEO and senior executives would be the primary users of such a suite. Wealthy elderly individuals and empty nesters, who had sold their main residence in Wiesbaden, might also be interested in renting, especially since the hotel would provide full service amenities and security. Karl estimated that these apartments could achieve 85 percent occupancy by the end of the first year.

Karl commented:

Over the years, I've had several companies and private individuals ask me if they could rent a suite here at the hotel on a long-term basis. I've always declined in the past as it would have required that we reconfigure the structure of the suites and install kitchens. In addition, I think we would need to have a different entrance for more permanent residents who would be coming into the hotel with grocery bags.

The team figured that the cost of converting the guestrooms into apartments would be approximately 1.5 million Euros (see Figure 10.12). They projected that these full-service apartments would rent for 8,000 to 12,000 Euros per month (see Figure 10.13), a 15 percent premium over typical rents in the center city area. They also believed the annual income from apartment rental would generate a departmental profit margin of 80 percent, compared with the department profit of 72 percent on hotel rooms (see Figure 10.8). Although guests might spend less per day by making use of the apartment's kitchen or dining elsewhere in the area, they also would be more likely to entertain friends at the hotel and purchase services such as spa memberships. One of the elevators near

NAME (SIZE) OF APARTMENT	# OF APARTMENTS	CONVERSION COST	TOTAL COST PER APARTMENT
Standard 1 Bedroom (80 square meters)	12	65,000 Euros	780,000 Euros
Large 1 Bedroom (120 square meters)	4	75,000 Euros	300,000 Euros
Deluxe 2 Bedrooms (160 square meters)	4	90,000 Euros	360,000 Euros
			TOTAL: 1,440,000 Euros

Notes:
Conversion costs include planning fees and architectural expenses
One garage space per apartment is included in rental price.

Source: Company records

FIGURE 10.12 Conversion of Guest Rooms to Apartments

12 Standard 1 Bedroom Apartments	@ 8,000 Euros per month
4 Large 1 Bedroom Apartments	@ 10,000 Euros per month
4 Deluxe 2 bedroom Apartments	@ 12,000 Euros per month

Source: Company records

FIGURE 10.13 Nassauer Hof Projected Apartment Income

the garage could be adapted for apartment guest's use. "Let's weigh the benefits and risks," Karl commented. "Maybe this is a strategy we should consider."

The Future

Karl thought about the meeting he had just had with his executive staff. The team had accomplished so much, but now was not the time for resting on one's laurels. "Should the hotel enter into a franchise agreement with a global brand like Hilton International, InterContinental, Marriott, Starwood, or Fairmont Hotels & Resorts?" Karl wondered. "Or maybe we should expand our existing marketing agreement with The Leading Hotels of the World by joining an additional marketing consortium such as Worldhotels, Relais & Chateaux, or Preferred Hotels & Resorts? Maybe it's time for some "out-of-the-box" thinking. Is the franchise option a viable one, or should we stay independent and try to find ways to reach new markets? Is there any advantage in downsizing by converting some guest rooms into rental apartments? Or should we just accept lower occupancy rates as one of the challenges of our market niche?"

Karl reflected ruefully, "I know of so many other independent hotels that have the same problem we have."

Discussion Questions

1. Why does Karl Nueser believe that a re-evaluation of the overall marketing strategy of the Nassauer Hof Hotel is necessary? Do you agree?
2. Develop a SWOT analysis assessing the Nassauer Hof Hotel in its present competitive environment.
3. What is the Nassauer Hof Hotel's competitive advantage?
4. Identify the primary market segments of the Nassauer Hof Hotel.
5. Evaluate the present marketing mix of the Nassauer Hof Hotel.
6. Which of the strategies proposed by the management team do you recommend that Karl Nueser adopt? Explain.

References

Bowen, J., & Makens, J. (2006). *Marketing for hospitality and tourism*. Pearson International Edition.

EHotelier. (2016). German hotel market still leading in Europe. *eHotelier*. Retrieved from https://ehotelier.com/global/2016/10/21/german-hotel-market-still-leading-europe/

Hisrich, R., Peters, M., & Shepherd, D. (2005). *Entrepreneurship 8th Edition*. Singapore: McGraw Hill.

Hoskisson, R., & Hitt, M. (2006). *Strategic management concepts 7th Edition*. Mason, OH: South-Western College Pub.

Jaaskelainen, L. (2017) Accommodation industry in Germany - Statistics & Facts. *Statista.* Retrieved from https://www.statista.com/topics/3374/accommodation-industry-in-germany/

Landen, T., Schroder, N., & Bakker, D., (2016) Data And Expert Opinions about the German Hotel Market. *Colliers International, Fairmas & Revinate*. Retrieved from https://www.colliers.de/wp-content/uploads/2016/10/Hotel-Germany-Papers-10042016.pdf

Machl, S.S. (2017) Understanding German business culture. *Expatica*. Retrieved from https://www.expatica.com/de/employment/Understanding-German-business-culture_100983.htm

Platz, K.F. (2017). Hotel Nassauer Hof history and traditions. *Hotel Nassauer Hof*. Retrieved from http://www.nassauer-hof.de/en/hotel/our-history.html

Relevant Videos

10 Amazing Things About Germany!
https://www.youtube.com/watch?v=sTFNvbGQp7k

How to pitch startup presentations #entrepreneurship #Germany:
https://www.youtube.com/watch?v=kMKH3rgnDNo

Turning Entrepreneurial Failure into Opportunity | Made in Germany - Interview, Part 2:
https://www.youtube.com/watch?v=Y5USEVGg_oo

Hotel Nassauer Hof:
https://www.youtube.com/watch?v=vUCNCzYqlBE

Market researchers observe where we look | Made in German:
https://www.youtube.com/watch?v=Hatmm84sqm0

Investigative Report Presentation - Marketing in Germany:
https://www.youtube.com/watch?v=3GilgkDQcEY

Chapter Eleven

GLOBAL INTERNATIONAL ALTERNATIVE MODES OF ENTRY FOR ENTREPRENEURIAL FIRMS

CRYSTAL LUSTRY: AN ENTREPRENEURIAL COMPANY'S ENTRY INTO THE WORLD'S BIGGEST AND MOST COMPETITIVE MARKET

Jay Gronlund and J. Mark Munoz

Learning Objectives

1. *Prerequisites for successful market entry*—to recognize and prioritize the most important requirements for successful penetration, as the basis for deciding whether/how to research and allocate resources.
2. *Internal capabilities*—to realistically examine a company's strengths and vulnerabilities for such an expansion, ideally to leverage certain assets to create a convincing value proposition and to address key limitations.
3. *Entrepreneurial style vs. market needs*—to understand the advantages of quick, intuitive initiatives, matched with the risks and local knowledge one must consider in preparation.
4. *Market potential*—to outline the parameters for an overall assessment of possible sales, which will also define the maximum universe size balanced with a conservative approach that is focused and niche oriented, plus a realistic review of production capabilities, now and ramped-up, for the possibility of extensive volume.
5. *Local partnerships*—to describe clear, realistic criteria for selecting a local partner, cultivating a trustful working relationship, and respecting insights that reflect the local market conditions and business practices.
6. *Penetration and distribution strategy*—with intense competition and limited ways to reach consumers, to determine the key considerations when assessing various distribution channels in light of the resources of a company.

Key Words

Entrepreneurial firm
Global entrepreneurship

Internationalization
International market entry

Abstract

Crystal Lustry is a medium-sized Czech entrepreneurial firm that sought to make a market entry in one of the world's biggest and most competitive markets—the USA. Attempting to do business in uncharted territory, the company faced several market entry challenges. In this case, typical internationalization pitfalls of entrepreneurial firms are discussed. Drawing from the lessons, strategies for the success of global entrepreneurs are offered.

⦾ Crystal Making—A Rich Heritage

Glass making in the Bohemian region of the Czech Republic started centuries ago. Actually the tradition of craftsmanship in this region goes back to 400 CE, mainly for making jewelry out of metals. The natural resources have contributed to this artistic tradition, with the nearby Jezera Mountains providing rock crystal, sand, and limestone for glass making, plus ample wood supplies for fire and rivers for power.

In the 18th and 19th centuries, Bohemia had become the recognized center for the finest glass and crystal in the world. In 1856 the world's first high school for glass making was established here, and then in 1880, Europe's first school for designers of fashion jewelry was started. In 1895, Daniel Swarovski left Bohemia for Austria, where he founded his famous crystal company.

Company Background

Crystal Lustry is a Czech company focused on crystal making. It was established in Jablonec (in northern Bohemia) after World War II, when it absorbed several local glass-cutting factories, some with a rich history in this crystal-making craft. For example, one local factory had been making crystal chandeliers since 1724.

During the next 45 years, Crystal Lustry built on these age-old traditions and developed innovative glass-melting and glass-cutting techniques, mainly to create fine crystal for three different product lines: chandeliers, fashion jewelry, and crystal figurines. Crystal Lustry today has worldwide distribution of its fashion jewelry gems, mainly as a component for jewelry making. However, the distribution of its chandeliers and figurines remained concentrated mainly in Europe. In total, there are 11 production plants in the Czech Republic, with 5,000 employees in total.

Crystal Lustry started to expand this third line of small crystal figurines in the early 1990s. In 1995, Crystal Lustry selected an importer located in New York, The Blue Star Crystal Company, to build retail distribution of its line of crystal figurines throughout the U.S. Blue Star positioned this Crystal Lustry line as "Lead-Free Crystal Figures" to be more distinctive, assuming that consumers would be attracted to its apparent environmental benefits.

The U.S. Situation

Initial efforts to gain broad distribution in retail jewelry stores and other outlets throughout the U.S. did not fare well. There was also some confusion about the merits of its positioning as an environmentally safe product. Early in 1999, Crystal Lustry's management started to consider alternative approaches for penetrating the U.S. market with this line of crystal figurines. A New York-based consulting firm was hired to assess the overall potential for this business, and to recommend a new strategic direction for establishing a presence here.

This market assessment project concluded that the potential of the general "Gifts and Decorative Accessories" market was huge (total of $47.4 billion at retail prices), certainly large enough to sustain a profitable niche business. Within this category, the segment of collectibles (including figurines) accounted for a healthy 23 percent of total sales.

The distribution of this gift/accessory industry was very fragmented, however, with most of the sales generated by small specialty (i.e., "Ma and Pa" shops) stores—57 percent. The next largest distribution channel was via direct response or direct marketing—21 percent—which offered a more controllable strategic option for Crystal Lustry.

Competition

The main competition for this Crystal Lustry line of figurines was Swarovski, the Austrian based crystal company founded in 1895. Swarovski is a formidable competitor, with an excellent image and reputation for high-quality crystal and distribution throughout the world. This includes both retail outlets and "collectible" membership clubs purchasing crystal figurines via direct marketing solicitations.

The pricing for Swarovski crystal figurines was quite high for most collectibles, but given its widely recognized reputation, not unaffordable for most of these consumers. Generally, the Swarovski crystal figurines were priced about one third higher than comparable figurines from Crystal Lustry.

The Collectible Consumer

The typical consumer of collectible items generally have two basic passions: a high appreciation for fine, high-quality art (based on their perception), and also a strong interest for a *limited* supply of such art items, which will hopefully grow in value in the future. Many of these "collectible" consumers buy more than one type of product, and almost always display such items in their homes. Importantly, once these consumers are satisfied with their first purchase, they usually want to acquire more items in that particular product line.

The Crystal Lustry Management

The strength of Crystal Lustry has always been as a manufacturer of high-quality crystal products. During the Communist times (1945–1990) Crystal Lustry never had a need to develop its marketing skills, since the Soviet Union and nearby East European countries provided a ready market for their crystal products.

The current president of Crystal Lustry, Jaroslav Hejl, took over from his father and founder in 1985. He was 55 and had high ambitions of making Crystal Lustry a global player in the world of crystal. He had two sons who were educated at the University of Buffalo, and were being groomed to eventually manage the business on a broader scale. While his sons had some exposure to different cultures, Jaroslav's management style was still somewhat autocratic, controlling, budget-obsessed, and sometimes "hip-shooting," typical of the Cold War era where ruthless negotiating and steady manufacturing were the keys to success.

Jaroslav was very impressed with, even overwhelmed by the relatively large market potential of the U.S. gifts and accessories category, and wanted to dive right into this market immediately. However, the New York-based consulting firm convinced him to first prepare a comprehensive market entry assessment that would detail all the positioning, marketing, and local infrastructure needs for such a cross-border expansion.

The Market Launch

Jaroslav rejected recommendations to do any kind of research on how these Crystal Lustry figures should be positioned, priced, named, packaged, marketed, and so on. Instead, he relied on the subjective opinions of its new consulting partners in New York. The local team accepted this with the caveat that Crystal Lustry take a step-by-step development approach, with introductory programs to be tested in the market place. However, the enormity of the U.S. market continued to blind such sound advice, and Jaroslav rejected this suggestion.

With no money to support a marketing or awareness-building campaign and growing signs that the appeal of collectibles was waning, the New York consultants recommended that these crystal figurines be positioned mainly as novel gifts with the added benefit of becoming a "collectible," due to limited production of each type. Only a few unique figurines would be highlighted to provide a clearer focus, and the pricing would be about 20 percent lower than Swarovsky. Packaging, font style, graphics, and logos were all improved. The limited print advertising would leverage the heritage of this Czech craft, using the headline: "Introducing Crystal Lustry—Handcrafted Czech Crystal."

A key component of the market entry recommendation was to discontinue its focus on distributing and supporting sales via retail stores. It simply did not have the resources or know-how to make this distribution channel work for them. Instead, it was recommended to use a more controllable channel, direct marketing, in two ways: free standing inserts (FSIs) in Sunday newspaper supplements in certain regions in the U.S., and a direct mail campaign offering a catalogue and purchase invitation to a select list of consumers of collectible items.

Both methods were measurable and improvements could be made from each campaign. The FSIs would reach a huge audience, so only a small response rate (0.05%) would be enough to generate sufficient revenues. The more targeted direct mailing campaign required a higher response (1.0%) to payout, but this goal was still estimated to be feasible.

What Happened—Market Launch Results

The initial response for both direct marketing campaigns failed to reach their targets. Without any allocation for follow-up research, the New York consulting team could only speculate on the reasons why. Their preliminary conclusions were that:

- The demand for collectibles and especially crystal figurines were softer than estimated (declining sales of Swarovski figurines later confirmed this);

- The medium of FSIs and its audience were not a good match for the high quality, specialty image of these crystal figurines;
- Building an attractive brand identity and awareness takes time, ideally with initial research, small-scale testing and continued updating and improving for a gradual roll-out approach.

The reaction by Jaroslav was impulsive. He immediately closed down the warehouse and fulfillment operation in Philadelphia, withdrew all inventory and fired the New York consulting firm.

Discussion Questions

1. What are the key assumptions behind foreign market potential assessment?
2. As a niche player, how should Crystal Lustry be positioned?
3. With limited resources, what kind of research should be conducted?
4. What should global entrepreneurial firms consider when reviewing possible distribution channels?
5. With these lessons, how should global entrepreneurs approach this market entry?

References

Barkema, H.G. Bell, J.H., & Pennings, J.M. (1996). Foreign entry, cultural barriers, and learning. *Strategic Management Journal, 17* (2), 151–166.

Crystal, E. (2007). Introduction: E-crystal. *Crystal chandeliers.* Retrieved from http://www.lollimemmoli.it/en/crystal-chandeliers/VLADIMIRO_oval

Elango, B. (2004). Geographic scope of operations by multinational companies: An exploratory study of regional and global strategies. *European Management Journal, 22,* 431–441.

Guillen, M., & Garcia-Canal, E. (2009). The American model of the multinational firm and new multinationals from emerging economies. *Academy of Management Perspectives, 23* (2), 23–35.

Hamel, G. & Prahalad, C.K. (1985, July/August). Do you really have a global strategy? *Harvard Business Review,* 139–148.

Johanson, J., & Vahlne, J.E. (1990). The mechanism of internationalization. *International Marketing Review, 7*(4), 11–24.

Jones, M. (1999). The internationalization of small high-technology firms. *Journal of International Marketing, 7*(4), 15–41.

Kuemmerle, W. (1999). The drivers of foreign direct investment into research and development: An empirical investigation. *Journal of International Business Studies, 30,* 1–24.

Lechner, C. & Dowling, M. (2003). Firm networks: external relationships as sources for the growth and competition of entrepreneurial firms. *Entrepreneurship & Regional Development, 15,* 1–26.

McDougall, P., & Oviatt, B. (2000). International entrepreneurship: The intersection of two research paths. *Academy of Management Journal, 43* (5), 902–906.

Morris, H., & Kuratco, D.F. (2001). *Corporate entrepreneurship: Entrepreneurial development within organizations.* Harcourt College Publishers: Orlando, FL.

Plunley, D.J. (2000). *Global ecommerce: The market, challenges, and opportunities.* Irvine, CA: Bowne Global Solutions.

Shane, S. (1994). The effect of national culture on the choice between licensing and direct foreign investment. *Strategic Management Journal, 15,* 627–642.

Stay, P. (2017). Glass and Crystal: Czech glass in Prague. *Prague Stay.* Retrieved from https://www.prague-stay.com/lifestyle/category/12-shopping-in-prague/74-glass-and-crystal-czech-glass-in-prague

Trade 2.0, P. (2014). Business etiquette. *Passport to Trade.* Retrieved from http://businessculture.org/passport-to-trade-2-0/

Wang, J., Gong, J., Rohani, S., & Gao, Z. (2017). Recent developments in the crystallization process: toward the pharmaceutical industry. Science Direct, 3 (3), 343-353.

Welch, L.S., & Luostarinen, R. (1988) Internationalization: Evolution of a Concept. *Journal of General Management, 14* (2), 34–55.

Relevant Videos

Czech Business Etiquette:
https://www.youtube.com/watch?v=Dc9B6Q_CUhc

Chemistry Experiment: Making Crystals:
https://www.youtube.com/watch?v=71bvKydh5gk

Welcome to Czech Republic:
https://www.youtube.com/watch?v=CUnN8WwYF0U

10 FACTS ABOUT CZECH REPUBLIC | GoFacts:
https://www.youtube.com/watch?v=8LvF7R8WCYE

FUEL JET PRO: DEVELOPING A MARKET ENTRY STRATEGY

George Puia, Ph.D.
Mark Potts, J.D.
Saginaw Valley State University

Learning Objectives

1. *Explain* the benefits and risks of alternative forms of direct market entry.
2. *Discuss* the basic strengths and weaknesses of joint ventures and direct foreign investment using evidence from the case.
3. *Assess* and quantify the sources of risk in the alternative foreign market entry strategies.
4. *Describe* procedures and processes that a firm can use to maintain unity during a potentially divisive decision process.
5. *Evaluate* potential economic gains from alternative entry strategies.

Key Words

Market entry strategy
Equity joint venture
Foreign direct investment

Country risks
MNC

Abstract

Fuel Jet Pro, Inc. (FJP) is a designer and manufacturer of automotive fuel injection systems. Like many firms in the auto industry, they see China as the market of the future. FJP's managers are divided as to which of two entry strategies that they should pursue. The first alternative was to develop a joint venture with a Chinese firm; the second was to build and operate their own factory in China. They need to decide on an entry strategy and do it in a way that preserves team unity.

The Dilemma

Fuel Jet Pro, Inc. (FJP) is a designer and manufacturer of automotive fuel injection systems. FJP's primary business has been in specialty high-performance fuel injectors. The need to become global has become increasingly clear to FJP, and in autos, that meant being in China.

FJP saw two clear alternatives. The first alternative was to develop a joint venture with a Chinese firm; the second was to build and operate their own factory in China. When the management team began to discuss these alternatives, it was clear that FJP's managers did not agree on a common strategy.

One group, which included an outside consultant, argued strongly for an equity joint venture. A joint venture required FJP to raise less than half the equity it would need to operate independently. Some FJP executives disagreed. One executive was concerned that FJP might be creating a competitor. After all, the Chinese could opt out of the venture in five years and leave with a thorough knowledge of FJP's products and processes. Further, they could begin exporting back to the U.S. and give FJP a real run for their money. The research and development group was the most adamant in their opposition to the joint venture. They held concerns that China would not honor FJP's intellectual property. The patented technologies and trade secrets could easily spill over to other Chinese firms. The research and development group proposed that FJP should build its own factory, and hire and train Chinese workers to staff it. However, some managers are skeptical. In their view, this strategy demands more time and higher cost. FJP's management team is struggling with the alternatives. What entry strategy should FJP choose? Since the management team is divided, how should the CEO unite the management team behind the decided entry strategy?

Company Background and Structure

As their name implies, FJP's product injects gas into a cylinder where it is ignited by a spark to drive pistons. Their products have been used in high-end specialty vehicles, e.g., prototype alternative energy concept cars and luxury autos. The domestic injector market is changing rapidly. Biodiesel and ethanol has given FJP an entirely new set of competitors. Fuel Jet Pro began operations in the mid-1980s. The auto industry was under considerable pressure from the Environmental Protection Agency (EPA) to reduce emissions. Controlling fuel-air mix with injectors helped in that process. While fuel injectors had been around for decades, the German firm Bosch introduced electronically controlled injectors in 1982. The new control systems allowed for more sophisticated controls.

FJP began linking injectors to an auto's onboard computer system. At first, only luxury cars could justify onboard computer systems; as the market matured, even the smallest cars used them. Injection systems for small cars became a commodity product; to compete, you needed to have the lowest price. As a smaller player in a large market, FJP focused on high-end users in the U.S. and Europe.

By 2000, the luxury market had evolved into a two-tiered market. At the lower end, autos from $40,000 to $65,000 had become more standardized; there were fewer opportunities to make above-normal profits. High-end carmakers were still searching out ways to differentiate their autos, a good opportunity for FJP. By 2008, a newer and more profitable segment had emerged: custom and prototype cars. In California, a large number of firms emerged that customized cars to specific customer needs. These custom cars were more than just re-decorated autos; they often had a chassis from one car, with an engine from another, and custom interior and exterior features. The small volume, high-priced custom market was a great fit with FJP's expertise.

At the same time, a new alternative fuels industry was developing. Car designers in the U.S. were feeling pressure to improve fuel economy and environmental performance. The fuels included ethanol-based systems like E-85, and bio-diesel systems. Bio-diesel was particularly interesting to FJP. Makers were efficiently brewing ethanol from sugar beets and blending with oils ranging from used frying oil from fast-food chains to soy oil from pressed soy beans. The resulting fuel was environmentally friendly and renewable; however, it required better injection technology. Car designers were ordering multiple configurations of expensive injector systems to test new fuels.

The Structure of the China Market

Like most auto suppliers, FJP was keenly aware of developments in China. Putting 1.4 billion Chinese into autos was going to create decades of massive industry growth. Manufacturers plan to build the bulk of these autos in China, at Chinese costs, to meet the needs of the low-cost market. FJP saw another opportunity emerging. The top two percent of the current China market represented a potential 8 million advanced cars. Further, with China's ultimate need to move to renewable resources, they were going to want advanced injection systems.

Research led FJP to believe that there was a growing economic nationalism in China; Chinese consumers wanted to buy advanced products from Chinese firms. China, with its long-term orientation, recognized it would not be able to be a low-cost manufacturer forever. Many scholars believed that by 2040, the aging Chinese population and the lack of young people resulting from the one-child policy would burden the country with enormous social costs for healthcare and social support systems. The demographic shift in China was too far into the future to worry about. FJP could produce at low cost now for China and reduce its costs for its U.S. customers as well. One key to China's future was to develop local high-technology businesses that could serve China, but that could also export from China.

After reviewing market opportunities with their consultant, FJPs management team has become enamored with the Chinese markets. The current market is smaller than the U.S., but the market has 12–16 percent compound annual growth. The FJP challenge is to design an effective entry strategy. It is clear that Chinese customers will not pay U.S. prices for FJP's injectors. To meet market prices, FJP needs to produce its product in China. Additionally, it was clear that China wanted to build local high-technology firms that can export from China.

As a result of the trade imbalance, many Chinese businesses were sitting on large sums of U.S. dollars that they needed to spend or invest. Since the Chinese were looking for investors, it would be relatively easy to find capital.

There were other benefits as well: the joint venture would give them local partners who understood the China market, and more importantly, who had relationships with Chinese political leaders at the local and regional levels. No one understood the Chinese market as well as the Chinese; having local partners meant that they would have access to local opinions when it came time to create the next generation of products.

Discussion Questions

1. What factors should Fuel Jet Pro consider in making this decision?
2. What are the potential benefits and risks of building and operating their own production facility?
3. What are the benefits and risks of developing a joint venture?
4. Based on your analysis, which entry strategy should FJP choose?
5. Since the management team is divided, how should the CEO unite the management team behind the decided entry strategy?

References

Beamish, P., & Lupton, N. (2009). Managing Joint Ventures. *Academy of Management Perspectives, 23*(2), 75–94.

Capital, A. (2016). Value Investor's Daily Macro: Jet Fuel and The Rate Hike. *Seeking Alpha*. Retrieved from https://seekingalpha.com/article/3976611-value-investors-daily-macro-jet-fuel-rate-hike

Chung, M.L., & Bruton, G. (2008). FDI in China: What We Know and What We Need to Study Next. *Academy of Management Perspectives, 22*(4), 30–44.

Crystal, E. (2007). Introduction. E-crystal: *Crystal chandeliers.*

Economics, T. (2017). China Foreign Direct Investment. *Trading Economics*. Retrieved from https://tradingeconomics.com/china/foreign-direct-investment

Enterprises, E. (2017). China: Foreign Investment. *Santander: Trade Portal*. Retrieved from https://en.portal.santandertrade.com/establish-overseas/china/foreign-investment

Foley, J.F., (2004), *The Global Entrepreneur: Taking your business international,* 2nd ed., New York, Jamric Press International

Gutterman, A.S. (2008). *A short course in international joint ventures,* 3rd ed., Novato, CA: World Trade Press.

Huang, L.Y. and Carraher, S. (2008), China, in, Carraher, S.M. and Welsh, D.H.B., eds. *Global Entrepreneurship*, Dubuque, IA: Kendall Hunt.

Ming, C. (2017). Asia markets tread water as investors keep an eye on China's Party Congress. *CNBC* Retrieved from https://www.cnbc.com/2017/10/17/asia-markets-china-party-congress-rio-tinto-and-dollar-in-focus.html

Nadeem, N. F., Farahmand R., Tagni R., & Wagdy A. (2003). Investing in China's economic development zones: A managerial guide. *International Journal of Management,* 20(2), 223.

Pastore, R. & Rosenblum, A. (2012). The Jets of the Future: How NASA and aircraft engineers intend to shape the future of air travel. *Popular Science*. Retrieved from https://www.popsci.com/tags/may-2012

Prime, P. (2009). Evaluating Risk in China: Does Location Matter?. *Academy of Management Perspectives, 23*(1), 82–84.

Puck, J., Holtbrügge, D., & Mohr, A. (2009). Beyond entry mode choice: Explaining the conversion of joint ventures into wholly owned subsidiaries in the People's Republic of China. *Journal of International Business Studies, 40*(3), 388–404

Roy, J., & Oliver, C. (2009). International joint venture partner selection: The role of the host-country legal environment. *Journal of International Business Studies, 40*(5), 779–801.

Shippey, K.C. (2008). *Intellectual property rights*, 3rd ed., Novato: CA: World Trade Press.

Stay, P. (2017). Glass and Crystal: Czech Glass in Prague. *Prague Stay*

Trade 2.0, P. (2014). Business etiquette. *Passport to Trade.*

Wang, J., Gong, J., Rohani, S., & Gao, Z. (2017). Recent Developments in the Crystallization Process: Toward the Pharmaceutical Industry. *Science Direct*, 3 (3), 343-353.

Relevant Videos

Electronic Fuel Injection System Working:
https://www.youtube.com/watch?v=xG1w3l41lmQ

20 Tips on Chinese Culture for Successful Business:
https://www.youtube.com/watch?v=H6g7tUcoF3l

China was top destination for foreign direct investment last year, topping U.S.:
https://www.youtube.com/watch?v=41uQkOrV3jl

Part Three

Area Studies

Chapter Twelve

ENTREPRENEURSHIP AND SECURITY: THE STATE OF ENTREPRENEURSHIP IN EASTERN EUROPE

The Early Days of "Perestroika": First-Hand Impressions

Dianne H.B. Welsh, The University of North Carolina at Greensboro

Learning Objectives

1. *Evaluate* the economic, social and political issues around a major change in government.
2. *Analyze* the leadership style present during the time of Perestroika.
3. *Evaluate* how international entrepreneurship played a role in the change of government.

Key Words

Economy   Soviet Union
Revolution

Abstract

This case describes the early days of the economic and social revolution in the former Soviet Union. The Soviet economy was in desperate need of stimulation when Mikhail Gorbachev outlined his blueprint for Perestroika in June of 1987. He described it as "a radical reform of economic management." In terms of international management, Perestroika's notion of cooperatives and factory independence are of particular interest. As an alternative to the rigid and cumbersome giant called the state system, private-sector, cooperatives were allowed to flourish. The reason behind this move included the need to further the competition that existed, increase entrepreneurship, and most of all, to increase services to increasingly disgruntled consumers. The case has implications for other emerging economies that time has shown repeat the same scenario.

Background

The Soviet economy was in desperate need of stimulation when Mikhail Gorbachev outlined his blueprint for Perestroika in June of 1987. He described it as "a radical reform of economic management." Mr. Gorbachev first used three slogans to characterize his reform plans: Uskorenie, Perestroika, and Glasnost. Perestroika, which means restructuring, and Glasnost, defined as openness, are now known to everyone. Uskorenie, which means acceleration, was dropped as it became increasingly evident it was impossible to accomplish. The Soviet leader's goal was to stimulate the economy through dramatic restructuring. This goal was translated into specific new directives in agriculture, alcohol consumption, banking, cooperatives, factory independence, foreign trade, and prices.

How this new Soviet system of Perestroika began can be characterized by first-hand impressions at the Leningrad airport. After the plane touched down about a mile outside the terminal, visitors were taxied by bus to where uniformed officers escorted them into well-formed lines to await customs agents. This one and one-half hour process gave one plenty of time to observe the surroundings. Cameras were positioned so that everyone could be observed at all times. The light marble parquet floor with black dividers looked very dull. The woman mopping it had only dirty water in her bucket. It seemed that the country had been out of any kind of soap for over six months. On the other side of the customs check was the luggage conveyor. The belt was badly worn and was missing parts. The luggage conveyor was much like the cars on the roads, in bad disrepair with bald tires. One or two suitcases appeared from behind the door in ten-minute intervals. After the tour group retrieved their luggage, they were directed into another line to declare possessions, and then they waited for an Intourist (USSR Official Tourist Agency) bus to take them to a hotel. Upon reaching the hotel, four hours had lapsed since the landing.

Much like the tourists' arrival just described, Perestroika's progress moved very slowly and clumsily in the Soviet economy. For instance, purchasers had to wait four to five years in advance to buy an automobile. The purchase price was equivalent to more than one and one-half times the annual salary of the average worker. Banks would not loan money for the purchase of a car. The major car manufacturer, Lada, produced 1,700,000 cars per year, far short of the demand. Used cars often sold at a much higher price than new ones because of availability.

Although Intourist profits were phenomenal, practically no service orientation existed. Since all foreigners had to book arrangements through them, choices rarely existed. Tourists were sold tickets to ballets, plays, operas, or museums primarily on a first-come, first-served basis. Guides were quick to learn to take whatever was available with no questions asked; otherwise they were likely to have to entertain their flock of tourists themselves for the day or be stuck in the hotel room. Favorite Soviet words seemed to be "impossible" and "never."

In terms of international management, Perestroika's notion of cooperatives and factory independence are of particular interest. As an alternative to the rigid and cumbersome giant called the state system, private-sector, cooperatives were allowed to flourish. The reason behind this move included the need to further the competition that existed, increase entrepreneurship, and most of all, to increase services to increasingly disgruntled consumers. Demand for services was constantly growing. The sale of consumer goods such as household appliances, clothing, and shoes was increasing. Although the availability of services more than tripled in the last 15 years, with the number of enterprises providing services nearing the 300,000 mark, supply still lagged far behind demand.

Far too many people were employed in factories and on farms, and not nearly enough in services. Perestroika had to somehow shift millions of people from overmanned factories into its underdeveloped service industries. The managers of factories had traditionally focused on maximizing output, rather than maximizing profit. The more they produced, the more the system rewarded them by a bigger bonus, even if it involved using inputs (such as materials and labor) unprofitably. Labor was cheap and the factories tended to hoard labor. Extra workers were needed for "storming" periods at the end of the month or year when there was a rush to meet target plans. Soviet managers were well aware that they would be rewarded on the tonnage of tractors produced rather than on the number or quality of those produced. In reality, many plant managers and their employees actually preferred the old system, because it guaranteed superfluous jobs, rewarded inefficiency, and held no one personally accountable.

The 1987 Law on State Enterprise was aimed at giving factories more independence. Although the law has since reimposed state control on some food and household items, especially those needed by children and pensioners, factory managers under Perestroika were allowed considerably greater control over production and wages, thereby reducing state bureaucratic power and control. Under the old system, all factories received specific orders from the government central planners. Under the new system, state orders were used only for key industrial products. Factories producing other goods, especially consumer items, were increasingly allowed to make their own decisions regarding what to produce and where to sell it. However, two important links were missing from the law. One was a price mechanism that reflected the real demand for goods so managers would have an idea what to produce and in what quantity to satisfy customers. The other missing link was that the new law failed to put an end to state control over the supply of raw materials.

The Law of State Enterprise decentralized control by introducing a measure of worker self-management. This followed the Leninist philosophy of power in the hands of the people. Workers were given the right to elect their managers, and had a say in the way their firms spent the money they earned. By the late 1980s, the USSR State Committee on Statistics reported that one out of every five directors and one out of every ten managers had been elected by the workforce instead of appointed from above. About the same time, the first report of the recently founded Center for the Study of Public Opinion was published. The findings of a survey of managers and workers found that 20 percent of the workers and 35 percent of the "business executives" responded negatively to the idea of electing managers. The main argument against electing managers was that the principle of one-person management (unity of command) would be violated, and that managers could be replaced without sufficient grounds. This was felt to have an adverse impact on discipline, labor productivity, and pay. Between 65 and 80 percent of the respondents said there was a real danger of "replacing a serious matter with playing at democracy."

Years of educating people in one ideology certainly did not give way to the development of new thinking overnight. The ever-widening democratization in the political sphere did have a considerable effect on the activities of all managers. For example, managers had to be taught participative forms of supervision to adjust to this change. But not only managers had to be retrained—workers also had to be oriented to this new way of thinking. Democratization of the workplace was believed to be permanent. A recent survey conducted by the Institute of World Economy and International Relations of the Academy of Sciences showed that 60 percent of the top executives of 1,000 large Soviet enterprises believe that in the future their enterprises must function solely as public corporations. Perestroika demanded a new type of manager for this political and economic thinking—energetic, entrepreneurial, and democratic.

The Soviets developed a multi-dimensional strategy for providing this badly needed management development. It included education abroad, executive education programs, and private management-consulting firms. At the elite level was the Academy of the National Economy, founded in 1978 in Moscow. It had two objectives. The first was to upgrade existing top managers. Five hundred managers a year went through three months of coursework. The second, greater objective was to train future managers. This involved 100 candidates a year on a two-year, four-term postgraduate course. Most of those going through this course were about 40 years old and served as senior managers or engineers, heads of departments from national ministries, or deputy ministers from Republic ministries. Probably nine out of ten Soviet Managers today are graduate engineers, with a few gaining an added administrative qualification.

According to the head of the Academy of the National Economy, Yevgeni K. Smirnitski, the Academy conducted an intense program that included seminars, role-playing, computer gaming, and private consultation with economic reformers. Much of this training was open to the press and was charged with heated debates. Participants were urged to speak openly about their concerns, including the top-down changes that were being enacted. A popular topic for discussion was how to balance workers' demands for higher wages and benefits against increased pressure from government to operate the plant profitably. Other topics included: decentralized planning, participatory management, property rights, international trade, economic theory, computer technology, and scientific management.

A survey conducted by the Institute of World Economy asked 1,000 Soviet managers to list, in order of importance, their greatest training needs. More than 30 percent answered human resources management. Other responses included: essentials of Western management (23%), international marketing (17%), and accounting and finance (15%). The survey reflected the urgent need to activate the human factor by concentrating on the management of the human side of Soviet organizations.

On the manager as well as the worker level, Gorbachev's Perestroika introduced a wide range of financial incentives as motivators. These included piece-rate incentives, lump-sum payments, and group incentives—all tied to the productivity gains. Both Khrushchev and Brezhnev had tried to introduce such incentives into the Soviet economy. However, incentive payments were of little value to managers and workers because no high-quality, desirable goods were available on which to spend this extra money. Gorbachev was the first leader in Soviet history to recognize the importance that high-quality consumer goods and services could have as a driving force of economic reform. Unfortunately, the reforms led to improvements in quantity, but not quality, of Soviet goods and services. Some analysts forecasted that there would be a short-term decrease in industrial output because of trying to improve product quality. At the organizational level (in both manufacturing and service industries), job enrichment and additional worker training were badly needed to enhance the level of quality.

The Soviet managers under Perestroika tended to be pragmatic, non-ideological, and ambitious. Many did not remember World War II, and they were small when Joseph Stalin died, so they did not directly experience frighteningly oppressive political and economic conditions. Young Soviets wanted a better life-style. They were aware of Western consumerism and life styles and they liked it. As a result, the Soviet value system began changing. Gorbachev's reforms were based on offering incentives to feed these new values. A restructuring of social-ism was off and running, not just a transformation into a for-profit economic system. Personal responsibility for the USSR's progress had to involve all its citi-zens. Freedom per se was not the topic at hand—but economic independence. Such independence could only be attained through planned management of the human side of society in general and organizations in particular. This was deemed to have the ultimate effect on the bottom-line results of Perestroika.

Discussion Questions

1. What is the present status of Gorbachev's Perestroika? How would you describe his leadership approach? What lessons could be learned from Perestroika in managing a modern MNC?
2. As a Soviet manager, how would you communicate to workers the importance of product quality? Which should come first: the production of world-class consumer goods or the use of high quality consumer goods to encourage the production of improved-quality Soviet products?
3. What incentives might motivate Soviet employees in addition to financial ones? Would there be differences for managers and workers?
4. From the information in the case, how would you evaluate the way that the Soviets developed their managers under Perestroika? Based on their stated needs and what you think they currently need, what would be the content of an ideal training program?

References

Harrison, M. (2017, November 7). The Soviet economy, 1917-1991: Its life and afterlife. CEPR's Policy Portal. Retrieved from https://voxeu.org/article/soviet-economy-1917-1991-its-life-and-afterlife

Johnston, M. (2016, February 17). Why the USSR collapsed economically. *Investopedia*. Retrieved from https://www.investopedia.com/articles/investing/021716/why-ussr-collapsed-economically.asp

Miller, C. (2017, February 22). The struggle to save the Soviet economy: Mikhail Gorbachev and the collapse of the USSR. *The Heritage Foundation*. Retrieved from https://www.heritage.org/international-economies/event/the-struggle-save-the-soviet-economy-mikhail-gorbachev-and-the

Non-Non-Libertarian. (2016, March 26). The Soviet Union: GDP growth. *Nintil*. Retrieved from https://nintil.com/2016/03/26/the-soviet-union-gdp-growth/

Rose, J. (2015, January 24). Paul Samuelson's repeated predictions of the Soviet Union economy catching up with the USA. *Utopia*. Retrieved from https://utopiayouarestandinginit.com/2015/01/24/paul-samuelsons-repeated-predictions-of-the-soviet-union-economy-catching-up-with-the-usa/

Relevant Videos

Glasnost and Perestroika:
https://www.youtube.com/watch?v=S9XtYPy4kM8

The Fall Of The Soviet Union:
https://www.youtube.com/watch?v=zadkWw702_M

NM2201 Russian Business Etiquette:
https://www.youtube.com/watch?v=0IduIle5r9Y

Russian Business Culture:
https://www.youtube.com/watch?v=zFCxjST0vtw

Doing business in Russia: What business leaders need to know?:
https://www.youtube.com/watch?v=gD0GYyF6Szg

A ROMANIAN ENTREPRENEUR'S SUCCESS— FLORIN TALPES—ON THE HYPERCOMPETITIVE CYBER SECURITY GLOBAL MARKET

Mariana Dragusin and Raluca Mariana Grosu
The Bucharest University of Economic Studies, Romania

Learning Objectives

1. *Understand* and identify the main challenges that an entrepreneur has to face when going global with his or her company.
2. *Understand* the entrepreneurial opportunities associated with the fast growing cyber security global market.
3. *Understand* and identify the additional barriers to be overcome by an entrepreneur with a centralized economy background/education.
4. *Identify* capital competencies corresponding to an entrepreneurial mindset.
5. *Understand* and identify types of entrepreneurial strategies used by the entrepreneur in the case study.

Key Words

Global entrepreneur
Entrepreneurial opportunity
Intellectual property rights protection
Worldwide distribution channels
Resource-Based Theory (RBT)

Cyber security global market
Antivirus software
Re-branding
Industrial Organization (IO)

Abstract

Targeting the global cyber market is a very ambitious and courageous goal for an entrepreneur, especially when coming from a former communist country… Becoming one of the top 5 leaders of such a dynamic market might seem an unrealistic dream, but it was one that came true for the Romanian visionary entrepreneur—Florin Talpes. The case briefly reveals his inspiring story: the transformation of a talented math teacher and researcher, acting in a centralized economy with no business knowledge nor programming background, into a well-known successful high-tech entrepreneur.

Learning Objectives

1. *Understand* and identify the main challenges that an entrepreneur has to face when going global with his or her company.
2. *Understand* the entrepreneurial opportunities associated with the fast growing cyber security global market.
3. *Understand* and identify the additional barriers to be overcome by an entrepreneur with a centralized economy background/education.
4. *Identify* capital competencies corresponding to an entrepreneurial mindset.
5. *Understand* and identify types of entrepreneurial strategies used by the entrepreneur in the case study.

Key Words

Global entrepreneur
Entrepreneurial opportunity
Intellectual property rights protection
Worldwide distribution channels
Resource-Based Theory (RBT)

Cyber security global market
Antivirus software
Re-branding
Industrial Organization (IO)

Abstract

Targeting the global cyber market is a very ambitious and courageous goal for an entrepreneur, especially when coming from a former communist country… Becoming one of the top 5 leaders of such a dynamic market might seem an unrealistic dream, but it was one that came true for the Romanian visionary entrepreneur—Florin Talpes. The case briefly reveals his inspiring story: the transformation of a talented math teacher and researcher, acting in a centralized economy with no business knowledge nor programming background, into a well-known successful high-tech entrepreneur.

◎ Dilemma

After decades of extreme communist regime and a centralized economy, the Romanian revolution at the end of 1989 opened unexpected new horizons. It was a tipping point for Florin Talpes and his wife, two mathematicians with a prior relatively short work experience as teachers and then dedicated researchers at the Bucharest Central Institute of Informatics. The pair decided to follow a different professional path only one month after the historic event. Confident in their expertise, they quit their stable jobs to take the path of entrepreneurship, a path that was very uncertain and unknown for them at the time.

The story of the first small company, setup with other colleagues, was short lived. After only 6 months the couple founded Softwin (name inspired by their twin children), a company that specialized in developing IT services and solutions, and they got their first project with a French company by pure chance. The expansion into the French, German, and Swiss IT rising markets brought their firm not only new opportunities, but a major challenge too: delivered floppy disks infested with unknown viruses from Bulgaria. The "answer" was the development of the company's first antivirus software, called AntiVirus eXpert.

It was the mid '90s and in a nascent cyber security market the main "star" was the American frequently updatable Norton Antivirus. It took one year for Florin Talpes to realize that they needed to shift the company's focus from software and outsourcing towards security solutions in compliance with an emerging major market trend. The change was accompanied by supporting actions at different levels of the organization. One of the actions was to "build" improved versions of antivirus, under the name AVX, with the ability to self-update, scan and monitor all files downloaded by the user. AVX became the first antivirus product with personal firewall features included and solutions for all instant message applications. Another important "move" was the purchase of the "avx.com" online domain in order to penetrate the US market. Owning that online domain was considered enough to cover the intellectual property rights. Shortly after launching the 6th generation of AVX antivirus—a copyright protected product—the company was warned of trademark infringement by a large American electronic components company. The high costs from the lawsuit lead Mr. Talpes to give up all his claims. He realized that adequate intellectual property protection across borders was crucial for his business.

The "lesson" learned pushed him to make a major shift in his original business model. This is how Bitdefender became the Softwin's spin-off, dedicated to developing advanced solutions for cyber security and it grew along with the fast paced market. The new venture's main product, actually the rebranded and improved antivirus—Bitdefender, reached the market in 2001. This was not the best timing considering the global dotcom bubble crash that took place between 2000 and 2002. However the new company managed to slowly make its way into several important markets including the United States, Japan, and Australia by using worldwide distribution channels. A growing team of creative and dedicated IT pioneers had continuously and carefully improved and diversified the company's products for all the targeted segments: end consumers (family included), businesses, and specialists in the field. Florin Talpes' firm launched the first commercial antivirus for the server version of Linux Samba 3 (2003), the anti-spam technology (2004), and introduced the HiVE technology (2005) and Active Virus Control (2009), to name only a few older examples. But in order to reach over 500 million users all over the world as of 2017, to be ranked among the first ten global vendors of Windows anti-malware application, and to get the highest prize of "Product of the Year" awarded by the renowned AV-Comparatives Testing Platform twice, once in 2013 and another time in 2015, "exceptional, innovative products" are not enough! These exceptional and innovative products had to be backed by exceptional, effective, and interrelated strategies in all functional business areas—human resources, research and development, selling, marketing, legal, financial—and developed and refined in each stage of the business.

Florin Talpes was always aware that attracting and keeping experts is essential for a business acting in a hypercompetitive environment. In an industry were top IT specialists are rare and in a country with high "brain drain" compared to more advanced economies, retaining the best people was a real challenge. The team at Bitdefender was formed by meticulously selecting Romanian and foreign professionals of different ages. Florin Talpes attentively invested in his team members' professional and personal development. The Human Resource Department was always considered an integral part of the company, with complex responsibilities that included recruiting, motivating, and stimulating employees to be innovative while ensuring that they had a friendly environment to work within.

One of the most difficult tasks for Florin Talpes as an entrepreneur was to find the appropriate legal, marketing, and selling experts in a country with a history of over 40 years of a centralized economy, in which these and most other related concepts were largely unknown. The company ended up directly targeting the United States as a pool of specialists highly skilled in those domains. In more recent years, the marketing and selling sectors of the business have gradually relocated to Romania, along with the development of national specialists. They have also expanded internationally—95% of the company activity today is oriented towards the international market.

Last but not least, the visionary entrepreneur—Florin Talpes—is also giving back to the community he belongs to through involvement in meaningful educational and corporate social responsibility programs.

Discussion Questions

1. Is cyber security a viable area for business in the 21st century? Why or why not?
2. What are the main challenges that a company has to face when going global? Are there, in your perception, additional drawbacks for an entrepreneur from a former centralized economy?
3. What were the psychological capital competencies that contributed to the development of Florin Talpes' global mindset?
4. What specific elements of the "industry organization type" approach and that of the "resource-based theory (RBT)," to entrepreneurial strategy can be identified in this case study?
5. Do you think a patent is always required for a software related invention/innovation? Comment on the way Florin Talpes solved the problem of his AVX product in the U.S. market.

◎ Case Update

At the present, with its network of over 500 million users in more than 150 countries, Bitdefender is the world's largest security delivery infrastructure based on innovative solutions. In 2016, AV-TEST, one of the most important independent organizations charged with assessing and rating antivirus and security software, awarded Bitdefender Endpoint Security Version 6.2 the best performance award, and in January-February 2017, Bitdefender Endpoint Security Version 6.2, Windows 7 was rated the best antivirus software for Windows Client Business User. There is an intention of going public with Bitdefender which was discretely announced by the company's owner and CEO, Florin Talpes.

Further details about Mr. Talpes and his companies, Softwin and Bitdefender, lay in the numerous interviews published in different national and foreign newspapers publicly available on the Internet. A comprehensive story is also provided by the only book (until now) about successful Romanian entrepreneurs, called *Cei care schimba jocul (The Game-changers)*, written with passion and dedication by Mona Dirtu and Andreea Rosca and published in 2014 by Publica Publishing House. Technical features and characteristics of Bitdefender products can be found on the company's well-structured official website, www.bitdefender. ro, on websites promoting and comparing cyber security solutions, on posts of IT bloggers, and also on cyber-security forums. Even a simple Google search reveals abundant additional information.

Relevant Videos

Bitdefender Cybersecurity Spotlight: What is Ransomware?
https://www.youtube.com/watch?v=WZ6Zkqp-iJk

Bitdefender Internet Security 2017 Review
https://www.youtube.com/watch?v=qPLTn2osHI0

Global cybersecurity market will be worth $170 billion in 2020 – report
https://www.youtube.com/watch?v=r5jx6d7xRIM

Chapter Thirteen

LATIN AMERICA

Kurotel Medical Longevity Center and Spa: Setting a Global Standard of Excellence[1]

Janet L. Rovenpor, Carolyn E. Predmore, and Frederick D. Greene, Manhattan College

Learning Objectives

1. *Analyze* conditions in the global spa industry and determine future opportunities.
2. *Determine* Kurotel's current strategy by selecting one of Michael Porter's generic strategies: cost leadership, differentiation, cost focus, or differentiation focus.
3. *Identify* the challenges facing the Silveira family regarding their spa's rapid diversification of services and possible expansion overseas.
4. *Describe* the human resource needs in a business that continuously strives to exceed customer expectations.
5. *Assess* possible conflicts of interests between the need to treat clients for medical problems and the desire on the part of clients to enhance their appearances.
6. *Discuss* how relationships between family members could have a positive or a negative impact on the viability of a small business.
7. *Compare* the services offered by Kurotel with the services provided by other global competitors such as Canyon Ranch (USA) and Baden Baden (Germany).

Key Words

Brazil

Family business

Global spa industry

International expansion

Kur Method

Kurotel

Abstract

Dr. Luis Carlos Silveira and his wife, Neusa, were the founders of the Kurotel Medical Longevity Center and Spa in Gramado, Brazil. They developed a unique approach to providing guests with high-quality care and opportunities for both exercise and relaxation. The world-renowned spa catered to the whole person, making sure treatment plans included exercise, dietary menus, hydrotherapy, phytotherapy, spirituality, and emotional balance. The Silveiras became interested in opening another spa in a new location. In this case study, students are asked to determine appropriate countries and international entry options for the launch of a second spa.

[1] We wish to thank Hannelore Leavy, Executive Director of the Day Spa Association and International Medical Spa Association and Adriane Kinzel, International Liaison for Kurotel Longevity Center and Spa, for their assistance. We also thank our students, Flavia Barbery, Jasmine Brown, Katlyn Reh and Elizabeth Ryles, for their research on the global spa industry.

The Opportunity

The founders of a world-renowned spa, Kurotel, would like to pursue growth opportunities in international markets. Dr. Luis Carlos Silveira and his wife, Neusa, opened the spa in Gramado, Brazil in 1982. The couple's approach towards well-being and happiness was unique at the time. They developed a new concept in which they would offer preventative medical services before clients became ill. Most modern-day medical services treated patients after they had become weak with disease and complained of illness-related symptoms. The Silveiras were interested in operating a five-star hotel, not a hospital, to promote long-lasting health among its guests.

From a small wellness center, with only 10 apartments and a handful of employees, Kurotel grew to a 6,000 square-foot complex with 35 apartments/suites and 130 employees, including physicians, dentists, nutritionists, psychologists, fitness experts, biochemists, beauty therapists and nurses. It built a stress control center, a cosmetics factory, pharmacy, and a state-of-the-art medical clinic. An additional 14,165 square-foot water station and spa, the largest facility dedicated to water therapies in South America, was opened in 2009. It is equipped with a pool (treated with ozone and water jets), organic bistro, 18 wet rooms, and 18 treatment rooms. Today, Kurotel receives an average of 200 guests a month.

Kurotel has won many prestigious awards. For several consecutive years, it was voted as Best Spa in Brazil by readers of *Viagem & Turismo*; it was honored with the *Spa Finder Crystal Award* for the best spa on the South American continent; it was cited as the *South America Leading Spa Resort* by World Travel Awards; it was listed as one of the 100 best spas in the world by Bernard Burt and Pamela Price. In 2007, 2008, 2009, and 2010, Kurotel received the prestigious *Conde Nast Johansens Award for the Most Excellence Spa in South America.*

How could the Silveiras leverage their 28 years of experience managing and operating such an outstanding spa? The couple, along with their four daughters—Mariela, Evelise, Rochele and Barbara—has been invited to speak about their philosophy and methods all over the world. They were regarded as experts with considerable knowledge of national and international markets. Expansion into overseas markets presented an exciting opportunity to take advantage of the Kurotel brand and to fulfill the founders' dream of promoting health and happiness to as many clients as possible in as many locations as possible.

The challenges facing the Silveiras were many. Should they open up a spa in another South American country? Would they be better off launching a spa in the U.S. or Europe? Once the founders decided on the most appropriate country, they would need to consider the best international entry option. Should they license their brand to another company in the host country? Would it be more beneficial to seek a joint venture partner, or to go solo? Finally, the Silveiras would need to make sure that the managers of the new spa were well trained and adhered to Kurotel's founding principles and high quality standards.

⊘ The Kur Method

In 1971, Luis Carlos and Neusa Silveira, newly graduated from medical school, began to study a system for healing that was first discovered by a Bavarian priest, Sebastian Kneipp, in the 19th century. The system, which was named the Kneipp Cure, included five basic regimens: exercise, nutrition, herbalism, spirituality, and hydrotherapy. Kneipp himself became one of the founders of the Naturopathic medicine movement (Hoheb, 2009b).

The Silveiras developed the Kur Philosophy as a modern application of the Kneipp Cure. Instead of herbalism, they use phytotherapy. They also added emotional balance to the original five components of the Kneipp Cure. As Rochele Silveira, COO and one of the four daughters of the founders, explains, "The Kur Method offers a new perspective on life, which facilitates our patients to reflect on their lifestyle, leave a sedentary way of life behind, and repair the damage from unhealthy choices. The Kur Method encourages harmonization of body, mind, and spirit by controlling stress levels, relaxing and adopting new habits and attitudes that promote well-being" (Hoheb, 2009b).

Kurotel's mission is "Better Health, Greater Life" (see Figure 13.1). It is committed to treating the guest as a whole with 24-hour attention to preventative health, using traditional methods such as hydrotherapy combined with the latest

Mission

BETTER HEATH, MORE LIFE—Kurotel promotes and stimulates people to be committed to a healthier lifestyle, predictive and preventive medicine, resulting in positive choices. We give due value to life in quantitative (longevity) and qualitative (vitality and well-being) senses. The health comprehension is global, in bio-psycho-social environments.

Values

Pioneerism: Kurotel looks forward to the adoption of new ideas. It is a pioneer in innovation in its market segment.

Liability: Our actions are based upon the conviction of offering and prescribing the best for our customers and other interested people.

Refinement: We excel in perfection of what we do; mainly in the differentiated treatments we offer our clients.

Respect for the Client: At Kurotel we do not impose limits. There are, of course, therapeutical prescriptions, which respect the clients' right to freedom and privacy.

Customization: Every customer is unique and he/she must receive customized attention.

Dedication: We persevere in doing well what we believe in.

Source: http://www.kurotel.com.br

FIGURE 13.1 Kurotel's Mission and Values

cutting-edge technologies. An interdisciplinary team comprised of physicians, physiotherapists, nutritionists, psychologists, biochemists, and beauty specialists care for guests. The ratio of professionals to client is 3.5 to 1, ensuring an individual, personalized experience. Kurotel offers many programs for weight loss, stress management, smoking cessation, optimal aging, healthy longevity, and post-partum and executive health. Morning activities such as hiking, aerobics, and stretching are offered. Afternoons are reserved for customized training and relaxation.

A Brief History of Kurotel

The Kurotel wellness center opened in 1982. The name, "Kurotel," which combines the German word for "kur" (which means "cure") with "hotel" is a tribute to the origins of the spa's philosophy. The main building was inspired by Portuguese colonial homes and was situated among the hydrangea blooms in the city of Gramado, in the state of Rio Grande do Sul (see Figure 13.2). The city was famous for its beautiful mountainside and lush natural surroundings. The purpose of the facility was to operate as a pampering spa, a state-of-the-art medical center, and luxurious resort (Hoheb, 2009a).

In 1983, the Silveiras opened the Kur Pharmacy in order to produce phytotherapic pills and dietary supplements. In 1984, the couple launched Kur Cosmetics to make the products that were used in Kurotel's therapies. A biochemist worked with a pharmaceutical company to test and develop a line of creams, lotions, and aromatic compounds. Guests could now purchase products for use at home. In 1985, a stress control center, which also offered psychological services, opened.

In 1997, Kurotel added a spa complex in order to provide aesthetic and beauty treatments in addition to its health services. In 2000, it started a Kinder Kur plan designed especially for mothers and their newborn infants. In 2001, it added a longevity center and spa with a medical team providing geriatric, genetic, and preventive medical services. In 2009, Kurotel opened the Kur Water Stations and Spa. Dr. Luis Carlos Silveira said it "was designed to benefit guests of all ages and fitness levels. Water therapies can increase balance, coordination, stability, muscular strength, and flexibility while protecting joints from strain or injury" (Hoheb, 2009a).

The Management of Kurotel

Dr. Luis Carlos Silveira and his wife, Neusa, serve as co-chairs of Kurotel's Board of Directors. Neusa has a graduate degree in Social Work from the Catholic University of Pelotas. The couple's four daughters are involved in the management of Kurotel. They are all board members and serve different functions. They oversee everything from logistics and operations to fiscal management and the hiring of personnel.

Dr. Mariela Silveira is a Research Physician at Kurotel. She received her medical degree from the Brazilian Lutheran University. She also has a post-doctorate degree in Nutrology from Sao Paulo University and an advanced certification in Acupuncture. Mariela is a spokesperson at international spa conventions for Kurotel's predictive and preventive medicine. She is also the director of the day spa. Rochele Silveira is a marketing executive and director of Kur Cosmetics. Barbara Silveira is the director of the Kur Pharmacy and Evelise Silveira is the medical director of Kurotel with a doctorate in geriatrics and disease prevention.

The Client

Kurotel is the spa of choice for motion picture stars, business people, and politicians. Its target clientele is high-income individuals. They tend to be married and between the ages of 40 to 70. There are more women than men. The clientele is mostly from South America, but Kurotel also receives visitors from North America, Europe, Africa, and Asia. A weeklong spa package might cost US$ 4,400 per person (see Table 13.1 for a price list). It includes lodging, pool and fitness access, daily nutritional guidance, medical assessments, daily vital signs checkup, daily group exercise classes, consultation with a beauty therapist, and more. It is also possible to use just the day spa or half-day spa. Kurotel has its own magazine, which is sent to 13,000 guests four times a year.

Upon arrival at Kurotel, a guest registers and is directed to the nurse station where his or her weight and blood pressure are taken. After the first medical consultation to discuss recent illnesses, surgeries, and overall health conditions, the physician might recommend blood tests for cholesterol and glucose unless the guest has brought recent lab results (see Figure 13.3 for a list of requested exams). The staff member prepares a holistic treatment plan along with the guest, who is an active participant in the process. The plan includes activities, treatments, and dietary guidelines.

A medical-nutritionist team was assembled at the spa and charged with developing the Kur Longevity Diet (KLD) in 2005. It is based on the dietary habits of the world's longest living people and consists of low-calorie-density food and low glycemic index/rate food. The diet combines the best ingredients used in food preparation in countries from around the globe, including Omega 3 fatty fish from Okinawa, Japan; soy and green tea from Asia; grapes from San Marino, Italy; olive oil from Crete, Greece; and the Brazil nut from Brazil. The chef makes light use of oils, butter, salt, honey, and caffeinated tea. The restaurant does not serve dairy products, coffee, food with trans fatty acids, alcohol, juices, soft drinks, sugar, or refined grains.

Throughout the Kurotel property, careful attention is paid to soothing lights and color schemes. Guest rooms are kept impeccably clean, with neutral colors and natural light coming in from large windows. Music is important, too. The founders of Kurotel are known for surprising guests with popular singers, such as the Brazilian artists, Eliana Pittman and Danilo Caymmi.

Accolades from satisfied clients abound. One blogger on the Global Spa and Wellness Web site, describes how she was made to feel "exceptionally special" the moment she arrived at Kurotel. Adriane Kinzel, Kurotel's International Liaison, greeted her personally. There had been a delay in the arrival of the guest's flight, but she was so impressed that an entire schedule had already been developed for her that she immediately got immersed in the spa's treatments. Another guest from England said, "I've been to many places in the world and Kurotel is the place where I've found the peace that I didn't find anywhere else. My life has changed here. I'm a stronger, better, and more relaxed person, with a positive view on life. I lost 12 kg and won new self-confidence" ("Kurotel 5-Time Winner," 2009).

Courtesy of Kurotel Medical Longevity Center and Spa

Sustainability

Kurotel follows sustainable and responsible practices to protect the environment. It uses a cistern to collect and treat rainwater for local reuse. Since exact portions of food are served to guests, there is little waste. Whatever is left over from the restaurant undergoes a composting process and is returned to the soil in an outdoor garden. To consume less energy, rooms have motion sensors to control room lighting.

The Global Spa Industry

Consumers from around the world have become increasingly interested in health, wellness, and the enhancement of mind, body, and spirit. The core spa industry caters to them by offering a wide variety of services, including massages, facials, body treatments, salon services, water-based treatments, health assessments, and retail products for home use. As a result, the number of spas, as well as total industry revenues, has increased rapidly over the years. In 2007, there were an estimated 71,672 spas operating in the global economy, with spa revenues totaling $46.8 billion and spa employment reaching 1.2 million persons ("Global Spa Summit," 2008).

The core spa industry is divided into five categories, which are Day/Club/Salon Spas, Destination Spas and Health Resorts, Hotel/Resort Spas, Medical Spas, and other Spas. In day/club/salon spas, trained professionals offer massages, facials, and body treatments during daily operating hours in private treatment rooms ("Global Spa Summit," 2008). A club spa offers its services in a facility primarily dedicated to fitness and exercise; a salon spa provides its treatments in conjunction with beauty services (hair, makeup, and nails). Destination spas/health resorts offer a full-immersion spa experience for all guests, with overnight stays and prepaid meal plans ("Global Spa Summit," 2008). They run fitness programs, weight loss programs, and educational classes.

Spas at hotels/resorts cater to tourists and business people. They complement a hotel stay or a wide range of other activities (e.g., golf and skiing) at a resort ("Global Spa Summit," 2008). Services are paid for on an á la carte basis. Medical spas require the oversight of a licensed healthcare professional. Services include Botox injections and laser treatments. The "other spa" category includes mobile spas, cruise ship spas, and mineral/hot spring spas ("Global Spa Summit," 2008). Day/club/salon spas represent the majority of spas around the world, accounting for 63 percent of all spa facilities. However, hotel, resort, destination, and health spas command higher average revenues than day/club/salon spas ("Global Spa Summit," 2008). Taken together, spas in three regions—Europe, North America, and Asia-Pacific—account for over 90 percent of total spa industry revenues (see Table 13.2). The five largest spa revenue-generating countries are the United States, Japan, Germany, France, and Italy, accounting for 55 percent of industry revenues worldwide. German medical insurance providers cover Kur therapies prescribed by physicians. Patients can visit a center for three weeks, every three years ("Spa," 2010). In the Asia-Pacific region, spas are considered relatively new but have increased at a rapid rate. This specific region is dominated by large hotels and resorts, which cater to international tourists.

Latin America-Caribbean is the fourth largest region in the world in terms of spa revenues ($2.5 billion in 2007) and in terms of spa numbers (5,435 spas). Latin American-Caribbean countries are strongly focused on a beauty culture, which explains the higher revenues generated by day/club/salon compared to hotel/resort spas. Even poor women feel entitled to cosmetic surgery; the government medical insurance in Brazil will pay for it (Edmonds, 2007). In contrast, the hotel/resort spa sector dominates the industry in the Middle East and North Africa region ("Global Spa Summit," 2008).

Spas in each geographic region have their own unique characteristics. The European spa industry has well-established traditions involving bathing and wellness. These date back to ancient Roman times. Natural and water-based solutions are used for therapeutic, curative, and preventive treatments ("Global Spa Summit," 2008). Three popular spas, which have been recently refurbished and renovated, include Bath in England (a UNESCO World Heritage site), Spa in Belgium, and Marienbad in the Czech Republic (Carlin, 2007). The North American spa industry is one of the most innovative. New business concepts, such as mobile spas, sea spas, and discount spa chains, have been introduced in the marketplace. The Canyon Ranch spas in Tucson, Arizona and Lenox, Massachusetts attract affluent guests who spend an average of $900 a day and have access to massages, nutrition consultations, diagnostic blood tests, and bone scans (McGinn, 2007).

In Asia-Pacific, many spas have evolved from Japanese "onsens," Indian ayurveda centers, and Thai and Chinese massage therapies. Thailand was recently called "Asia's spa capital" (Emmons, 2009). From just one spa in 1992, the country now has 585 spas. Guests can visit urban spas, holistic medical centers, luxurious destination spas, and island wellness centers (Emmons, 2009). Many spas in the Middle East-North Africa region are offshoots of "hammams," or Turkish baths. Because of poverty in many African nations, spas are found mostly in upscale tourist destinations ("Global Spa Summit," 2008).

A. Kurotel's Natural Suite

B. Kurotel's Fitness Center

C. Kurotel's Medical Team

FIGURE 13.2 Photographs of the Kurotel Medical Longevity Center and Spa.

TABLE 13.1 **Kurotel's Price List**
Recommended stay: 1 week, Minimum stay: half-week

ROOMS	SINGLE	DOUBLE	SINGLE	DOUBLE
Colonial Suite with balcony	4,400	8,355	5,055	9,955
& Kur Chalet	5,938	10,400	6,827	11,961
Special Suite with balcony	6,294	11,011	7,238	12,661
Natural Suite	7,777	12,622	8,944	14,516
Royal Suite	9,405	14,888	10,816	17,122

Notes:

Rates for weeklong stays are in U.S. dollars and range from 4,400 to 17,122 + 10 percent (tax service), depending on room type. Rates for half-week stays are charged at 50 percent of the weeklong stays. Rates for double occupancy are quoted per two guests in a room.

Check payment forms. We request a 30 percent deposit in 48 hours to guarantee the reservation.

Cancellation policy: cancellation with funds returned will only be accepted with 12 days prior notice. Changing dates with 7 days prior notice. Any other cases no funds will be returned.

Ground Transfers—We can arrange the transfers back and forth to Porto Alegre Airport, upon request. These costs are not included in the package.

Source: Company documents

Kur Lifestyle Plan

Clients over 12 years old

- Complete haemogram, sodium, potassium, glucose, uric acid, triglycerides, total cholesterol and fractions, urine test. Validity of 3 months.

- TSH–Validity of 3 months—For those who monitor the thyroid dysfunction, it is important to be able to compare current results to previous results.

Clients over 30 years old

- Ergometric (ECG) Test—Validity of 6 months: Through this test, is possible to investigate if there are any heart disorders that could represent risk during physical exercises. It is extremely important for your safety.

Clients with diabetes (Any age)
- Glycated Hemoglobin—Validity of 3 months

Clients with hepatic disorders (Any age)

- Transaminase GOT and GPT—Validity of 3 months

Note: After the clinical evaluation the physician may ask you for other exams, if necessary. If you have radiological lab results, please bring them with you, they are important for the treatment prescription.

Source: Company documents

FIGURE 13.3 Requested Exams

TABLE 13.2 Global Spa Facilities by Region, 2007

	ESTIMATED TOTAL NUMBER OF SPAS	ESTIMATED TOTAL SPA REVENUES (US$ BILLIONS)	ESTIMATED TOTAL SPA EMPLOYMENT
Europe	22,607	$18.4	441,727
Asia-Pacific	21,566	$11.4	363,648
North America	20,662	$13.5	307,229
Middle East-North Africa	1,014	$0.7	20,938
Latin American-Caribbean	5,435	$2.5	82,694
Africa	389	$0.3	7,273
Total	71,672	$46.8	1,223,510

Source: Global Spa Summit, Global Spa Economy 2007. (2008, May). Prepared by SRI International.

Discussion Questions

1. How is Kurotel as a business defined now, and how does that definition factor into plans for international expansion for the Silveiras?
2. Understanding what the company is—what are the differential advantages of the Kurotel methods?
3. How should Kurotel continue to expand to reach more of the global population with its message of better health habits?
4. How should the ownership/management structure be constructed—knowing that the original spa's success may have been due to its organic development on site with family ownership and supervision?
5. What are the entrepreneurial implications of the Kurotel business for the Silveiras?

References

Bachrach, J. (2006, July). The girls from Ipanema. *Allure*, 148.

Carlin, D. (2007, January 11). Europe's spas sparkle again. *Business Week* Retrieved from https://subscribe.businessweek.com/pubs/BW/BWK/BWKRelaunch_US_PaidSearch_June2017.jsp?cds_page_id=216736&cds_mag_code=BWK&id=1519062218996&lsid=80501143389035220&vid=1&gclid=EAlaIQobChMl1fGK2sOy2QIVgonIChO-XAoTEAAYASAAEglO6PD_BwE#theseErrors

Carroll, R. (2010). A bright future: The transformation of Brazil: Ready for take-off: A sustained period of stable government and a responsible fiscal policy has helped Brazil's economy to spread its wings and reach for the sky. *The Guardian*, p. 1. Retrieved from https://www.theguardian.com/us

Edmonds, A. (2007). 'The poor have the right to be beautiful': Cosmetic surgery in neoliberal Brazil, *Journal of the Royal Anthropological Institute*, 13: 363–381. Retrieved from http://www.cghi.nl/uploaded_files/.../Edmonds_JRoyAnthrInst_2007.pdf

Emmons, K. (2009). Thailand—Spa capital of the world. *PR Newswire*. Retrieved from https://www.prnewswire.com/

Global Spa Summit, Global Spa Economy. (2008). *SRI International*. Retrieved from https://www.globalwellnessinstitute.org/industry-research/

Hoheb, C. (2009). A balanced approach to spa going. *Les Nouvelles Esthetiques & Spa.* Retrieved from http://www.lneonline.com/spa_of_the_month/archive/?200909

Hoheb, C. (2009). The Kur Method—A philosophy for optimal wellbeing in body, mind and soul. *Heath and Tourism Magazine*. Retrieved from http://healthtourismmagazine.com/articledetail.php?issue=issue-2&article=Kur-Method

Johansson, J. (2009). *Global Marketing*. NY: McGraw-Hill/Irwin.

Kuratko, DF (2009). *Entrepreneurship*, 8th edition. South-Western, Cengage Learning.

Kurotel. (2017). Longevity Medical Center and Spa. *Kurotel*. Retrieved from https://www.tripadvisor.com/Hotel_Review-g303536-d647353-Reviews-Kurotel_Longevity_Medical_Center_Spa-Gramado_State_of_Rio_Grande_do_Sul.html

Kurotel 5-Time winner. (2009). Luxury spa finder best spa award. *Company Press Release*.

Machl, S.S. (2012). Understanding German business culture. *Welcome to Expatica*. Retrieved from https://www.expatica.com/de/employment/Understanding-German-business-culture_100983.html

McGinn, D. (2007, October 15). Spa makeover; Canyon Ranch is the ultimate in health resorts. *Newsweek*, *150* (16): E6. Retrieved from http://www.newsweek.com/spa-makeover-102827

Petersen, H.D. (2013). Global Spa & Wellness: Industry Briefing Papers. *Wellness Summit*. Retrieved from http://www.globalwellnesssummit.com/industry-resource/industry-briefing-papers/

Spa: Sanus per aquam an old Roman cure. (2010). How to Germany, Chuck Emerson Media Services. Retrieved from http://www.howtogermany.com/pages/spas.html

Trade, P. (2014). Business etiquette. *Passport to Trade*. Retrieved from http://businessculture.org/passport-to-trade-2-0/

Relevant Videos

Brazil's beauty industry boosts economy:
https://www.youtube.com/watch?v=pANhNi4lfec

Spa Industry Boasts $100 Billion in Revenue Annually:
https://www.youtube.com/watch?v=M5qokPPtk_Y

Top 5 Interesting Facts About Brazil:
https://www.youtube.com/watch?v=5ad8Muc3HUI

Brazilian Business Etiquette:
https://www.youtube.com/watch?v=UIX6XCoPF0g

Chapter Fourteen

CHINA

CORPORATE ENTREPRENEURSHIP OF FOREIGN MULTINATIONALS IN CHINA: A COMPARISON OF MOTOROLA AND NOKIA IN THE CELLULAR PHONE INDUSTRY

Nir Kshetri, The University of North Carolina at Greensboro

Learning Objectives

1. *Analyze* the environmental conditions affecting corporate entrepreneurship of foreign multinationals in China.
2. *Demonstrate* an understanding of the competitive environment in the Chinese technology industries.

Key Words

Code division multiple access (CDMA)
GSM (Global System for Mobile Communications)

Diffusion of an innovation
Internet

Abstract

This case examines the corporate entrepreneurial environment in the Chinese technology industry and compares corporate entrepreneurial strategies of two foreign multinationals in the cellular phone industry in China: Motorola and Nokia. The case focuses on the early stage of cellular phone diffusion. It also sheds light into many unusual and idiosyncratic features of the corporate entrepreneurial environment in China, especially in the high-technology industry, and illustrates various constraints and opportunities that foreign multinationals face.

Introduction

"We're going to be number one in the second half of this year. We would want to maintain that position and probably grow from that," said Colin Giles, general manager of Nokia's mobile phone division (CNETAsia 2003). He was referring to China, the biggest mobile market in the world, in mid-2003. Nokia, the world's biggest handset maker, was losing its grip in China for a long time. In 2003, Nokia wrestled against its competitors in China by rolling out 15 new models (CNETAsia 2003). It also launched code division multiple access (CDMA) phones in the Chinese market in August 2003. Motorola's Chief Operating Officer Mike Zafirovski said Motorola would respond by accelerating its plan to introduce 14 new phones designed for the Chinese market; by entering in the

TABLE 14.1 **Market Shares of Major Players in the Global and the Chinese Mobile Market**

WORLD		CHINA		
VENDOR	MARKET SHARE (2003 Q1, %)	VENDOR	MARKET SHARE (2002 Q3, %)	MARKET SHARE (2003 Q1, %)
Nokia	35.5	Motorola	28.9	20.6
Motorola	15.5	Nokia	25.7	16.7
Samsung	12.3	TLC	7.4	11.4
Siemens	7.4	Samsung	6.8	
LG	5.2	Siemens	5.1	
Other	24.1			

Source: International Data Corporation (IDC) for the global data. Data for the Chinese market are from various sources.

"third and fourth tier" cities and by increasing the R&D budget in China by 30 percent (Charny 2003).

China, together with the U.S., Japan, and South Korea, was one of the few major handset markets where Nokia lagged behind its competitors. Motorola and Nokia historically dominated the Chinese handset market, and still occupied the top two slots in the early 2000s (see Table 14.1) but were experiencing tough competition from local handset makers as well as those from Japan, Korea, and Taiwan. What is more, the Chinese government had set a target to increase the combined shares of its domestic handset makers to 85 percent by 2006 (Merritt 2003).

Motorola and Nokia in China

Oviatt and McDougall (2005) define international entrepreneurship as "—the discovery, enactment, evaluation and exploitation of opportunities across national borders to create future goods and services." Entrepreneurial firms such as Motorola and Nokia are tapping the global market for growth. Nokia opened its first office in China in 1985 and sold the first NMT450 (Nordic Mobile Telephones/450) analog cell phone system in 1986 (Chinanex.com 2003b). It started selling GSM[1] digital phones in 1991 (Törnroos 2003). Motorola, on the other hand, entered the Chinese market in 1987, two years after Nokia, by setting up an office in Beijing. In 1992, it established Motorola (China) Electronics Ltd. in Tianjin and began the production of beep-pager, mobile phone, two-way radio, wireless communications facilities, semiconductor, automobile, and electronics[2]. Being the first company to introduce pagers in China, "Motorola" means pagers

---

[1] Global System for Mobile phone communications (GSM) was the first commercially available digital standard mainly used in Europe and Asia.

[2] See http://www.motorolacareers.com/moto.cfm?cntry=China

for most Chinese.[3] In the early 1990s, China became a lucrative market for Motorola as Chinese consumers heavily bought its pagers for convenience as well as a symbol of social status.

Both companies have been selling CDMA[4] phones in the Chinese market. In December 2001, Motorola introduced its first CDMA phone, V8060, in the Chinese Market. During the trial of China Unicom's CDMA network, V8060 was found to be the preferred choice of 80 percent of customers.[5] By early 2003, Motorola had captured about a third of the CDMA handset market. In March 2003, Nokia announced that it would begin production of CDMA handsets. Nokia launched its first phone running on the CDMA standard in August 2003 and became the second foreign company making CDMA handsets. Its CDMA phone, 2280, was specifically designed for China Unicom.

By 2001, the investment by Motorola and Nokia in China amounted to US $3.4 billion and US $2 billion respectively. In 2000, Motorola became the largest foreign investor in China by overtaking General Motors (UltraChina.com 2000). Its cumulative investment is expected to reach US $10 billion by 2006.[6]

By early 2003, Nokia had 22 local offices, five joint ventures (JVs), two research centers, and a reseller network with 900 outlets in China. In March 2003, the company announced that it would form a new JV for handset production, which would replace four handset JVs—two in Beijing, one in Guangdong, one in Jiangsu. The new JV will be the largest handset manufacturer in terms of combined production and exports (Chinanex.com 2003b). Capitel, one of Nokia's JV partners in China, however, is seeking to expand its own branded handset business, which has made the JV relationship weak (Dean 2003). In December 2001, Nokia also opened a "Xing Wang (StarNet) International Industrial Park" with a Chinese partner. The U.S. $1.2 billion Park will also be used to manufacture handsets and other products by Nokia's part suppliers (Chinanex.com 2003b). Similarly, Motorola's operations in China consist of one wholly owned factory, one holding company, eight JVs, 18 R&D facilities, and 26 sales offices (Chinanex.com 2003a). In 1998, Motorola moved its North Asia headquarters from Hong Kong to Beijing. Although Motorola is facing problems in its relationship with a Chinese JV partner, Eastcom, it has the advantage of maintaining a wholly owned subsidiary (Dean 2003).

Motorola and Nokia are also among China's biggest exporters. Motorola (China) Electronics was China's fifth-largest exporter in 2001 with exports of U.S. $1.61 billion. Its exports in 2002 increased to U.S. $3.6 billion. Similarly, Nokia's JVs in Beijing and Dongguan were in seventh and eighth place, with exports of U.S. $1.02 billion and $832 million respectively.

---

[3] See http://www.welcome-to-china.com/biz/gen/7bp.htm

[4] CDMA (Code Division Multiple Access) technology allows carrying many conversations over one frequency. It does so by sending all communications in groups of bits mixed altogether and tagging each group, belonging to a specific communication, with a different code. CDMA is mainly used in North America (see http://cellphones.about.com/library/glossary/bldef_cdma.htm).

[5] See http://www.motorola.com.cn/en/news/2002/01/0107_02.asp

[6] See http://www.china.org.cn/english/2001/Nov/21765.htm

Motorola began to build a nationwide distribution network in 1997. By 2000, the company had over 300 hand-picked agents. Motorola has also divided China into several regions with different developing strategies.[7] In selected Chinese cities, Nokia cut distribution costs by directly supplying handsets to large regional distributors and retail outlets (Bolton and Wei 2003). Some players in the Chinese handset market, however, have even more efficient distribution systems. For instance, Bird, a local handset manufacturer, has branches in every Chinese province to sell directly into retailers (Dean 2003). Nokia's distribution system, however, has been designed for GSM handsets. Analysts argue that CDMA handsets require different distribution channels from GSM phones (Dean 2003).

Motorola and Nokia have designed phones with Chinese appeal. For instance, Motorola's Accompli, which was manufactured in China, was the first handset with Chinese character recognition.[8] Similarly, Nokia's 6108, a pen-based GSM handset designed for the Chinese market, allows users to write messages in Chinese on an input tablet concealed beneath a flip. It was designed by Nokia's Beijing R&D centre (PMN 2003). In mid-2003, Nokia also announced that it would introduce two entry-level handsets—1100 and 2300—and a cheaper-to-operate network in countries like India, China, Russia, Thailand, Brazil, Indonesia, Vietnam, and the Philippines.

According to a survey conducted with Chinese university students by *ChinaHR.com* in early 2003, Motorola ranked 7th among the most popular employers[9]. The same study ranked Nokia in 15th place. Motorola also has a good reputation among local consumers and the government. In 1999, *Fortune* magazine named Motorola as the second most admired foreign company in China. According to Christopher B. Galvin, chair and CEO, Motorola's aim is "not to be the biggest but the best foreign investor in China" (UltraChina.com 2000). The company, for instance, has formed alliances with local state-owned enterprises in the production of semi-conductors. In 1999, it purchased U.S. $1 billion worth of equipment with 730 local enterprises. Motorola has over 75 percent of managers who are Chinese, and 40 percent of the managers are female. The company has also helped to establish 27 Motorola Hope Primary Schools and donated U.S. $1 million to eight institutions of higher learning. All the profits earned in its local operations in recent years have been reinvested back in local establishments (UltraChina.com 2000).

The Chinese Mobile Market

The combined fixed and mobile connections in China increased from 6.8 million in 1990 to 472 million by mid-2003. An estimate of Pyramid Research suggests that the number increased to 950 million or a penetration rate of 75 percent

---

[7] See Motorola to Improve Sales Network, Sci-Edu, November 25, 2000, http://fpeng.people-daily.com.cn/200011/25/eng20001125_56097.html

[8] See Motorola Accompli 008 Product Review, 25-Mar-2001, http://www.mobiletechnews.com/info/2001/03/25/070116.html

[9] See http://www.rieti.go.jp/en/china/03040201.html.

by 2008. The Mobile network is growing much faster than the fixed network (see Figure 14.1). The number of mobile subscribers in China increased from 18 thousand in 1990 to 234.5 million by mid-2003. In 2003 alone, an estimated 52 million mobile phones were added in China compared to 33 million fixed phones. The number of mobile phone users in China passed the fixed phone users in 2003. Estimates suggest that China accounted for U.S. $8.4 billion (Liu 2003) of the U.S. $60 billion global mobile market in 2003 (Kahn 2003).

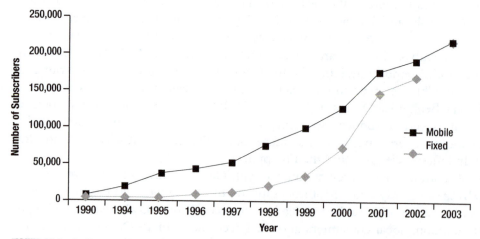

FIGURE 14.1 A Comparison of Mobile and Fixed Network Growth in China

Figure 14.2 compares the growth of Chinese mobile market vis-à-vis those of Japan and the U.S. The Chinese mobile market became the biggest in Asia by overtaking Japan in 2000 and became the world's biggest in 2001. Mobile penetration in China is, however, much lower than both countries (Figure 14.3).

Although GSM standard dominates the Chinese market, CDMA is growing more rapidly. The Chinese CDMA market has also become highly competitive. There are 19 players licensed to make CDMA handsets (Dean 2003). Even before its launch in January 2001, there were 500,000 people registered to get CDMA connection. By the end of 2002, the number crossed 7 million. By April 2003, China Unicom's CDMA network had 9 million customers, and is expected to reach 20 million by the end of 2003. CDMA network's second-phase of construction is expected to ensure the China Unicom's capacity to 30 million subscribers and the network is expected to upgrade from 2G to 2.5G.[10]

R&D and technology related factors such as R&D investment, technology diffusion, patent systems and standards, technological cooperation between firms, broadband access and university/industry interface affect corporate entrepreneur-

---

[10] Second generation (2G) refers to digital wireless standards that concentrated on improving voice quality, coverage, and capacity. It was originally designed to support voice. 2.5G builds upon the 2G standards by providing increased bit-rates and bringing limited data capability.

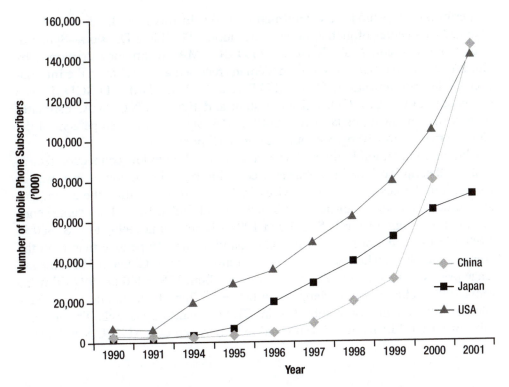

FIGURE 14.2 Growth of Mobile Subscribers in China, Japan, and the U.S.

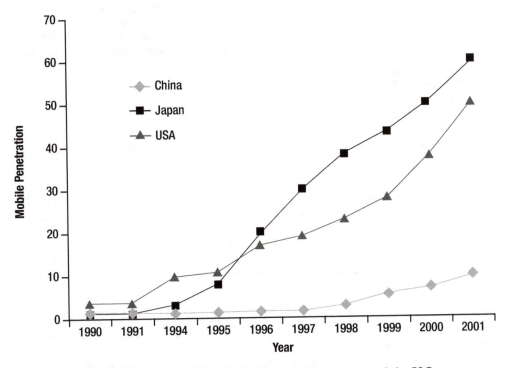

FIGURE 14.3 Penetration Rates of Mobile Phones in China, Japan and the U.S.

ial performance (Ahmad and Hoffmann, 2008). In this regard, China has also emerged as a center of global mobile innovations. The Time Division—Synchronous Code Division Multiple Access (TD-SCDMA) technology developed by China's Datang Mobile and German Siemens received approval from the International Telecommunications Union (ITU) as a 3G[11] standard. TD-SCDMA is a competitor to the U.S. CDMA2000 system and Europe's WCDMA. Estimates suggest that following its launch, TD-SCDMA would capture 30 percent of the Chinese market and 10 percent outside China (Einhor 2003).

Fierce competition in the mobile sector has resulted in low connection fees as well as subscription fees for mobile services. Monthly subscription rates as well as connection charges for mobile services in China are lower than the average of lower-middle income countries as well as the world (Table 14.2). The average connection fee declined from U.S. $600 in 1994 (Tsuchiyama 1999) to U.S. $60 in 1999. Fixed-line connection, on the other hand, is more expensive than both the averages. Similarly, when handsets were first introduced in China in 1994, the average price was U.S. $850, which decreased to about U.S. $200 in 1999 (Tsuchiyama 1999). The increased competition between China Unicom and China Mobile has resulted in heavy subsidies in CDMA handsets as well. The average subsidy per CDMA handset is estimated to be between U.S. $193–U.S. $300.[12]

TABLE 14.2 **A Comparison of Fixed and Mobile Charges in China and the World**

	CHINA	LOWER-MIDDLE INCOME COUNTRIES AVERAGE	WORLD AVERAGE
Mobile network (1999)			
Connection ($)	60	90	86
Monthly subscription ($)	6.04	20.99	21.40
Tariff per minute (peak) ($)	0.05	0.25	0.27
Tariff per minute (off-peak) ($)	0.05	0.18	0.18
100 minute basket ($)	10.87	39.69	38.15
Fixed network (1998)			
Residential connection ($)	226	133	109
Business connection ($)	226	212	155
Residential monthly subscription ($)	1.9	4.8	6.9
Business monthly subscription ($)	2.9	8.8	11.5
Cost of 3 minute local call ($)	0.01	0.05	0.09
Subscription as a % of GDP per capita	3.1	3.8	7.5

Source: ITU (1999).

[11] Third generation (3G) mobile technology will provide wide-area coverage at 384 kbps and local area coverage up to 2 Mbps and thus supplements standardized 2G and 2.5G services with wideband services.

[12] See China Becomes World's Leading Mobile Phone Market!, http://www.fiducia-china.com/News/2002/2102-1625.html

Various multilateral trade agreements under the World Trade Organization (WTO) regime have further facilitated the diffusion of mobile technology in China. Under General Agreements on Trades in Services (GATS) commitments of the WTO, China has promised to eliminate restrictions on foreign ownership in telecom services. Under the Information Technology Agreement (ITA), China is required to eliminate tariffs on key IT products. The average tariffs on ITA products were reduced from 12.5 percent in 2001 to 3.4 percent in 2002; and tariffs on 83 percent of ITA products were eliminated by January 2002. Before China's accession to the WTO, tariff rates were 12 percent for cellular phones, 18 percent for batteries, and 20 percent for pagers (Leopold 2000). In January 2003, China eliminated handset import tariffs.

Chinese Consumers

The demand for cellular phones is also related to psychological "stock of habits" of Chinese consumers. In the mid-1980s, for instance, the penetration rates of consumer durables in China were about the same as South Korea, Japan, and the then-USSR (Sklair 1994). In terms of the technology achievement index constructed by the UNDP (2001), China's rank 45 (out of 72 economies considered) puts it in the group of "dynamic adopters" of new technologies and ahead of several countries with higher per capita GDP than China.

Mobile phones have also fulfilled rapidly increasing telecom demand in China. Liberalization since the early 1980s led to a greater freedom for Chinese to move around and to work away from hometowns. Compounded by the arrival of offshore investors and an increasing number of tourists, telecom demand rose rapidly[13]. While mobile phones are supplements to fixed phones in developed economies, they are substitutes for fixed telephones for low-income economies such as China (ITU 1997). According to the Wireless World Forum, mobile phones have now become the *de facto* tools of communication among Chinese youth.

Analysts have predicted that purchases of upgraded handsets by China's existing mobile phone users will soon exceed sales to first-time buyers. China Unicom's CDMA technology is targeted to quality conscious consumers. The 2.5G CDMA technology has higher voice quality; is safer for users because of low radiation; provides high security; and has a data transmission rate of up to 10 times faster than 2G networks.

Chinese consumers also seem to place more emphasis on social status, and the mobile phone's association with social status has thus helped accelerate its diffusion. For instance, the really small wireless phones initially did not sell well in China because they were "too inconspicuous" and did not offer adequate opportunity to show off. The public attitude toward small wireless devices has, however, changed in recent years.

---

[13] In the first half of 2003, the revenue of China's telecommunications industry amounted U.S. $220 billion up 12.1 percent from the same period in 2002.

Chinese Government and the Environment for Corporate Entrepreneurship

While some argue that the Chinese government has exercised its power over its firms in a "chaotic way," which has hindered corporate entrepreneurship in the country (Gilboy 2004), the state seems to have played an important role in stimulating entrepreneurship in the cellular telephone industry. In general, observers have noted that the government's policies are friendly to entrepreneurs as long as they structure their strategies to integrate governmental agenda (Pei 2006). In China, the base of regime legitimacy is shifting from Marx Leninism to economic growth (Chen 2002; Zhao 2000). Chinese leaders have set economic growth as the top priority (Zhao 2000). China arguably has "inbuilt" and "government-fostered" mechanisms to promote entrepreneurship (Monro 2007). Forecaster Gerald Celente put the issue this way: "China is invigorated with a sense of entrepreneurship that is supported by its government, while in the USA, such a spirit is on the decline" (USA Today December 26, 2006).

The Chinese government also has the ambition of providing every household with a telephone. To achieve this objective, top priority was given to build R&D capacity in mobile telephony in the late 1990s and corporate entrepreneurship was encouraged in this sector (Niitamo 2000). During the 1990s, China spent U.S. $10 billion to build a national mobile network (Goodman 2003).

We might detour briefly to point out that there are various forms of capitalism. Baumöl, Litan and Schramm (2007) have proposed four prevalent forms of capitalism, and demonstrated how each form contributes to economic growth: (i) entrepreneurial, (ii) big firm, (iii) state directed and (iv) oligarchic. Specifically, some developing countries such as China have found state-guided capitalism as a way to promote entrepreneurship and achieve economic growth.

The heavy investment was supplemented by a series of programs designed to accelerate telecom development. They include extensive re-engineering of and intense competition in the mobile sector. China Unicom was formed in 1994, which competes with China Telecom, then-monopoly Chinese Telecom Company. Unicom is licensed for mobile, paging, data, Internet, and long-distance (James 2001). The two companies are involved in a price war in the cellular market (Wilhelm 2000). China Mobile, China Unicom, and a number of Internet service and content providers are also forced to adapt to the rigorous disclosure requirements of the NYSE, NASDAQ, and Hong Kong's Growth Enterprise Market and to cut off redundant workers (McDaniels and Waterman 2000).

◎ Nokia: A Profile

A forest industry enterprise was established in 1865 in Southwestern Finland by mining engineer Fredrik Idestam.[14] Finnish Rubber Works founded in 1898, and Finnish Cable Works founded in 1912 were merged together with Idestam's enterprise in 1967 to form Nokia. In the early 1980s, Nokia acquired Swedish

---

[14] See http://www.nokia.com/nokia/0,8764,32884,00.html

companies Mobira, Salora, Televa, and Luxor, and strengthened its position in the telecom and consumer electronics markets. In 1987, Nokia acquired the consumer electronics operations and part of the component business of the German Standard Elektrik Lorenz and Oceanic, a French consumer electronics company. In the same year, Nokia also purchased Maillefer, a Swiss cable machinery company. By acquiring Ericsson's data systems division in the late 1980s, Nokia became the largest Scandinavian IT company. In 1989, Nokia expanded its cable industry into Continental Europe by acquiring the Dutch cable company NKF. Since the beginning of the 1990s, Nokia has concentrated on its core business, telecomm, by divesting its information technology and basic industry operations.

By early 2003, Nokia was making about 40 different models of cell phones (Pringle 2003). According to the senior vice-president of Nokia's Asia-Pacific, Nokia envisages an "MIS (mobile information society) that will be based on three cornerstones—digitalization, mobility, and the Internet" (Litchfield 2000). In 2002, Nokia ranked sixth among the most valuable brands in the world, with estimated brand equity of U.S. $30 billion.

By the end of 2002, Nokia had established 17 production facilities in 9 different countries, and R&D facilities in 14 different countries. Such facilities allow it to switch rapidly from one product to another. For instance, following a last-minute delay to a new color-screen model in summer 2002, Nokia bridged the gap by lowering the production of an existing phone by 50 percent in its factories in Finland, Germany, and China (Pringle 2003).

Motorola: A Profile

Galvin Manufacturing Corporation, founded in Chicago in 1928, changed its name to Motorola, Inc in 1947. Its first product, a "battery eliminator," allowed users to operate radios directly from household current, thereby eliminating the needs of batteries supplied with early models of radios. In the 1930s, the company moved into car radios under the brand name "Motorola." In the 1940s, it also started government work and opened a research laboratory in Phoenix, Arizona, to explore solid-state electronics. By the late 1960s, Motorola became a world leader in military, space, and commercial communications, had built its first semiconductor facility, and was a growing manufacturer of consumer electronics.

Motorola expanded into international markets in the 1960s and also began shifting its focus away from consumer electronics. In the mid-1970s, it sold its color television receiver business to focus on high-tech markets in commercial, industrial, and government industries.

By the late 1980s, Motorola became a major supplier of cellular phones. Cell phone business, however, accounts for a smaller proportion of its total business compared to Nokia (Table 14.3). Moreover, its operating profit for the cell phone business is declining (Table 14.4). The company deployed the world's first commercial CDMA network in Hong Kong in 1995. By early 2003, Motorola had been awarded with over 100 CDMA contracts and is the largest CDMA equipment supplier in Asia.[15]

After its merger with General Instrument Corporation, Motorola strengthened its position in cable modems and set-top terminals. Motorola also delivers embedded chip system level and end-to-end network communication solutions[16]. In 2002, Motorola ranked 74th among the most valuable brands in the world with an estimated brand equity of U.S. $3.4 billion.

TABLE 14.3 **A Comparison of Motorola and Nokia's Global and Chinese Businesses**

	NOKIA	MOTOROLA
Global		
Sales (2002, U.S.$, billion)	30.8	$27.3
No. of employees (2002)	52,000	55,000
Cell phone's share in the overall business (2003)	80	43
China		
Sales (2002, U.S.$ billion)	3	5.7
No. of employees (2002)	5,000	13,000
Cumulative investment (2001, U.S.$, billion)	2	3.4

Source: Author's research from various published sources.

TABLE 14.4

Profit and Loss Statements of Motorola and Nokia

	NOKIA		MOTOROLA	
	2003 Q3	2002 Q3	2003 Q3	2002 Q3
Overall				
Revenue (U.S.$, billion)	8.00	7.13	6.8	6.47
Operating profit (U.S.$, million)	1388.68	1204.25		
Operating profit margin (%)	17.3	16.9		
Net profit (U.S.$, million)	960	711	116	111
Cell Phone Business				
Revenue (U.S.$, million)	6547.30	5564.82	$2900	2700
Operating profit (U.S.$, million)	1464.40	1233.90	147	241
Operating profit as a % of revenue	22.4	22.2	5	8.9

Data for Nokia are from http://www.nordicwirelesswatch.com/wireless/story.html?story_id=3365.
The values in Euros are converted into U.S. dollar with exchange rates at the end of the respective periods. Other sources for Nokia data include Dallas Business Journal (2003), Hines (2003).
Data for Motorola are from Drucker (2003) and Gray (2003).

---

[15] See http://www.motorola.com.cn/en/news/2002/01/0107_02.asp

[16] See http://www.motorola.com/content/0,,115-110,00.html

○ Concluding Comments

Market conditions related factors, such as competition, access to the domestic and foreign markets greatly influence firms' entrepreneurial performance (Ahmad and Hoffmann 2008). In this regard, for technology multinationals such as Motorola and Nokia, rapid growth of emerging markets such as China and India have undoubtedly provided important opportunities.

In prior theoretical and empirical research, scholars have noted that contexts and environment play important roles in determining entrepreneurial behavior (FORA 2006; Tan 2002). The operating environment for entrepreneurs is arguably more complex in emerging economies such as in India and China than in developed economies (Stewart, May, and Kalia 2008). In prior research, scholars have also found that entrepreneurs scan more frequently developing countries than developed countries, due to the complexity of the environment in the former group (Stewart, May, and Kalia 2008). One complexity in China is related to the state-guided capitalism as a way to promote entrepreneurship and achieve economic growth. This case illustrated how Motorola and Nokia had to deal with this and various other complexities in the Chinese cellular market.

Questions for Discussion

1. Consider an emerging market other than China and compare it with China in terms of various characteristics for corporate entrepreneurship in technology sectors.
2. How do emerging markets such as China differ from industrialized countries such as the U.S. in terms of the environment for corporate entrepreneurship in technology sectors?
3. Why and how has the Chinese government promoted corporate entrepreneurship in the cellular technology sectors?

References

Ahmad, N., & Hoffmann, A.N. (2008). A Framework for Addressing and Measuring Entrepreneurship. *OECD Statistics Working Paper, 2,* 1-36.

Baumöl, W.S., Litan, R.E., & Schramm, C. J. (2007). *Good Capitalism, Bad Capitalism, and the Economics of Growth and Prosperity.* New Haven and London: Yale University Press.

Bolton, Jamie M and Wei, Yan (2003). Distribution and logistics in today's China. *The China Business Review,* 30(5), pp. 10–17

Charny, B. (2003). In China, Motorola gets boxed in. *CNET News.com.* Retrieved from https://www.cnet.com/news/

Chen, A. 2002. Capitalist development, entrepreneurial class, and democratization in China. *Political Science Quarterly, 117*(3), 401–422.

Dallas Business Journal (2003). Nokia third-quarter profit up 35%. *Dallas Business Journal.* Retrieved from https://www.bizjournals.com/dallas/subscribe?csrc=6350&ana=ps_dal_wbsbga

Dean, T. (2003) Nokia under Fire, *BDA Consulting,* Retrieved from https://www.bdaconsultinggroup.com/

Drucker, J. (2003, August 6). Leading the news: Motorola reports slim profit rise amid weak prices. *Wall Street Journal,* A.3.

Einhor, B. (2003). Master of innovation: China aims to close its technology gap with Korea and Japan. *Business Week Online.* Retrieved from https://subscribe.businessweek.com/pubs/BW/BWK/BWKRelaunch_US_PaidSearch_June2017.jsp?cds_page_id=216736&cds_mag_code=BWK&id=1519063835437&lsid=80501143389035220 &vid=2&gclid=EAlalQobChMlkLOV4cmy2QlVUEsNCh1jiQw7EAAYASAAEgKbtvD_BwE#theseErrors

Fairfax Media. (2017). China's central bank sends warning about 'hazardous' financial risks. *The Sydney Morning Herald.* Retrieved from http://www.smh.com.au/business/china/chinas-central-bank-sends-warning-about-hazardous-financial-risks-20171105-gzfdx7.html

FOR A. (2006, October). Quality assessment of entrepreneurship indicators. København, Denmark: The National Agency for Enterprise and Construction's Division for Research and Analysis International Consortium for Dynamic Benchmarking of Entrepreneurship, 2(16), 1-185.

Gilboy, G.J. (2004). The myth behind China's miracle. *Foreign Affairs.* 83(4), 33–48.

Goodman, P.S. (2003) China calling with cell-phone standard; competition worries western providers. *The Washington Post.* E.01.

Gordan, K. (2017) Smartphones industry: Statistics & Facts. *Statista.* Retrieved from https://www.statista.com/topics/840/smartphones/

Gray, S. (2003, April 3). Motorola reports gain in third-quarter revenue. *The Washington Post,* E05.

Hines, M. (2003). Nokia sees growth in profits, handset market, *CNET News.com.* Retrieved from https://www.cnet.com/news/

ITU. (1997). *World telecommunication development report: Trade in telecommunications.* Geneva, Switzerland: International Telecommunications Union

ITU. (1999). *World Telecommunications Development Report.* Geneva, Switzerland: International Telecommunications Union.

James, D. (2001). China's sizzling circuits. *Upside, 13*(1), 60-67.

Kahn, G. (2003). Selling cell phones with mixed messages. *Wall Street Journal,* February 27, p. *B5.*

Kshetri, N. (2008). *The rapidly transforming Chinese high-technology industry and market: Institutions, ingredients, mechanisms and modus operandi.* Sawston, UK: Chandos Publishing.

Leopold, G. (2000). Guarded telecom sector seen as plum Chinese prize. *EE Times.* Retrieved from https://www.eetimes.com/

Litchfield, N. (2000). Mobile phones put the Net in every pocket. *Business Times.* Retrieved from https://www.washingtonpost.com/

Liu, J. (2003). Nokia expects to pass Motorola in China. *The Washington Post.* Retrieved from http://www.washingtonpost.com/wp-dyn/articles/A26704-2003Jul22.html

McDaniels, I. K., and Waterman, J. (2000). WTO: a done deal?. *The China Business Review, 27*(6): 22–27.

Merritt, R. (2003). China cell phone makers seen challenging Nokia, Motorola. *EE Times.* Retrieved from https://www.eetimes.com/

Monro, A. (2007). "Mysteries of the East." *New Statesman, 136*(4826), 58–59.

Niitamo, V. (2000). Making information accessible and affordable for all. *Wider Angel*. Retrieved from https://www.pervalentin.com/wider-angel

Oviatt, B.M., & McDougall, P.P. (2005). Toward a theory of international new ventures. *Journal of International Business Studies, 36*(1), 29–41.

Pei, M. (2006). *China's trapped transition: The limits of developmental autocracy*. Boston, MA: Harvard University Press.

PMN. (2003). Nokia introduces pen-based handset in China. Retrieved from http://www.publicmedianet.org/

Pringle, D. (2003). How Nokia thrives by breaking the rules. *Wall Street Journal*, A.7.

Schell, O. (2017). A deal-maker goes to China. *The New York Times*. Retrieved from https://www.nytimes.com/2017/11/06/opinion/trump-xi-jinping-china.html?rref=collection%2Ftimestopic%2FBusiness%20and%20Economy%20in%20China

Sklair, L. (1994). The culture-ideology of consumerism in urban China: Some findings from a survey in Shanghai. *Research in Consumer Behaviour, 7,* 259-292.

Stewart, W. H., May, R. C., Kalia, A. (2008). Environmental perceptions and scanning in the United States and India: Convergence in entrepreneurial information seeking? *Entrepreneurship: Theory and Practice, 32*(1), 83–106.

Tan, J. (2002). Culture, nation, and entrepreneurial strategic orientations: Implications for an emerging economy. *Entrepreneurship Theory and Practice, 26*(4), 95–111.

Törnroos, J.-Å. (2003). Nokia Mobile Phones & the Chinese Market–Managing culturally based strategic nets. Abo, Finland: Åbo Akademi University, Department of Business Administration.

Tsuchiyama, R. (1999). The cellular industry in China: politics, rewards, and risks. *Pacific Telecommunications Review,* 2nd quarter, 149-160.

UltraChina.com. (2000). Why Motorola invested additional RMB16 billion in China. Retrieved from https://umfchina.com/

UNDP (2001). *Human Development Report 2000.* New York: United Nations Development Program.

USA Today. (2007). What's in the cards for 2007? Retrieved from https://www.usatoday.com/

Webber, R. (2016). Why the confusion of the cell phone market has caused millions to switch. *Forbes Financial Council*. Retrieved from https://www.forbes.com/sites/catescottcampbell/2017/09/18/podcast-yes-you-are-an-expert/#725f2ecd1a3a

Wilhelm, K. (2000, July 13). Mobile muddle. *Far Eastern Economic Review, 163:24,* 73-83.

Zhao, S., 2000. Chinese nationalism and its international orientations. *Political Science Quarterly, 115*(1), 1–33.

Relevant Videos

Motorola History:
https://www.youtube.com/watch?v=1b_YDHHE1PE

Nokia | The Rise And Fall [Part 1]:
https://www.youtube.com/watch?v=yyRb_4-cquc

China innovation: Big breakthrough in the quest for innovation:
https://www.youtube.com/watch?v=0yi8jYfYvUo

China technology 2017:
https://www.youtube.com/watch?v=w__im7a3D9s

WHAT WORKS IN BEIJING, DOESN'T WORK IN BEIJING? THE USE OF PAY FOR PERFORMANCE IN CHINA

Sherry E. Sullivan, Bowling Green State University
Shawn M. Carraher, Minot State University

Learning Objectives

1. *Enhance* the student's understanding of international operations. The case offers students with a complex view of multinational operations and requires them to consider the interplay between cultural distance (e.g., differences in values) and organizational context (domestic versus foreign ownership).
2. *Enhance* the student's ability to critically examine whether Western HR practices can (or cannot) be used in non-Western countries.

Key Words

Collectivistic Culture
Individualistic Culture

Iron Rice Bowl
Pay for Performance System

Abstract

Diana Princely and her Chicago-based HRM team were under pressure to enhance their organization's new facility in Beijing, China. After gathering information on changes in China's economy, working environments, and compensation systems, it was decided to introduce merit-based rewards. Despite China's collectivistic culture, the team found evidence that such merit-based systems had been successful in Chinese domestic organizations and were increasingly being used in such organizations. However, one year after recommending the use of a pay-for-performance system at the Beijing facility, Diana and her team were still trying to determine why the system had failed.

Although at first blush this situation appears to be a relatively straightforward case of cultural distance (i.e., value differences), it is much more complex. This case involves the interplay of cultural distance and organizational context (i.e., domestic versus foreign). Previous research has demonstrated the effectiveness of pay-for-performance systems in domestic firms in China. The decision-making team in the case, however, lacked any empirical evidence regarding the use of pay-for-performance systems in foreign-owned firms in China. Recent research (e.g., Du & Choi, 2010) found that the use of pay-for-performance systems in China was influenced not only by the country's collectivistic culture but also by whether the workers were employed by a domestic or a foreign organization. Drawing from the fascinating study completed by Du and Choi, it can be surmised that PowerMax's use of a pay-for-performance system in Beijing may have failed because the workers did not trust their foreign managers and owners. The highly complex pay-for-performance system may have highlighted the value incongruence between the Chinese workers and the foreign owners. The system may have been perceived by the Chinese work-

ers as unfair, making the workers question the link between performance and rewards. What has worked in the past in China does not necessarily work anymore—especially when it comes to compensation issues. The expectations of workers in China have been changing.

Diana Princely looked out of her office window at the panoramic view of the Chicago skyline, wondering how she and her talented team had made such a serious miscalculation. One year ago today, her firm had introduced a pay-for-performance system at their Beijing facility. Diana, the Vice President of Human Resource Management (HRM) for International Operations at PowerMax Multinational, still wasn't sure why the well-established practice of pay-for-performance had failed so miserably.

The implementation of the system was the result of numerous strategic planning sessions in which her HR team had discussed possible ways to enhance the performance of the employees at the new Beijing facility. Although neither Diana nor any member of her team had yet to travel to the new facility, as a long-tenured HR professional, she was well aware of the old adage: what works in Chicago—or New York or Phoenix—doesn't always work in Beijing—or Bombay or Cairo. At her request, three of her team, James Kowalski, Sally McCafferty, and Jamal LeBron, each provided a briefing about the changes in China's economy, work environment, and compensation systems.

James described how in less than two decades, China had transformed herself from a developing nation to the fourth-largest economy on the planet. In the next decade, it is predicted that China will become the second-largest economy in the world. Many well-known multinational corporations (MNCs), including Motorola, Hewlett-Packard, and Delphi Corporation, were among the first foreign organizations to invest and conduct business in China. While many MNCs have reaped numerous benefits from the great opportunities to be found in China, others have faced great obstacles and some have even terminated their operations in China.

James also described troubling incidents in which the Chinese government was accused of unfairly assisting domestic organizations in negotiations and disputes with foreign companies. Under the Chinese system, individuals involved in business disputes can be detained for up to 12 months without any formal charges. Once detained, these individuals are typically cut off from any direct communication with their friends and members of their employing organization. For example, in 2004, Apex Digital accused Changhong, a state-owned company and China's largest TV manufacturer, of owing them $470 million. Changhong used its influence to have David Ji, a partner in Apex Digital, detained. During his detainment, Ji was interrogated as well as threatened with bodily injury, life in prison, and execution. Seven months after his detainment, Ji was formally arrested. It was not until after Apex and Changhong reached a partial agreement that Ji was released on bail[1].

---

[1] For more details on this case, see Kahn, J. (2005, November 1). Dispute leaves U.S. executive in Chinese legal netherworld. *New York Times*. http://www.nyt.com.

Following James' discussion of the economy, Sally detailed changes in China's work environment. Prior to the economic reforms in the 1990s, a career in China was viewed as the means by which individuals contributed to the welfare of society. Young Chinese didn't choose jobs based on what interested them but were placed in jobs as dictated by the needs of the state. Workers were provided with an "iron rice bowl," whereby lifetime employment was guaranteed by the state or the employing firm.

In contrast to the highly individualistic culture of the U.S. in which emphasis is placed on individual choice and personal achievement, in China's collectivistic culture, people place greater value on the welfare of the group, family relationships, and personal enlightenment. The importance of family and political connections in the Chinese work environment is evident in the concept of guanxi. Guanxi is the granting of favors to others with the expectation that they will be returned in a different form in the future. Guanxi goes far beyond the Western concept of network building. In the practice of guanxi, trust is an essential ingredient, and this trust usually takes a great deal of time to cultivate and cement. Because of the importance of guanxi, nepotism and political party affiliations often influenced an employee's compensation and organizational advancement opportunities. Individuals with important connections were usually richly rewarded regardless of work commitment or performance.

While political and family connections are still important in China, individuals in today's workforce are no longer guaranteed lifetime employment. Pay-for-performance systems were introduced in China to help reduce workers' dependency on lifetime employment. This more market-driven economy has resulted in Chinese workers becoming more proactive in managing their careers. For example, individuals working in state-owned enterprises, which offer stronger employment protection than other firms, often lament their relative lack of job mobility.

After Sally's discussion of guanxi and the changing work environment in China, Jamal detailed changes in compensation practices. Traditionally, Chinese workers' compensation was linked to factors such as seniority, status, and education, rather than performance. Unlike in the U.S. where workers tend to value equity norms and merit-based reward systems, employees in collectivist cultures like China tend to value equality norms and rewards based on group membership. Furthermore, not only is China a collectivistic culture, but the culture is based on Confucian principles and the ideology of communism. All of these influences suggest that Chinese workers would find pay-for-performance systems to be incongruent with their values.

Since the Chinese government's 1978 economic reforms, however, the country's wage system has dramatically changed. Despite China's collectivist culture, a growing number of public and private Chinese firms have successfully introduced merit-based systems. The use of bonuses has become a common practice in domestic organizations in China, even in state-owned enterprises. A 1996 study of 10 state-owned enterprises found that the majority of these organizations compensated workers using a basic wage, with additional pay for the acquisition of technical skills and meeting productivity goals (Warner, 1996). In China, the use of piecework pay and bonuses as a percentage of total wages rose from 3.1 percent in 1978 to 23.3 percent in 1993. A 2002 study reported that 40 percent of the total pay of urban Chinese employees was based on pay-for-performance systems (Chiu, Luk, & Tang 2002)[2].

Diana and her team examined the information provided in the briefings. They discussed the options available to enhance the performance of the workers at the Beijing facility. While production levels in Beijing were good, the level of productivity had yet to meet projections. The grapevine had it that some Power-Max executives were already advocating the closing of the Beijing facility. Under pressure to quickly find a solution, Diana and her team recommended the use of the company's pay-for-performance system in PowerMax's Beijing facility.

Discussion Questions

1. Diana Princely and her team had examined changes in China's economy, work environment and compensation systems, finding that domestic firms in China had successfully introduced pay-for-performance systems. Why did PowerMax's implementation of pay-for-performance systems in their Beijing operations fail?
2. What could PowerMax have done differently in their decision-making and introduction of the pay-for-performance system to increase the likelihood of success?
3. What would you do differently than PowerMax had done in order to be successful in opening a similar type of business in China? What type of business might you desire to open in China?

---

[2] The reference for the 1996 study is: Warner, M. Human resources in the People's Republic of China: The 'three systems' reforms. *Human Resource Management Journal. 6*(2), 32–43. The reference for the 2002 study is: Chiu, R. K., Luk, V. W.M., & Tang, T. L.P. Retaining and motivating employees: Compensation preferences in Hong Kong and China. *Personnel Review, 31*(4): 402–431.

Additional Readings

Professors using this case may find the following list of references, especially the Du and Choi article, useful.

Chiu, R. K., Luk, V. W.M., & Tang, T. L.P. (2002). Retaining and motivating employees: Compensation preferences in Hong Kong and China. *Personnel Review, 31*(4), 402–431

Du, D. J. & Choi, J. (2010). Pay for performance in emerging markets: Insights from China. *Journal of International Business Studies, 41*, 671–689

Fernandez, J. A., & Underwood, L. (2005). Succeeding in China: Voices of experience. *Organizational Dynamics, 34*, 402–416.

Forret, M., Tu, H., & Sullivan, S.E. (2007). The awakening dragon: An investigation of firm type and its relationship to the work outcomes and attitudes of Chinese managers. In L.L. Neider & C.A. Schriesheim (Eds.), *Research in management: International perspectives* (Vol. 6). Charlotte, NC: Information Age Publishing.

Hofstede, G. (1980). Motivation, leadership, and organization: Do American theories apply abroad? *Organizational Dynamics, 9*(1) 42-63.

Hofstede, G. (1993). Cultural constraints in management theories. *Academy of Management Executive.* 7(1) 81–93.

Kahn, J. (2005, November 1). Dispute leaves U.S. executive in Chinese legal netherworld. *New York Times,* http://www.nyt.com.

Li, J., & Wright, P.C. (2000). *Guanxi* and the realities of career development: A Chinese perspective. *Career Development International, 5*, 369–378;

Tu, H., Kim, S.Y. and Sullivan, S.E. (2003). Investment strategies of small and medium size firms in China. *International Journal of Small Business, 1*, 51–60.

Warner, M. (1996). Human resources in the People's Republic of China: The 'three systems' reforms. *Human Resource Management Journal, 6*(2), 32–43.

Relevant Videos

https://www.youtube.com/watch?v=zUhAylUJ_Gc

https://www.youtube.com/watch?v=MxuVYv-qn70

https://www.youtube.com/watch?v=hJPop4_vlwU

https://www.youtube.com/watch?v=aFL6gPEimSU

INDEX

CPSIA information can be obtained
at www.ICGtesting.com
Printed in the USA
FSHW02n1025251018
53268FS